HEELLOY
Modern Poetry and Songs of the Somali

HEELLOY
Modern Poetry and Songs of the Somali

John William Johnson

HAAN Publishing, London

Published by
HAAN Publishing
49 Effra Road
London SW2 1BZ

Ⓞ John William Johnson 1996

NEW EDITION 1996

ISBN 1 874209 81 2 (PB)
ISBN 1 874209 12 X (HB)

Printed and bound in Great Britain by HOBBS the Printers
Cover design by David Bird

First edition printed by Indian University, Bloomington 1974, with the title *Heellooy Heelleellooy: The Development of the Genre Heello in Modern Somali Poetry*
ISBN 87750 174 2

NOTE TO THIS EDITION
When this material was first published in 1974, the new Somali National Orthography had not yet come into common usage. The Somali spellings in this edition have been completely updated to conform to that orthography.

Once again,
To Muusa, who started it all,
To Goosh, who finished it up,
To Wisop, who keeps it going.

CONTENTS

FOREWORD TO THE FIRST EDITION

Any outsider who comes into close contact with Somali culture soon discovers that the art of poetry is one of its dominant features. The Somalis themselves take it for granted that this should be so, and are by no means astonished when someone refers to them as a nation of poets. In their hierarchy of values a talent for poetry can place a person at the very apex of public acclaim, alongside national leaders and heroes; in fact the status of a poet in Somali society would inspire their counterparts in modern Europe and America with envy.

The richness and the diversity of Somali poetry are vast, but so far little has been made available in translation to the world outside. Among the numerous genres the *heello* is the least documented, and Johnson has done a great service to Somali studies and world literature by editing, annotating, and translating the poems provided in this volume. Furthermore, by reconstructing from oral testimonies the history of the genre he contributes to our knowledge of the cultural history of the Somali nation in the turbulent period extending from the Second World War to the eve of the Revolution of 21 October 1969.

In the choice of his poetic material and oral testimonies Johnson is particularly fortunate; he succeeded in winning the confidence and cooperation of some of the most renowned practitioners and connoisseurs of poetry in Somalia.

The documentation which the book provides is of particular relevance in this period of rapid change, and as time passes its historical value will increase. Since the Revolution there have been spectacular developments in Somali poetry, and new modes of artistic expression are now emerging. Future historians of Somali culture will be grateful to Johnson in their researches: one day they themselves will be tracing the origins of some of these innovations in the way he sought the origins of the *heello* by going back to the *belwo*, a genre which already seems very remote to the younger generation of today.

The transcripts of tape recordings which provide the book with its Somali texts were made with great care. It differs from the national orthography only in that it uses "z" instead of ' for the glottal stop. Like the national orthography, the transcription used in this book does not mark tone. The reasons for this are simple: tone in Somali is related to grammar and is thus predictable from the structure of the sentence. The rules of this correlation are subconsciously known to a Somali speaker, while a foreign reader will find guidance in several existing publications. In Somali there are no pairs of words which are within the same grammatical category and yet are distinguished by tone alone.

Johnson's book presents to the public only a part of the literary material which he collected during his researches in Somalia. The publication of the material not included in the book would also be of great importance to Somali studies and certainly deserves all support and encouragement.

B . W. Andrzejewski

FOREWORD TO THE 1996 EDITION

It is a great honour and pleasure to be asked to write the foreword of the book entitled *Heelloy: Modern Poetry and Songs of the Somali* on the occasion of its second edition. This book is the first to describe the most interesting history of this form of Somali sung poetry accompanied by music. Professor Johnson's research accurately documents the developments of modern Somali poetic song. My words which follow simply serve to outline and support his in-depth analysis and to reflect his findings against some of my personal experiences.

The Somalis are by nature deeply religious, and the birth and acceptance of the modern *heello* had to overcome the antagonisms and resistance of tradition and of religious leaders. In its infancy the *heello* was considered to be something completely against Somali and Islamic culture. For those of us who were involved, it was a creative and recreational pursuit. We would gather in a house in the evenings to compose and to play and to sing. But the music of the *heello*, the clapping and unconstrained enjoyment of it, and the ill-famed houses where women danced to it were not acceptable, the behaviour therein being considered far beyond the limits which were set for young people. By custom, traditional songs and dances were always performed by young people in the open air, in full sight of their elders; anything else was looked upon with deep suspicion. The prevailing attitude to be overcome is appropriately summed up in the saying quoted by Professor Johnson:

> *Haddii aan sacabka xeeli ku jirin, maxaa habeenkii loo tumaa?*
> If there is no hidden purpose in the dance, why is it done under cover of darkness?

I vividly remember the night when religious resistance reached a climax. A well-known sheikh climbed onto the roof of a building in Hargeysa where we were enjoying a *heello* party, with music, singing, clapping, and some ladies dancing. It was midnight, not a normal time for a religious service, and the sheikh was calling people to prayer. The neighbours came running to see what was happening. The sheikh started to preach to the gathering assembly about the evils of these new habits and how they must be stopped by any means possible, for it was a great sin to stand by and watch young people going astray. The crowd became so incensed that had we not scattered and run for our lives that night, I think some of us would probably not have seen the morning.

However, the incident proved to be a turning point for us, forcing us to think about what we were trying to do and leading to some important changes. At that time we were still using the name *balwo* to describe the newly born form of song, and this term was helping the opposition. The earliest composers began their songs with the words, "*Balwooy, balwooy, hoy balwooy. . .*"—derived from the word *belo*, meaning 'calamity' or 'misfortune' in Arabic. But in Somali usage, the word had acquired the implication of profligacy in matters of sex, womanizing, drinking, and so on. Thus we see that the name *balwo*, which had negative connotations in Somali, was adding to the unacceptability of the '*balwo* movement' in respectable society. It provided the religious leaders with ammunition to have it suppressed and outlawed.

So we changed the name to *heello* and began the first few bars of the song not with '*balwo*' but with the acceptable, traditional invitation to dance '*heelloy heellelloy. . . .*' We also worked hard to improve upon the lyrics, which, to be honest, I have to describe as being at that time generally meaningless, weak, and inferior. Professor Johnson cites one such poem which deals with a punctured tyre. They dealt with trite and insignificant subjects, and we were reviled and ridiculed by older people, especially by the poets and literary minded. Early examples of the *balwo* were composed not by established figures in society, but by hopefuls dreaming of a bright future, by young government servants, and by truck drivers and their assistants as a way of passing the time on long journeys away from home. We determined to polish the poetry and minimize any grossly improper meanings or innuendo so that the songs would be worthy of respect from all Somalis, both old and young, and would be suitable for performing at social gatherings such as weddings. We introduced themes other than love, and marches and patriotic songs began to be composed.

It was now the 1950s, and national independence was very much on the agenda; the *heello* became the natural vehicle for freedom songs which expressed the people's aspirations. In the end the popularity of this once 'forbidden' music and song swept over the country like an unstoppable tide.

Somali oral culture stretching back into the mists of time is filled with poetry, chants, work songs, and children's rhymes. The appearance on the scene in the middle of this century of poetry sung to a melody and which became known as *heello* stands on firm foundations, and it has established its own legitimacy. It has produced its own hall of fame of exponents and devotees, a long line of famous and respected figures, male and female, singers, composers, musicians, fanciers, and actors proud to be associated with it. Professor Johnson names many of them, including Cabdi Sinimo, Khadiija 'Balwo'; others to be remembered are Busaad, Aadan Dacay, Yuusuf 'Qodban' Sharif, Belaayo Cas, Maxamed Aadan 'Ayban,' and Abdo Sofi.

In every age there have been people who supported new artistic ventures and who by luck or vision helped to nurture new cultural trends. In spite of massive resistance, there were those—some from government circles, some who were opinion leaders—who lent their approval and muscle, and in some cases their financial backing, to what we were about. Among those were Xaaji Axmed Naaleeye, a wealthy businessman of Hargeysa and mentioned in Professor Johnson's text, Jaamac Nuur Dacar of Djibouti (ex-French Somaliland), Calwan from Aden Colony, and Warsama 'Sayaad,' a fish merchant also from Aden. There was Yuusuf Xaaji Aadan, a government school teacher, a graduate from the Sudan, a poet in both Somali and Arabic, and a supporter of our cause, himself a composer in the genre. Maxamed Axmed Cali, often referred to as the 'Father of Education' in our country, was a courageous supporter of liberal causes; he was someone who seemed to recognize our potential, and he gave encouragement to me personally.

Finally, I should like to express appreciation for the work which Professor John Johnson did in collecting, translating, and explaining the popular poetry and songs of the Somalis. As one who has been involved with the *heello* movement all my life, I do read with pleasure his accurate account of the first decades of development of this genre, and I am extremely glad that this very useful and important record cites 'Muusa' and 'Goosh'; I, too, would like to honour the names of 'Macallin' (Teacher) Goosh Andrzejewski and Muusa Galaal, two giants in the history of the preservation and exposition of the Somali verbal art in all its forms.

After more than half a century, the *heello* is a well-established and flourishing form of expression among Somalis. In the 1960s, '70s, and '80s, Somali artistes were hosts to and hosted by artistes from many other countries. Cultural exchange visits with, and participation in international festivals in China, the Sudan and Egypt, Senegal and Nigeria,

(East) Berlin, Paris, Rome, Moscow, and Sofia provided stimulus and cross referencing of musical expression in particular. In more recent times, the scattering of Somali society throughout the world following our national social trauma has informed much of the lyric expression of the day. My hope is that the republication of this study will encourage others to build on the foundation of information so ably laid by Professor Johnson.

Abdilahi Qarshi
London, 1996

PREFACE TO THE FIRST EDITION

Modern Somali poetry, manifested in the genre called *heello*, I is at once an expression and outgrowth of a new period of history, and a potentially strong influence on changing Somali society. The present study attempts to describe the development of this poetry, its structure and imagery, and the social and historical setting from which it arose.[1]

The characteristics of form and content of the *heello* come from four major sources. First, it is within a traditional group of genres, here called the Family of Miniature Genres, that the history of the modern poem begins, especially with the last miniature poem to develop: the *belwo*. Second, the modern poem has acquired characteristics from Somali classical poetry. Third, it has borrowed some features from abroad. And finally, it has acquired some of its structure from its intrinsic development through time. An historical approach, beginning with the *belwo*, is probably the most fruitful way to deal with the question.

The *belwo*, begun sometime between 1943 and 1945 in the British Somaliland Protectorate by a man called Cabdi 'Sinimo,' is the immediate forerunner to the *heello*. The product of a period of heightened change precipitated by World War II, the *belwo* offered a new medium of expression. It was an immediate success with Somali youth and progressive urban populations, as well as with the "new elite" of the country, but it encountered opposition from the more conservative religious leaders and elders.

The changes brought about by World War II that helped to develop the *belwo* also brought it into its next form, the *heello* Form A, which was actually a tacking together of many *belwo* into one large poem. Hargeysa, the last capital of the British Somaliland Protectorate, became the focal area for this change. Political and patriotic themes made their way into the text of the new poem, and its form also altered drastically. Its next step of development, the *heello* Form B, then became a major tool for the new elite, as cries for independence (usually hidden in the imagery of the new poem) could be heard regularly from radios and tape recorders in local tea shops. By the end of its first period of development in late 1954, the light *belwo* had been transformed into the much longer *heello* and had adopted the traditional imagery of Somali classical oral literature, as well as the use of musical instruments imported from abroad.

In 1955, political events surrounding the transfer of part of the British Somaliland Protectorate to Ethiopia led to political protests from the Somalis and to the second period of the *heello*. With this period a fresh and concerted effort was made by the new elite to attain independence, and their unique genre of poetry had almost replaced traditional verse in urban society.

With the advent of independence in 1960 came the development of the third period of the *heello*, characterized by the addition of innovative, matured ideas as themes in modern poetry. Antigovernment poems, as well as those debating the role of women in the new society, could be heard. The use of the *heello* in the theater and on the radio continued to drive it forward. Important internal political events found their expression in it, as did the original and still dominant theme of love. Today the *heello* continues to develop in Somalia.

This book was researched while I was a volunteer in the United States Peace Corps in the Somali Republic (now known as the Somali Democratic Republic) from June 1966 until July 1969. Much of the work was done, beginning in July 1968, under the direction of B. W. Andrzejewski, Reader in Cushitic Languages at the School of Oriental and African Studies, University of London. Dr. Andrzejewski was in Somalia on a year's research leave and gave me valuable help in the study of the structure of the Somali language. Although I had studied spoken Somali since March 1966, his assistance was essential for the specialized skill of the translation of texts.

There are three sources for this book: poetry, interviews, and published works. Most of the poetry was collected and translated by me and my informants, although a few of the poems (and this is noted when it occurs) are from the unpublished collection of Muuse X. I. Galaal, translated by him and edited by me and another former Peace Corps volunteer, Michael Cushman Walsh. Observations on the development of modern poetry are made from the entire body of collected poems, although only a carefully selected set of examples appears in the text.[2] These poems were obtained from tapes made for use on the radio stations in Somalia, as well as from individuals who either recorded the poems on tape for me, or dictated them to me as I transcribed. Some of the transcription was done by Cumar Aw Nuux, who also carefully checked the entire collection for its accuracy in transcription.

In addition to the interviews and conversations I collected, Somalis were also asked to comment on the development of their poetry, for there is a large body of oral history of art concerning the development of modern poetry. Although the information obtained in this manner cannot be final, general ideas and opinions on the direction of development can be obtained. Some of the information was conclusive. All Somalis with whom I spoke, for example, agreed that modern poetry developed from a genre called the *belwo*. It must be remembered, however, that memory sometimes fails on minute points and that opinions vary. Fortunately, the memories of people in oral societies are used much more often than those of persons who can make notes in writing. For this reason, they may be more accurate than the memories of literate men. Copies of these interviews, together with some newspaper articles and the transcription of a radio program, have been deposited at the School of Oriental and African Studies, University of London, where they can be consulted by arrangement with the Department of Africa.[3]

I have attempted to translate the poetry in as complete a manner as possible. In so doing, each line of poetry underwent four processes:

The first step is to transcribe the text accurately so that each morpheme is properly accounted for. I have not used a phonetic or phonemic transcription, but rather an orthographic system which is used by most Somalis who employ the Latin script. This system represents the majority of the symbols finally chosen as the national orthography by the Somali government.[4] Furthermore, this system is very practical to use with a typewriter, and I have employed it in this book. It was originally devised by Armstrong in 1934, and has undergone minor adjustments by such people as Muuse X. I. Galaal, Shire Jaamac Axmed, and B. W Andrzejewski. An account of how these variations relate to one another can be found in Andrzejewski, Strelcyn, and Tubiana 1966. The variation of the system used in this book is outlined in Muuse X. I. Galaal 1968.[5] One adjustment has been made by me. The symbol < ' > has been replaced by < z >, representing the glottal stop / ʔ /, in order to avoid visual confusion with the raised comma.

It should be noted that prior to the adoption of an official orthography, proper names and certain commonly used words were written in very rough, ad hoc transcriptions, either following the English, French, or Italian conventions—for example, Jama, Djama, Giama, for Jaamac. In this book the orthographic system previously mentioned is used throughout. Popular spelling of Somali can be found in the Appendix of Somali Proper Names.

Having taken care to spell correctly, a morpheme by morpheme translation then follows in step two. Step three is a literal translation of the line, while step four is a translation that takes the whole of the poem into consideration and attempts to provide a literary version in English. Except for some of the short poems, I have not attempted to imitate the alliterative system employed in Somali poetry. I have also noted all references which would remain obscure to the non-Somali even when translated. In some cases, Somali words are employed in the text and then explained in the notes.

In order to save space and to render the poetry less monotonous in translation, line repeats have been omitted from the text. They have been indicated, however, by italicized notes on the line where they occur, and by numbering the lines to account for them. All refrains at the ends of stanzas are indented, and when a refrain is repeated after each stanza in a poem, it is given in full only the first time it appears. (See the poem on pp. 7-11 for clarification.)

The translations were done with two informants, Maxamed Jaamac Galaal and Axmed Cali Abokor. Maxamed, who was a student in the National Teachers College in Somalia, was graduated from the National Teacher Education Center, one of the best secondary schools in the country. He had taught for a year in intermediate school before entering the college. Axmed was a research official in the cultural division (Department Five) of the Ministry of Education. Having graduated from Sheikh Secondary School, Axmed served for a while as a teacher in northern Somalia and as headmaster at Laas Caanood Intermediate School before going to Muqdisho to enter the cultural division. Both informants spent their early lives herding camels in the traditional manner of northern Somalis. Both have a good command of English; Axmed especially is proficient in the specialized language used in traditional Somali poetry and has collected a considerable amount of traditional poetry. I am greatly indebted to these men for their help.

Although the limitations of this book are not so great as to prevent it from being written, they nevertheless cannot be ignored. Cultural differences between Somali society and my own prevent an understanding of many subtle points. For example, it was not uncommon for me to praise the aesthetic aspects of a poem which appealed to me only to find that my informant was not similarly impressed.

Another obvious limitation in the recording of this study is the scarcity of relevant documents. I should like to stress, however, that the lack of a script is in no way a limitation to the composition and development of poetry among the Somalis.

The lack of information on the influence that southern Somalia had on the development of modern poetry presents yet another limitation. Although the *belwo* is a northern genre, and although the greater part of the development of modern poetry was accomplished in the north, some influences—more correctly, some parallel development—from the south can be noted. The poetry performed by Axmed Naji, for example, is considered distinctly southern by my informants, but this emerged after the modern poem had evolved.

A serious difficulty also arises from the fact that no one has yet succeeded in formulating the rules of Somali scansion. We do not even know what the units are of which the actual verse patterns are composed, but it seems almost certain that Somali scansion differs radically from that used in Arabic or European languages. Several scholars have tried to establish the rules of Somali scansion (Muuse X. I. Galaal, Andrze-jewski, Maino, and others) but have failed thus far, in spite of the fact that Somalis readily recognize different meters, though they cannot state what these meters consist of. It has been suggested by A. M. Jones, an eminent specialist in African music, that the rules of Somali scansion, whatever they are, might be discovered through analyses of rhythm with the methods employed by specialists in non-European music.[6]

Finally, the most serious difficulty I faced in the book was nomenclature. Trying to find the appropriate term in English for a Somali word or for some problem not named at all in Somali was very tiresome. The most important specific difficulty here was the problem of whether to call the genres of Somali verbal art under discussion poetry or song.[7] Although it is often recited, all Somali poetry can be sung and many genres have their own characteristic melodies. This verbal art is, nonetheless, what we as Westerners would readily recognize as poetry. Moreover, all these genres have been referred to as poems by scholars in the past. When one comes to modern poetry, the problem is most acute, and even the Somalis have difficulty. Sometimes the modern poem is referred to as the *heello* (a poetic term), and at other times it is referred to as a *hees* ("song"). Furthermore, in my search through musical terminology in English, I could find no useful term that would describe the *heello* without also introducing ambiguous connotations. Although I do *not* consider the problem solved, it is obvious that a decision had to be made. Since this book deals primarily with the poetic aspects of the *heello* and very little with the musical side, I have chosen to call it poetry and not song. Although necessary references to some musical features are made, the nomenclature surrounding the *heello* in this book, therefore, is drawn from literary criticism and not from ethnomusicology.

Although it would be impossible to mention everyone, I should like to acknowledge several people for their help in the preparation of this book. Appreciation is due to my informants in the translation of the poetry, Maxamed Jaamac Galaal and Axmed Cali Abokor, and in the checking of the spelling, Cumar Aw Nuux. I would also like to thank all the informants of the interviews, especially Muuse X. I, Galaal and Xasan Sheekh Muumin. For direction and advice on the preparation of the manuscript, for assistance in learning the grammatical structure of Somali, and for permission to quote from his books and articles, as well as for continual encouragement, I should like to express especial gratitude to B. W. Andrzejewski. Thanks are also due I. M. Lewis for permission to quote from his *Modern History of Somaliland from Nation to State*, and Saadia Touval and the Harvard University Press for their permission to quote a passage from Touval's book, *Somali Nationalism*.

John William Johnson
London, 1974

NOTES

1. Although mentioned in a few works, modern Somali poetry has not yet been described for Western scholarship. Considering its central role in Somalia today, I feel that this absence marks a blank space in the study of Somali oral art. Hopefully this book will reduce this gap in some measure. The genres which have received some treatment are the *belwo* (Maino 1953; Laurence 1954; Andrzejewski 1967), and the *heello* (Andrzejewski and Lewis 1964).

2. The entire collection is made up of 24 *wiglo*, 16 *dhaanto*, 10 *hirwo*, 3 *dheel* (*baal-baal*), 79 *belwo*, 1 unidentified miniature poem, 85 *heello*, and 3 *gabay*. Copies of the poems for which a tape was available have been deposited in the tape libraries of the School of Oriental and African Studies, University of London, and the Archives of Traditional Music, Folklore Institute, Indiana University.

3. Poetry not used in this book has also been deposited at the School of Oriental and African Studies, University of London, and may be consulted under the same arrangements.

4. For a detailed description of the debate on written Somali, see Andrzejewski 1962, and Andrzejewski, Strelcyn, and Tubiana 1966.

5. One correction should be made in this publication. On p. 4, where the orthography is explained, under the symbol "C, c" for "glottal fricative," one should read "pharyngeal fricative."

6. As this revised edition goes to press, scansion rules for Somali poetry are known. Moreover, Jones has been proven partially correct, for there are complex relationships between Somali scansion rules and the music to which it is recited. For detailed descriptions of these rules, see the bibliography under Johnson (1979, 1980a, 1980b, 1985, 1988, 1993, 1996, and ca.1996).

7. This problem is apparent in other scholarly works in this field. Compare the following quotes from Andrzejewski and Lewis 1964, p. 51:

    The *heello* is represented in this book by a sequence of poems under the title *Twelve modern love songs*.

    . . . It is represented in our collection by the poem *Independence Song*.

See also the interesting discussions on this subject in Finnegan 1970, pp. 75-76 and p. 241.

PREFACE TO THE 1996 EDITION

So many changes have occurred in Somalia since this book was first published in 1974 that at first thought it seemed major revisions would be necessary if this book were to be republished. However, historical studies need not be revised unless theoretical approaches change, and that has not happened. This book is about the historical development of the genre *heello*, and those facts remain the same. Therefore, the book is revised only by replacing the orthography chosen for the first edition with that chosen by Somalis to be their national script. I have also edited a few places where the orthography was mentioned to conform to this change. "Revised edition" thus refers only to the orthography.

Why has the book been republished? I have been asked on so many occasions where one might get a copy, only to have to reply that it was out of print. With the emergence of Haan Associates Press, it has now become easier to make Somali materials available to the public. It was also thought that the large number of diaspora Somalis might want to read the history of the development of one of their important poems. Finally, it is my hope that by exposing the reading public in Britain and America to the artistic creativity of the Somali people, a more objective and positive view of Somalis might emerge in place of the one engendered by the negative headlines, which have resulted from the civil war on the Horn of Africa. At any rate, it is my fervent hope that the book will be well received by a new generation of Somalis and Somali scholars, and it is also my hope that Somalia will soon recover from the upheaval of the 1990s.

John William Johnson
Bloomington, 1996

1

INTRODUCTION

The Social Context

Poetry has many uses within Somali society. Among its other functions, it is employed as a running commentary on the latest news, a lobbying pressure device for social and political debates, a record of historical events, a revered form of aesthetic enjoyment, and an expression of deep feelings about love. The poet is a prominent public figure who commands a following, and his prestige corresponds to his poetic abilities. For as long as Somalis can remember, the poet has enjoyed this high status, and in spite of all that is new in Somalia today, he is in no danger of losing this status. In fact, his poetry has adjusted itself to modern influences and is presently enjoying a renaissance. Having thus evolved, the main genre of modern poetry, the *heello*, now commands the attention formerly reserved for the traditional genres, at least among the urban and elite segments of Somali society.

Contemporary Somali poetry is a product of the "new elite" of the country; that is, it has arisen and developed inside that part of the Somali social system which was heavily influenced by the colonial administration and has become the ruling segment of the modern Somali nation-state. The roots of this development, however, are well within the traditional way of life.

There are four main economic systems on the Horn of Africa, each of which has a separate influence upon the social structure of the Somalis involved in them. These systems are: the pastoral nomad, the agriculturalist, the town dweller, and the coastal merchant.[1] It must be emphasized from the beginning that all these peoples consider themselves Somalis and share a basically similar culture. They all speak the same language. Like every language, it is divided into dialects. To date, studies have defined three main dialect types.[2] All of these people share a common religion, Islam. Furthermore, the geography of their land is fairly uniform. Muuse Galaal has said: "The Somalis go as far as their camels go,"[3] stopping at the highlands of Ethiopia and Kenya. In fact the geography does vary to some extent, but not appreciably. All these peoples, moreover, relate to each

1

other through a patrilineal, agnatic genealogy system which enables every Somali to relate to all of his countrymen and defines his responsibilities and liberties within traditional society.[4]

The four economic systems mentioned above are the main traditional ones, and they include the greatest part of the Somali population. It must be noted, however, that there are several other groups that differ from these four, but their contribution to modern poetry is minimal and they need not be discussed here. In fact, of the four main economic systems (and the societies which surround them), it was from the traditional poetry of the pastoral nomad that modern poetry developed. Not only has the nomad contributed most of the imagery, but the very genres from which the *heello* developed come from pastoral society. Moreover, the nomad's dialect is employed in almost all modern poetry.

Although the nomad's contribution to modern poetry is great, it is at first glance somewhat paradoxical that the immediate predecessor of the *heello*, a genre called *belwo*, first emerged inside the society of the town dweller in northern Somalia. This development will be covered in detail in Chapter 3, but suffice it to say here that the *heello* itself is a development from traditional pastoral poetry that has lived all of its life inside the new elite segment of Somalia. In short, by the time it had become a secure genre in Somalia as a whole, poets from all four main groups—and some of the minor ones as well—were contributing to its composition and development.

Detailed works on the history and social structure of the four main economic systems have already been written.[5] Lewis's study (1965) has, moreover, covered the history of the new elite through 1963; and since it is this segment of society from which the *heello* emerged, more consideration must be given to it.

It must be made clear from the beginning that all of the traditional economic systems mentioned above still exist today. There is, however, a present day social group whose members come from all segments of Somali society but whose lives are no longer inextricably tied to the traditional segment from which they came. This group we have already referred to as the new elite, because its members are increasingly involved in the control of the political and, to some extent, economic future of their country.[6]

The new elite is a segment of society not based on an economic structure and not having a long cultural background as such. Its heritage is, however, drawn from the traditional economic segments, and this heritage is often used as propaganda. (As we have pointed out, the art form of the elite, the *heello*, is rooted in the tradition of the pastoralist, but it has other characteristics too, such as its use of musical instruments, which have been imported from other cultures.[7]) This group, many of whom have been formally educated to some degree, is made up of several subsegments of the population: politicians; members of the army and police who now control the politics of the country; the educated government civil servants; and a substantial number of people, educated abroad, many of whom are idle because of the scarcity of jobs in their fields.[8] There is also a segment of professional poets, reciters, and musicians.

Although the economic and social backgrounds of the four traditional groups differ from the backgrounds of the new elite (and often their formal educational background also differs), the social contacts between them are not as greatly removed as one might think. One need only look at the participation of Somalis in general elections. Great numbers of traditional Somalis have participated alongside the new elite in all of the country's elections. As we shall demonstrate presently, the themes in modern poetry are also a reflection of the ties, as well as the differences, between the new elite and the traditional segments.

There are, of course, attitudes which differ between the two segments. In present day Somalia the ancient system of tribalism, which represents older beliefs about personal and clan relationships, is being combated vigorously by the nationalists of the elite. Mention of clan names was common in some genres of traditional poetry but is almost completely absent in the *heello*. Other differences in attitudes could be mentioned, but since poetry is our main concern, let us compare a traditional *gabay*, a genre of Somali classical poetry, with a modern *heello*.[9] The differing points of view concerning the role of women in society can be clearly seen in the following poems.

Saahid Qamaan, the composer of the following *gabay* (Example 1), used a tone of instruction to the woman he wanted for his wife.[10] He begins his poem by giving an extensive list of clans (a practice definitely absent in antitribalist modern poetry) through which he has searched for a good wife. Having found the right one, he concludes the first stanza by lecturing her as he would a student. What follows is an instruction in the proper role of a married woman from the traditional point of view.

Example 1:

II.	13	Ma udgoona naag inan-gumeed, uudna shidanayn e,
	14	Mar haddii ubad yeelatona, Laga ba aayuus ye,
	15	Arwaaxaaga oogada biyaa, ubad ha moogaynin,
	16	Uskag naag leh waa necebnehee, yuusan Kugu oollin,
	17	Nin udgoonka jecel baan ehee, uunsiga ha deynin,
	18	Kolla haddaanad iga maarmihayn, idan ha moogaanin,
III.	19	Haddii inan La guursadoo tolkay, waw abtiriyaan e,
	20	Adyadiyo waxay Kuula iman, agabbar naagood e,
	21	Afka iyo ilkaa rumayga mari, oo indhaha kuulo,
	22	Adigaan ilwaad quruxsanayn, yaan LaGuu imanin,
IV.	23	Aqalkiyo ardaagiyo qoryaa, ilinta aad joogto,
	24	Aqlibiyo awaare isku kacay, sidatan geel ooddii,
	25	Yuu Kaa ahaanine kurtiis, ha isku awdnaado,
	26	Isku idibiloo wada adkee, ilaxidhkaan jiifo,
	27	Ha na igu itaaline ka yeel, meel ergada deeqda,
V.	28	Ilma-adeerraday iyo kuwaan, oday wadaagayney,
	29	Niman urursanoo ila fadhiya, haw irdho lazaanin,
	30	Uurkaygu suu damacsanyay, aniga oon sheegin,
	31	Aqligaa wax Laga fiiriyaa, garo ixtaadkayga,
VI.	32	Ammin gaabtay aaskoo dam yidhi, niman aguugaaya,
	33	Meeshay adduunyadu martiyo, adhiga foolkiisa,
	34	Irridday fadhiistaan galbeed, kama ajoodaane,
	35	Arwaahhooda waa uga tudhaan, Reer Ugaas-Magane,
	36	Dadka uma ekee yaan La odhan, Lama oqoonayn e,
	37	Anshaxooda baro haatanaa, LaGu ogaysiin e,
	38	Afarta hilqadoodiyo qardhaas, aqalka Kuu taalla,
	39	Alaabtaada oo idil adoo, urursadoo qaatay,
	40	U tagoo ogow inay yihiin, awrta Bah-Xawaadle,
VII.	41	Anoo maqan Islaan idin martiyay, niman i aanaystay,
	42	Aad ha odhan Allaa igu ogoo, aayahood ma hayo,
	43	Arli durugsan yay iigu iman, inaad asbaaxowday,
	44	Anoo aan ogayn dhuuni yay, igaga eed sheegan,
	45	Naagaa ugaaslee dadkiyo, ururi waayeelka,

4

VIII.46   Ayaan noolba tii qaylisa, waa ibliis darane,

     47   Irdho qaado aashaana soco, aayar hadalkaaga,

     48   Is ogow afkaaga na yasiro, edebtu waa doore,

IX. 49   Usha aniga oo Kugu dhuftaad, meelo ka ilduuftay,

     50   Inaad oydid inaad aammustaad, Kuu arrindhaantaa ye,

     51   Ayaaniyo ayaan naag xun baan, umalka daynayn e,

     52   Adoo uubatayn reero kale, yayan Ku ogaanin,

X.   53   Intaasaan afeef Kuu dhigoo, waano Kuu idhi ye,

     54   Hadduu Eebbeheen Kugu anfici, waa kitaab idile,

     55   Haddii aanad aqbalin xaajadaa, LaGu ogaysiiyay,

     56   Nin kaloo Ilaah Kuu baxshoba, kala awaaraynay.

II.   13   The wife of a man of low birth never smells well, because she does not burn incense for herself;[11]

     14   After she had given birth, [her husband] abandons her .

     15   [So] don't forget [to wash] your body regularly with water.

     16   [My clan] hates dirty women; [so] do not allow it of yourself .

     17   I am a man who likes sweet smells; do not stop [using] incense,

     18   As long as you are in need of me, do not forget the incense burner.

III. 19   If a girl is married [into] my clan, my relatives [always] check her ancestry;

     20   They come to you with prying [questions] and ridicule [used with] women.[12]

     21   Clean your mouth and teeth [with] a tooth brush,[13] and use eyeshadow [on your] eyes.[14]

           22 One should never come upon you [when your] appearance is not beautiful.

IV. 23   [It is shameful] for the antechamber,[15] and the area around your house where you stay

     24   To be untidy and dirty like a camel corral,

     25   [So take care that] it is not like this; let it be kept neat.

     26   Keep tidy and strong the bed chamber[16] where I sleep,

     27   But do not overdo it for me; let there be ample room for guests.

V.   28   Do not ignore the men who gather around and sit with me,

29   My cousins on my father's side and those with whom I share an ancestor.

30   [Let it be unnecessary] for me to tell you the wishes of my emotions;[17]

31   [You must] be sensitive; know my needs.

VI. 32   [Honorable] men will travel [to you] at sunset—

33-34   They appreciate sitting west of the gate [of the corral] where the animals, sheep and goats, pass.[18]

35   Be lenient with their persons: the Reer Ugaas Magan.[19]

36   They do not resemble [other] people; one [should] never say that they are not known [throughout the land].

37   You are informed [thus]: learn their behavior from this time forth.

38   [When] you have collected and put on all your [fine] clothes, and

39   The amulet and the four earrings which are in your dwelling,

40   Go [to them] and be aware that they are the noble men[20] of the Bah-Xawaadle.[21]

VII. 41   When I am away, [if] Moslems come to you as guests [in order] to visit me,

42   Do not say: "God knows that I have no sustenance [for you]."

43   [News] should not come to me in a distant place, that you have been disgraced.

44   While I am unaware [of their visit, I should] not be reproached about [the lack] of food.

45   Women have nobility; [therefore, you must] care for [my] people and the elders.

VIII. 46   The [wife] who nags every day is [like] the evil Satan.

47   Be careful, walk prudently, speak slowly;

48   Know yourself; speak gently, [for] politeness is noble.

IX. 49   If I hit you with a stick when you transgress,

50   Is it better [for] you to keep silent, than to weep.

51   A bad wife never ceases her anger, day after day.

52   Other people [should] not know when you cry.

X.   53   This I have told you as a warning and as advice.

        54   If God make you understand, [what I have given you] is a complete book.

        55   If you do not accept these arguments, which have been told to you,

        56   [Then] whomever God [may] give you [as a husband], we [must] separate [from each other].

The following modern poem deals with a topic which would be quite rare, if not unheard of, for a classical poem. The exchange between a man and a woman debating the role of women in modern Somali society must not mislead the reader. Although both sides of the question are given in the recitation, the poem was composed by a single poet.

Example 2:[22]

   I.   M: 1   Dumar waxa u fiicnayd,

           2   Tii doorkii Nebigii,

           3   Reer Laga dillaashee,

           4   Duufsaday iblaysku ye,

           5   Biyaha uu dul- joojee ,

           6   Hadhkeedii dad mooddee,

              (repeat, ll. 1-6)

         13   Aadan oon dembi lahayn,

         14   Daaqsiisay geedkee,

         15   Diinteenu sheegtee,

              (repeat, ll. 13-15)

         19   Inta Loogu daw-gelay,

         20   Jannadooy dabbaashaan,

         21   Dibadda Looga saaree,

              (repeat, ll. 19-21)

             25   Waa iga dardaaran e,

             26   Waxaan Kaaga digayaa,

             27   Dabka hura dhexdeenee,

                 (repeat, ll. 25-27)

F: 31 Waan idin dar-yeelloo,
    32 Idin daadahaynoo,
    33 Dusha idin ku qaadnee,
    34 Ruux idin ku daaloo,
    35 Dambarkiisa nuugteen,
    36 Haw deeqin caydee,
       (repeat, ll. 31-36)
    43 Carrabkiinoo daaha gala,
    44 Lama-dublaysaan,
    45 Sida aar dad-qaadee,
       (repeat, ll. 43-45)
    49 Idinkaa daliishaday,
    50 Dadka kala sarreeyoo,
    51 Ummadda kala dambaysee,
       (repeat, ll. 49-51)
      55 Dan bay innaga dhaxaysee,
      56 Daacad aan ahaanno,
      57 Aynnu wada dadaallee,
        (repeat, ll. 55-57)
II. M: 61 Dadkii raacay Nebigii,
    62 Kuwii diiday Shaafici,
    63 Maalintay is dilayeen,
    64 Doqorkii uu Sayid Cali,
    65 Intuu daray kufaartii,
    66 Daafacaayay Abu Jahal,
       (repeat, ll. 61-66)
    73 Ee dhiiggu daatee,
    74 Sida daad qulqulayee,
    75 Maydku daadsanaa degel,
       (repeat, ll. 73-75)
    79 Dabcigiinu waa kii,
    80 Hadba qolada debecdo,
    81 Aad ku digan jirteenee,
       (repeat, ll. 79-81)

85 Waa iga dardaaran e,

86 Waxaan Kaaga digayaa,

87 Dabka hura dhexdeenee,

    (*repeat, ll. 85-87*)

F: 91 Dayax dhaca habeen dam ah,

92 Iyagoon dembi lahayn,

93 Idinkaa dalaaqee,

94 Reer ay daruureen,

95 Idinkaa ka dira oon,

96 Dawgooda marininee,

    (*repeat, ll. 91-96*)

103 Dibnahoo qaniiniyo,

104 Dabkay taasu leedahay,

105 Ayaa idin ka daahan e,

    (*repeat, ll. 103-105*)

109 Xaqayaga aad daboosheen,

110 Damac yaad ku qaaddeen,

111 Ayaa idin ku deynee,

    (*repeat, ll. 109-111*)

    115 Dan bay innaga dhaxaysee,

    116 Daacad aan ahaanno,

    117 Aynnu wada dadaallee,

        (*repeat, ll. 115-117*)

I. M: 1 Of [all] women, the one who was best

2 Was the one [who lived during] the era of the Prophet [Aadan].[23]

3 Her dwelling place[24] was destroyed;

4 She was led astray by Satan.

5 He placed her by the stream,

6 [Where] she thought her shadow was someone else.[25]

    (*repeat, ll. 1-6*)

13 Adam, who had never committed sin—

14 She caused him to eat of the Tree [of Life].

9

15 So teaches our religion.
    (*repeat, ll. 13-15*)

19 [This] is the reason [that they], while

20 Swimming [peacefully] in Paradise,

21 Were expelled to the outside.
    (*repeat, ll. 19-21*)

  25 These are my last words [of warning]:

  26 What I shall warn you about is

  27 The fire[26] which burns between us.
      (*repeat, ll. 25-27*)

F: 31 We gave you assistance;

    32 We taught you to walk;

    33 We carried you on our backs [while you were yet too young to walk];
        (*repeat, ll. 31-33*)

    37 Refrain from giving insults to

    38 The ones who became fatigued for your sakes,

    39 And from whom you suckled the first milk [of your lives].
        (*repeat, ll. 37-39*)

    43 The tongue which you possess

    44 Speaks two [opposite] things [at the same time]

    45 [And is] like the male lion which catches people.
        (*repeat, ll. 43-45*)

    49 You have demonstrated that

    50 [Some] people are better than [others];

    51 And that some are not as good as [others].
        (*repeat, ll. 49-51*)

      55 There is a necessity which brings us together:

      56 Let us be honest;

      57 Let us work hard together.
          (*repeat, ll. 55-57*)

II. M: 61 The people who followed the Prophet [Maxamed]

     62 And those who rejected the Shaafici:[27]

     63 Fought with each other one day.

     64-65 While Sayid Cali[28] slew the infidels with his weapon,

66   And defended [his people against] Abu Jahal,[29]

   (*repeat, ll. 61-66*)

73   And blood which was spilt [was]

74   Like a rushing flood,[30]

75   Dead bodies covered the ground.

   (*repeat, ll. 73-75*)

79   Your character is like this:

80-81   You are always pleased to see a group of people become weak [and defeated].

   (*repeat, ll. 79-81*)

   85   These are my last words [of warning]:

   86   What I shall warn you about is

   87   The fire which burns between us.

      (*repeat, ll. 85-87*)

F: 92-93   You divorce them when they have committed no sin,

   91   On a dim night when the moon has set.

   95   You expel them from

   94   The houses which they [themselves] constructed.

   96   You do not allow them to have their rights.

      (*repeat, ll. 91-96*)

   105   You are not aware of

   103   The lips which are bitten [in anger],

   104   And the fire that [this ill treatment] causes.

      (*repeat, ll. 103-105*)

   111   You are in debt [to us for]

   109   Our rights which you hid;

   110   You have taken them with greed.

      (*repeat, ll. 109-111*)

      112   There is a necessity which brings us together:

      113   Let us be honest;

      114   Let us work hard together.

         (*repeat, ll. 112-114*)

Before we take up a discussion of the changes through which the modern poem has come, we must first consider the general characteristics of Somali poetry as a whole.

The Nature of Traditional Pastoralist Poetry

As previously stated, it is the traditional poetry of the pastoral nomad which contributed the most to the structure of modern Somali poetry. For this reason, we shall confine our statements to this type of traditional Somali poetry. Although less is known about the structure of poetry among the other main groups in Somalia, three important characteristics link the modern poem to the northerner's poetry: its form, its dialect, and its historical origin.[31]

For the most part, the form of the modern poem has been inherited from the traditional poetry of the pastoralist, and its dialect is from the same source. Furthermore, the modern poem has developed only since about 1948, and its origin in northern Somalia can easily be traced. The main feature which separates it from traditional pastoralist poetry, its musical setting, is borrowed not from any of the other traditional segments of Somali society, but from abroad. Its remaining characteristics are, as we shall see, the results of its own development in time.

We have considered the social setting from which the modern poem arose, and we shall later view its historical background in each of its periods of development. But if an adequate examination of the modern poem is to be made, its structural heritage must also be described, and it is in an examination of the pastoralist, traditional poetry that this structural heritage can be found.

The alliteration of traditional Somali poetry,[32] its poetic diction,[33] and its linguistic background[34] have all been adequately covered by Andrzejewski and Lewis (1964). Duplication of these topics is not necessary here. Most of the genres also have been well described, except for one group which shall be referred to in this book as the Family of Miniature Genres.[35] This group, which includes the genres of *wiglo*, *dhaanto*, *hirwo*, and *belwo*, is covered in detail in Chapters 2 and 3.

Somalis make a sharp distinction between poetry and prose. Differentiated from prose by its alliteration, among other distinctions, poetry is by far the more important form of literature to the Somali, and scholars, both foreign and indigenous, have concentrated most of their work on the poetry. Investigations into the social functions of the folk narrative remain to the scholar of some future date.[36] Although we are unable to assess the importance of prose in Somali literature, it remains quite evident that poetry is the most important medium of artistic expression. Even one type of proverb (*maahmaah*), which also plays an important role in Somali society,[37] is structured in verse.[38] Many social activities require poetry. At festivals and weddings, for example, one can hear a cantor and chorus chanting a special genre called *hees-cayaareed* ("dance-song") to which a crowd of youths will dance. Work is often done to the rhythm of poetry, and, as with the pounding of grain by women or the watering of camels and livestock by men, labor is lightened and paced by the chanting of verse.

In more serious situations, such as the relating of history by a clan elder, one also finds poetry occupying an important role. As the elder recites the history in prose, he intersperses his narrative with classical poems, or more frequently quotations from poems relevant to the plot. These poems will have been composed by the men involved in the period of history being related and are used as a proof or illustration of the reciter's version of the story. Likewise, historical recitation is sometimes used only to give the background to the chanting of a specific poem.

Traditional poems have played an important role in the actual unfolding of history on the Horn of Africa. Uprisings as well as peace have been pleaded for in verse.[39] Aside from his genius as a warrior and as a sheikh of Islam, the Sayid Maxamed Cabdille Xasan (the so-called Mad Mullah of Somaliland) was also a great poet.[40] At least one historian has recognized the value that the Sayid's poetic talent had for his movement.[41]

One of the Sayid's assistants (and the man who succeeded him as leader of the Dervishes for a short time after Maxamed's death) was entrusted with the duty of memorizing Maxamed Cabdille's poetry during his lifetime. Xuseyn Diiqle could be called upon for the appropriate poem whenever a political situation arose that required verse. In fact Xuseyn embodies the important Somali distinction between poet and reciter, which will be discussed later. But why was such a memorizer necessary when so many Somalis, the Sayid included, had a good command of Arabic script and could have devised a writing system for transcribing Somali poetry?[42] The answer to this question lies in the oral nature of Somali poetry.

Although Somalis have been exposed to writing through their religion since around the thirteenth century when historians believe Islam came to the Horn, they did not adopt writing for their own language until the early 1970s.[43] Everyone attending Koranic school learns at least some Arabic script, but for reasons unknown to me, this exposure to writing has never exerted any successful pressure upon the Somalis to reduce their language to script. Such pressure has been reserved for the twentieth century.[44] The art of Somali poetry has, therefore, remained an oral art. Only as an image in a few poems can one discover that Somalis even think about writing. (See above, p. 7, line 54, and the two poems on p. 64.) The composition, transmission, and performance (and thus preservation) of poetry have all been accomplished orally and without the resulting influence of pen and ink or printing press. Let us consider these topics in detail.

In many oral cultures, composition and performance are accomplished simultaneously. Using an elaborate set of formulae and with a number of years of study and practice behind him, the poet is able to compose his poem as he performs it.[45] This is not the case in Somalia. Somali poets rarely perform their work until composition is completely finished in private.[46] Few poets indeed—and the Sayid Maxamed Cabdille was one of these exceptions—were able to compose while performing. This is owing to the high degree of public criticism, probably caused by two factors. First, there are so many poets in Somalia, and second, almost every adult male is to some degree acquainted with the art of poetry.[47]

One may consider the transmission of oral poetry on two different levels: how poems are dispersed in space, and how they are dispersed in time. The spatial dispersion of oral poetry among the pastoralist must be considered within the context of a nomadic society. Pastoralist camps moving from place to place, travellers, men searching for new grazing areas, and the gathering of clans on festive occasions all lead to the dispersion of poetry from mouth to ear. In modern times, the radio and trade truck have added to the more traditional methods of dispersion, and the tape recorder is also used in the transmission of poetry; but, with the radio, this machine is more important for the modern poem, as we shall later see.[48]

The transmission of oral poetry in time is accomplished in the manner of any tradition: from the old to the young, from generation to generation. Poems of great popularity may last for several generations, while others will die with those in whose memories they are stored. The preservation of any one specific poem depends upon its being continuously performed, but first we must clarify one further point concerning transmission and then look to how the traditional poem is performed.

Because of the nature of composition in the Somali oral tradition (i. e., completion of composition before performance), and because of the prestige value of composing poems, Somalis are able to attribute any given poem to a specific poet. Thus the differentiation between poet and reciter is clearer than in some oral societies. Both positions are held separately in Somali society, and both carry their own prestige, though the poet is perhaps considered the more able. Some men have the ability to memorize vast amounts of poetry, as did Xuseyn Diiqle. Certainly the alliteration rule, scansion rules, and musical accompaniment greatly aid the reciter's memory.

There are several characteristics of the performance of traditional, pastoralist poetry which are basic to understanding the modern poem, as we shall later see. The classical genres, that is to say, those poems traditional Somalis consider highest in the rank of serious poetry and noble enough with which to discuss politics and important social considerations, are performed by and for men only. No musical instrument accompanies the recitation of these genres which can all be chanted. Indeed, only the women ever consistently used a musical instrument (a drum) to any important extent for traditional poetry in northern Somalia. The serious poem of the women (*buraam-bur*) is likewise performed by and for their sex only, but it should be pointed out that both sexes are acquainted with each other's poetry and often listen to it when chance permits.

Like the classical poetry, work songs tend to be segregated, for the work of the men and women keeps them separated most of the time. Here a cantor and chorus are often heard, chanting to the rhythm of the particular work being performed. Other forms of verse are less segregated. Dance songs, though most often composed by men, are performed for the benefit of both sexes. Standing in a circle, the crowd takes the lines of the chorus, while one person chants in the role of the cantor. Two or three dancers (sometimes one is a woman) perform in the center. One also finds verse in children's games.

Like the topic of transmission, preservation can be understood on several levels. Will a particular poem survive? Will it survive in its original form? And more broadly, will traditional poetry itself survive?

Heretofore, if a poem in the oral tradition was to survive, it had to be continuously performed. Even if it were merely being taught by one person to another, it had to be performed verbally, as the language was not written. In this sense, its performance *was* its preservation and vice versa, thus being transmitted to others, as we have seen. The tape recorder, of course, changed all this, but its impact on traditional poetry has been minimal compared to its impact on the modern poem. In the traditional setting in which the tape recorder plays no role, preservation and performance are one and the same.

On another level, one might ask if traditional poems survive in their original forms. Again we are limited in our conclusions because of the lack of research into variation in traditional Somali poetry. The entire question of variation in oral poetry, the study of which contributes to the uncovering of structural points, has been reopened in recent years by such people as A. B. Lord and Ruth Finnegan, and can no longer be ignored by scholars.[49] Certainly Somalis will argue heatedly over the "purity" of the version of a poem, but this approach may be somewhat naïve.[50] To be sure, specific poems are attributed by reciters to specific poets whether or not they are preserved in an actual morpheme by morpheme version. Nothing can be conclusively said until the question of variation in Somali traditional poetry is formally researched.[51]

On the broader level of the survival of traditional poetry as a whole, even less can be said conclusively. Some Somali scholars express the fear that it is dying. This fear can also be found among many members of the new elite. Several Somalis are at present engaged in a frantic scramble to record as much of traditional poetry as they can before it "dies." Here again, this may reflect a misunderstanding into the nature of Somali oral poetry. The so-called death may be a characteristic of the oral process itself. Something had to precede the *gabay*, from which the *gabay* could develop. Culture and its characteristic attributes are dynamic and in a constant state of flux. If traditional poetry is dying (and certainly one cannot condemn anyone for recording as much of it as possible before it disappears), one thing remains absolutely certain: the art of composing oral poetry in Somalia is not about to die. If a specific poem, or even a genre, does die, the art of oral poetry goes on, and indeed is enjoying a renaissance today with the arrival and development of the modern oral poem.

The Historical Development of Modern Oral Poetry

With the social context of Somali society and the nature of traditional pastoralist poetry described as background, it remains to give the history of the evolution of modern poetry in Somalia. The discussion which follows is general; the topics of each subsection become the subjects of the chapters to follow, where the growth of modern poetry is described in greater detail.

THE FAMILY OF MINIATURE GENRES   The evolution of modern poetry in Somalia begins in the Family of Miniature Genres, and it is here that the history of modern poetry must begin. The members of this family, the *wiglo*, *dhaanto*, *hirwo*, and *belwo*, are light poems, primarily (but not always) concerned with love. Considered frivolous and the domain of youths, poems from this family were almost never employed for such "noble" topics as politics and social debates.

Aside from the *belwo*, the origins of these poems are not known. The latest revival of the *wiglo* and *dhaanto* occurred during the Dervish War of the Sayid Maxamed Cabdille Xasan, but none of the Somalis I interviewed believe that these genres were conceived during this period (1900-20). The *hirwo* is thought to have arisen during the Ethio-Italian War of 1935, but some Somalis say it is older than this. The origin of the *belwo*, on the other hand, is known, and because of its special connection with the modern poem, it must be given special attention.

THE BELWO (1943-48)   The *belwo*, the last poem to develop in the Family of Miniature Genres, differed from the other members of this family in several ways. Beginning in the society of the town dweller, but sharing most of the characteristics of its sister genres, the *belwo* was considered soon after its invention to be a member of the Family of Miniature Genres by Somalis themselves, as will be explained later (p. 27 ff.).

The distinguishing feature of the *belwo* was that, unlike its sister miniature poems, it did not remain static in structure. As a genre, the *belwo* remains alive to some extent today, but during the late 1940s it began to develop in a way that had not happened with the miniature genres before it. At first the *belwo* became a longer poem, and, although it

17

was not yet in the structural state of the modern poem, it had acquired the name *heello*. With this state of artistic metamorphosis, the first period of the *heello* began.

THE HEELLO: PERIOD ONE (1948-55)   The hallmark of the first period of the *heello* was rapid structural change. Before the modern poem emerged around 1948, a period of artistic metamorphosis took place with the *belwo*. Although the result of this change was not, strictly speaking, the modern poem, it had acquired the name of the new genre, the *heello*. For this reason, the interim form, which was to continue alongside the modern poem for a few years before it disappeared, belongs to the first period of the *heello*.

Taking its name from the introductory formula to the miniature poem (see pp. 32-33), this medial form, which shall be referred to as the *heello*, Form A, was characterized by the tacking on of one *belwo* after another into one long poem. The formula was often chanted between each *belwo*, now the stanzas of the poem, to make it even longer. This new "mega-miniature poem" (see pp. 76-77)—if so paradoxical a neologism may be employed—would sometimes include as many as fifteen or twenty *belwo*.[52]

Eventually the formula was eliminated from between the stanzas and individual melody was added to each poem of the genre as the restrictive genre melody of the *belwo* was abandoned (see pp. 28-29). Possibly a result of the addition of more and more musical instruments (tambourine, flute, lute, and violin) individual, albeit Somali, melody may also have come directly from another form of the *heello* which emerged at this time, and which shall be referred to as the *heello*, Form B. The *heello* A and B were to continue side by side for a while, but the B form eventually eclipsed the A, which later disappeared entirely.

To Somalis, the two forms of the *heello* were members of the same genre, for they each bore the same name. The *heello* B (also called *hees*, "song"), however, differed in several ways from the *heello* A, and to determine a model for it is not easy.[53]

Unlike the A form, the *heello* B was composed by a single poet (or group of poets at the same time). A long poem, it was possible to develop the theme to a greater extent than in the miniature and mega-miniature poems. By now a musical setting and an individual melody had become regular features, as had the device of line repeating. A refrain was also coming to be characteristic of the *heello* B, sometimes sung by a chorus, sometimes by

18

the soloist alone. Moreover, alliteration gradually became unified for the entire poem, though unity of each stanza was only required at first.

Along with the new characteristics of structure, a definite change in theme occurred with the *heello* B. Politics was becoming a topic of frequent occurrence alongside love. As we shall see presently, some of the features of the *heello* were inherited from the *belwo* and some from outside Somali society altogether. But it was from the classical pastoralist poetry that the theme of politics came, and women were being allowed to chant and sing poems in which politics were discussed, a privilege without precedent in the traditional setting of Somali poetry.

With the addition of politics as a theme for the new genre, and with the use of it on the newly established radio stations in both North and South, the *heello* became firmly established as an art form. The new elite began to employ the *heello* in the drive for independence, which was in an embryonic state at this time. Matters continued thus until early 1955, when a political event of major importance occurred, which was to ensure the future of the *heello*. With this event, the second period of the *heello* began.

THE HEELLO: PERIOD TWO (1955-60) In November 1954, the British government agreed to turn over a section of the British Somaliland Protectorate to Ethiopia for the second time in history. We shall cover this political situation in detail in Chapter 5, but suffice it to say here that the agreement between Britain and Ethiopia led to a political crisis on the Horn. Riots and protests resulted, and an even more intensive drive toward independence began. As a reaction to the boundary shift, three Somalis from Boorame, a town in northwestern Somalia, composed a poem which was to herald the beginning of the second period of development for the *heello*. With the coming of this poem, "Jowhariyo Luula" (see pp. 98-101), many Somalis recognize the beginning of a new period of the *heello*. Although they do not agree on why this otherwise ordinary and typical *heello* was different—indeed other Somalis see nothing new about it at all—two of my informants and several other Somalis with whom I spoke do agree that "Jowhariyo Luula" was the beginning of a new period of the modern poem.

What was so important for the artistic development of the modern poem was that the *heello*, and no longer just the classical poems, was being used in a political situation.

From 1955, scores of *heello* were composed, and more and more poets were becoming attracted to the new genre.

THE HEELLO: PERIOD THREE (1960-PRESENT)   The third period of the *heello*, which began with the independence of the modern Somali state, is marked by the latest structural innovations and the addition of new topics which had now matured. Although some poetry attacking the semiautonomous Somali administration in the south had been composed before independence, such political themes now became much more common in the fully independent state. Domestic politics concerning acts by the new government and political developments under it also became new themes in the *heello* of this period.

Together with political themes emerged one which had now ripened in the social scene. Poems on the role of women in the newly independent country appeared. Moreover, the scope of themes from which the *heello* could draw its text now seemed limitless. Football (soccer) could be found alongside local politics and the still popular theme of love. The problem of choosing an orthography for writing down the Somali language provided the text of several poems, as well as topics on international political developments, such as the death of Patrice Lumumba and the Berlin Wall.

This period also marks the definite eclipse of traditional poetry by the modern poem. Although the former continues today among traditional Somalis—and the *gabay* does not appear to have lost any prestige—the *heello* seems to be more popular among the new elite of the nation-state as well as among its town dwellers. By the time of independence, one could find young elite Somalis who could no longer remember any *gabay* they had heard, but they could recite many *heello*. The *heello* of this period had acquired a more elaborate style, but this refinement occurred gradually, throughout the whole of the developmental periods.

CHARACTERISTICS OF THE HEELLO: ALL PERIODS   The historical approach to the development of modern poetry in Somalia does not cover all of its characteristics. Some themes from the early days are to be found throughout all periods, and certain aspects of structure also cover the entire period of development. Moreover, the impact of media such as the radio and tape recorder also covers the whole of these periods.

NOTES

1. Note that the term "coastal merchant"is here used for convenience and does not fully describe the sort of culture the name represents. Both the coastal merchant and the town dweller societies have merchant classes, skilled artisans, and other types of workmen. The difference between these two groups is historical rather than cultural. (See note 5 below.)

2. Information on Somali dialects can be found in Andrzejewski 1971, pp. 271-73; Andrzejewski and Lewis 1964, pp. 37-38; and Muuse X. I. Galaal and Andrzejewski, 1956 p. 1.

3. In private conversation as well as in many speeches.

4. See Lewis 1957b.

5. For the pastoralist, see Lewis 1955 and 1961, and Lienhardt 1964; for the argicul-turalist, see Lewis 1955, 1961 and 1969, and Cerulli 1959; for the town dweller, see Lewis 1955, 1955/56, 1961, and 1965; for the coastal merchant, see Cerulli 1959 and Trimingham 1952 and 1964.

6. Somalis themselves have used the term *Dhallin Yarada* ("The Youth") as a term in their own language for the new elite. This term is probably derived from the name *Ururka Dhallin Yarada Soomaaliyeed* ("Somali Youth League"), the main political party in the country until October 1969.

7. It must be pointed out that the elite also enjoy the traditional forms of poetry. Moreover, the *heello* has penetrated traditional society to some degree.

8. Recent reports indicate that some of these idle university graduates have been conscripted by the revolutionary government to teach school in place of the U. S. Peace Corps volunteers, who were expelled from the country in December 1969.

9. *Gabay.* One of the three traditional poems—the *jiifto* and the *geeraar* are the other two—considered the best form of serious poetry in traditional pastoralist society. In this book we shall refer to these three forms as classical genres. For a description of these and other genres of Somali poetry, see Andrzejewski and Lewis 1964, pp. 46-52.

10. This *gabay* is from the unpublished collection of Muuse X. I. Galaal. It was originally translated by him and edited by me and Michael Cushman Walsh. For this book it was translated again through the process described in the Preface.

11. "Burn incense for herself." This refers to the practice of women perfuming themselves with incense. Incense is placed into a burner (*dab-qaad*, literally, "holder of fire") and allowed to permeate her clothing so that she will smell pleasantly in the presence of her husband.

12. Young clansmen often come to a wife who has not been married into a clan for very long and put her to severe verbal tests on behalf of their clan. In traditional Somali society, the clan as a whole plays a part in the choice of women for its common good. Choosing a wife is not always left entirely to the individual.

13. *Rumayga*. "Tooth brush." A small stick used in cleaning the teeth by vigorously rubbing the teeth and gums.

14. "Eyeshadow." Somali women use a small silver bottle (*indha-kuul*) which holds eyeshadow (also called *indha-kuul*). The applicator, with eyeshadow on the end, is placed under the eyelid and moved back and forth until the eyeshadow has been applied to the entire eyelid.

15. "Antechamber." The area just outside the entrance of the portable nomadic hut (*aqal*). Fine mats are laid when guests come to visit. Tea is served and an animal is sometimes slain for the guests to eat.

16. "Bed-chamber." A special section for sleeping inside the hut, separated from the rest of the "rooms" by matting walls.

17. *Uurka*. "Emotion"; literally "stomach." One of the metaphorical seats of emotion in Somali poetry. See pp. 199-200.

18. The exact implication of this line is not understood by me. Presumably it means away from the smell of the animals.

19   *Reer Ugaas-Magan*. Subsection of the Daarood Ogaadeen, Reer Cabdille, the clan of the poet.

20. "Noble men." Literally "male camels." This is a metaphor of great politeness. The *awr* are the biggest, strongest males in the herd. They are used for breeding because of their fine quality. *Awr* also means male camel in general.

21. *Bah-Xawaadle*. Further subsection of the poet's clan.

22. Throughout this and other texts in this book, the following abbreviations will be used: M (male), F (female), C (chorus), and T (together).

23. *Nebigii*. "The Prophet [Aadan]," Adam, the first man created by God in Moslem theology. Lines 1 and 2 imply that the best of all women was Xawo (or Xawa, or Xaawa, from Arabic *Hawa* , "Eve").

24. *Reer.* "Dwelling place"; literally "family (smallest social unit)/married man/ camp," i. e., the Garden of Eden.

25. One of the traditional versions of the account of the fall of Adam and Eve told in Somalia. Satan took Eve to a stream while they were yet in Paradise. He told Eve that Adam had taken another woman. Eve did not believe Satan, but he said he would show her the woman. He commanded her to look into the stream, which she did. Seeing her own reflection, she thought she had seen the other woman. Eve asked the devil to prove what she had seen. He told her to return to Adam and tell him what she had seen. Then he commanded her to tell him to eat of the Tree of Life. If he refused to eat, it would mean that he loved the other woman; if he consented, it would mean that the reflection was false. Eve then went to Adam and did what was commanded of her by Satan. Adam, of course, ate of the fruit, and the two were exiled from Paradise forever.

26. *Dabka.* "Fire," i.e., conflicts. Somalis often express the belief that because of what Eve did, womanhood has been cursed, causing women to remain forever trouble-some to men on earth.

27. *Shaafici.* From Arabic, Shāfici, "Intercessor," a panegyric epithet applied to the Prophet Muḥammed and to some major Sufi saints. Here it is applied to the Prophet Muḥammed.

28. *Sayid Cali.* Somali equivalent of the Arabic forms *Sayyid cAli bin Abū Ṭālib*, the son-in-law and paternal cousin of the Prophet Muḥammed. Some Somalis claim that they are direct descendants of this great warrior and poet.

29. *Abu Jahal.* Somali equivalent of the Arabic forms *Abū Jahl*, one of the Meccan leaders who opposed the Prophet Muḥammed and was killed in the battle of Badr (A. D. 623). He was of the same clan as the Prophet. The poet uses the story of Abū Jahl as an allegorical analogy with women. Abū Jahl dragged down his followers by his infidelity, and they were destroyed. Eve dragged down Adam by her infidelity, and they were cast out of Paradise.

30. Note that in the original lines 61-74, a sequence of dependent clauses has been amended in translation to facilitate reading.

31. Research into the poetry of the other segments of Somali culture is far more limi-ted than that for the pastoralist. Preliminary research by Andrzejewski has revealed, however, that the poetry of the agriculturalist and the coastal merchant

does not differ drastically from that of the pastoralist and follows identical rules of alliteration.

32. Andrzejewski and Lewis 1964, pp. 42-43.

33. Ibid., pp. 43- 44.

34. Ibid., pp. 33-38.

35. All the names of the genres in this group are Somali. The term "miniature," however, is borrowed from Andrzejewski, 1967. Assigning this name to the group as a whole is my own innovation.

36. One collection of untranslated Somali stories has been done by Muuse X. I. Galaal and is entitled *Hikmad Soomaali* (ed. B. W. Andrzejewski. See Bibliography), but this work contains no data on the place of the folktale in Somali society. Some of these stories, as well as additional ones, have been translated by B. W. Andrzejewski 1964, but here again, there are no data given on their function in society.

37. For a discussion on the role of the proverb in Somali society, see Andrzejewski 1968.

38. The technical distinction between the poetic proverb (*maahmaah*) and the prosaic proverb (*odhaah*) is that of the Somali scholar Muuse X. I. Galaal. The general public in Somalia use these terms synonymously.

39. For a plea for peace, see the poem on pp. 128-34 of Andrzejewski and Lewis 1964.

40. Some of the Sayid's poetry can be found in Andrzejewski and Lewis 1964, pp. 66-102 and 150-51. Two Somali scholars have collected a vast amount of the Sayid's poetry which they have transcribed, but not translated, into English, and not published. These scholars are Muuse X. I. Galaal and Axmed Cali Abokor. Sheekh Jaamac Cumar Aw Ciisa (1974) and Yaasiin Cismaan Keenadiid (1984) have published large collections of the Sayid's poetry.

41. Hess 1968, especially pp. 104-07.

42. It might be mentioned in passing that some Somali scholars, notably Muuse X. I. Galaal, have pointed out that the Sayid in fact attempted to transcribe his poetry using the Arabic script. These scholars claim that he abandoned his attempts when he was unable to utilize the vowel system of the script. The Arabic script has only three vowel characters and three diacritical vowel symbols, and the latter are normally left out in letters, newspapers, and books, except in some theological works and elementary schoolbooks. Such symbolization is completely inadequate

for the Somali vowel system, and there is strong resistance in Somalia to the use of any additional symbols which were devised to augment the Arabic script. The Sayid did transcribe some of his poetry, but only that composed in the Arabic language. See Andrzejewski and Lewis 1964, pp. 150-51 and 161.

43. Trimingham 1952.

44. Although several scripts of Latin and Arabic extraction, as well as some which have been invented especially for Somali (Cismaaniya, Gadabuursi—see Lewis 1957a—a script invented by a former Somali District Commissioner of Baydhabo) have been and are presently being used by small groups of Somalis, none of these scripts has ever exerted any influence on the composition of oral poetry.

45. For a detailed discussion on the use of formulae as a means of composing oral poetry, see Lord 1960.

46. Andrzejewski and Lewis 1964, p. 45.

47. Ibid.

48. Ibid.

49. See Lord 1960, and Finnegan 1970.

50. Andrzejewski and Lewis 1964, p. 46.

51. This question has now been researched, at least to some degree. See Johnson (1980).

52. Laurence 1954, p. 7.

53. The fact that this genre has two names is due to its musical setting. The terms *heello* (based on the introductory formula for the miniature poem) and *hees* (based on the musical setting) are used interchangeably. I have chosen to employ the term *heello*, because this name emphasizes the historical background of the modern poem. Furthermore, the term *heello* is used more commonly than the term *hees* by the Somalis themselves.

2

THE FAMILY OF MINIATURE GENRES

The Nature of the Family of Miniature Genres

The present chapter will attempt to give the artistic background to the arrival of the *belwo* specifically and the *heello* in general. Moreover, it will also deal with some genres not covered in Andrzejewski and Lewis (1964), and will hopefully fill a gap in the study of Somali poetry as a whole.

The *wiglo*, the *dhaanto*, the *hirwo*, and the *belwo* are the four genres that make up the Family of Miniature Genres.[1] The names of these genres and the classifications of specific poems in a particular genre are Somali. The grouping of the four into one family, however, is my own innovation. Three characteristics of these genres justify such a grouping.[2]

To begin with, Somalis themselves claim that each miniature poem gave rise to the next one historically. Second, the structure of the poems of these genres serves not only to differentiate each genre from the next and from other types of Somali poetry, but also to group the four together. And third, the similar use of these genres in Somali society provides further evidence that together they constitute a larger division of Somali poetry. Let us further consider these three points separately.

There are of course no indigenous documents to aid the scholar in uncovering the origins of these genres. Moreover, little reference is made to them in works by foreign scholars, who have concentrated most of their efforts on genres having greater prestige in Somali society. Our conclusions here are based, therefore, on the oral history of poetic art believed to be true in Somali culture.

The origin of the *belwo* is the only genre that Somalis know about and agree upon; it will be covered in the following chapter. Of the remaining three, only the origin of the *hirwo* can be accounted for, and not all Somalis agree on this. Some believe the *hirwo* first appeared during the Ethio-Italian War of 1935-36, while others believe the genre is much older. In the midst of this confusion—this claim and counter claim—one opinion is agreed upon by all: the *wiglo* is the oldest and the *belwo* the most recent.

An important historical characteristic of these genres, and one which cannot be omitted from this book, is their popularity during periods of social stress Although its origin is unknown, the most recent revival of the *wiglo*, for example, was during the early years of the Dervish War of the Sayid Maxamed Cabdille Xasan. The *dhaanto*, its origin, like the *wiglo*, in an unknown past, was revived during the last years of the Dervish Movement. And the *hirwo*, if it did not actually arise during the Italian conquest of Ethiopia in which some Somali groups participated, was at least revived during this period. The *belwo*, arising and spreading in the social upheaval after World War II, also represents a period of storm and stress.

At present we shall deal critically with the structure of the miniature poem and give examples of its characteristics. What is needed here is a résumé of these characteristics to illustrate the grouping of the several genres into one family of Somali poetry.

As the name of the family implies, the miniature poem is short. Its usual length is from two to four lines, though single line poems have been composed as well as ones with six, eight, or even more lines. The *dhaanto* is sometimes found to be very long indeed when it is employed for religious purposes.[3] Usually, however, it is short, as are its sister genres. The length of the miniature poem also exerts an influence upon the type of poetic language possible in its verse. As we shall see, a complete poetic statement must be made in the most concise manner possible, a task which not only demands special skill, but also limits the poet in the development of a theme. Length also exerts an influence on the imagery of the poem, most of which is taken from pastoralism. This does not, however, eliminate images taken from modern phenomena.

Another important characteristic to be considered in drawing these genres together is the themes employed in their texts. By far the most common theme is private, individual love. Panegyric naming (see pp. 42-43) is employed to a high degree of development by all these genres.

The generic name of the modern poem, the *heello*, later to develop from the *belwo*, also comes from this family. The introductory formula (see pp. 32-33) is used with all four genres, although the *wiglo* and *belwo* may use their own formulae.

Finally we come to the key characteristic which joins the four genres into one group and differentiates each specific genre from the next: the melodies to which they are sung. There are two points to be clarified here. First, there are a limited number of melodies to which a poem in any given genre can be recited. Any *wiglo*, for example, can be recited to any of the melodies set aside for its genre, but not to any of the other melodies used for the *dhaanto*, *hirwo*, or *belwo*. This leads us to the second point. It is the melody to which a poem is sung which denotes the genre. This characteristic melody, and not any linguistic or prosodic rule, differentiates the genres within the family.[4]

This being the hypothesis, it should then hold that any one poem—despite its original melody (i. e., genre classification)—could be sung to the melodies of the other three genres. This is precisely the experiment I carried out successfully. One informant was able to take a miniature poem and with it demonstrate the characteristic melodies of all four genres.[5]

We have seen how history and structure contribute to the grouping of these four genres into one family; but how does their similar use in Somali society contribute to this grouping?

The miniature poem does not share the exalted status of classical or even modern poetry. It is employed most often by youth in circumstances where youth are to be found. The themes, however, are not always frivolous; nor is the miniature poem always composed by youths. There are many situations in which the recitation of such poetry is considered appropriate, but our interest remains with the modern poem. The following compilation of the uses of miniature poetry is, then, by no means definitive; it is only presented to give a general picture of where and when the miniature poem is used.

One important use of miniature poetry is with the dance.[6] Groups of youths standing in a circle will all join in with hand clapping while one man chants the poem and (usually) two people dance. Sometimes women are included in this activity.

Somalis enjoy challenging each other to poetic duels, and the miniature poem, like many genres of Somali poetry, is used in this verbal game.[7] The poet of the *hirwo* below presents his challenge as a riddle:[8]

> Waxaan hadhin hawlna Kuu qabanoo,
> Hortiina na jooga, soo heda eey.[9]

> That which will not leave you, [nor] do [anything] useful for you,
> And which remains [always] before you: find out [what it is].

and was answered by another *hirwo* with the same alliteration:

> War waxaan hadhin hawlna Kuu qabanoo,
> Hortaada na joogaa, waa hooseey.

> O man, that which will not leave you, [nor] do [anything] useful for you,
> And which remains [always] before you, is [your] shadow.

The Sayid Maxamed Cabdille Xasan employed the miniature poem to attract recruits to his Dervish Movement. One of his compositions, a *wiglo*, was used as a sort of recruiting poem for attracting followers:

> Ninkii diinta Eebbahay dhigan
> Dadaal ku dhintaa ye waa daw,
> Ninkii dabka qaatee duulee,
> Dagaal ku dhintaa ye waa daw,
> Anigu dadka waxaan la yaabaa
> Oo hadda na doqonnimo ku saaraa,
> Ninkii duunyo kaleeto foofsadayee,
> Ku daaqsada doobka caanaha eey.

> The man who learns the religion of God
> And dies with hard work, is honorable.
> The man who takes up weapons[10] for fighting
> And dies in battle, is honorable.
> But [of all] people, the one who surprises me,
> And whom I accuse of foolishness,
> Is the man who cares for another's animals, and
> Receives a vessel full of milk [as his reward].[11]

The practice of looking after another man's livestock was done by the poor in the Sayid's day, and it was to these people that he appealed in the poem. The implication here is that it is foolish to have servile employment when one could become rich by looting the camels of the enemies of the Dervishes.

As we stated earlier, the *wiglo* and the *dhaanto* had been revived during the Dervish movement in Somalia. Like the *geeraar*, it is said that the *dhaanto* was sometimes sung on horseback,[12] and some, no doubt, were, like the following pair, used to raise the *esprit de corps* of warriors:

> Hooy Jidlaanu nahoo ma joogi karree,   (*repeats*)
> Allow jidka roobka noo mariyeey,   (*repeats*)

> Hey you, we are the Jidle[13] who cannot wait [for battle];   (*repeats*)
> O Allah, let it rain for us on the way.[14]   (*repeats*)

And:

> Naa haddii raggu duulo, raar ma galoo,   (*repeats*)
> Hooy, dagaal-ramataanu leennahayey!   (*repeats*)

> Hey you, when men go [to battle], they do not enter the recesses [of a
>   house];[15]   (*repeats*)
> Hey you, we are fond of battle!   (*repeats*)

Somali men of religion often object to the use of the miniature poem, and we shall cover this point in more detail later.[16] Their objection to the miniature poem led one Islamic leader, Sheekh Caaqib Cabdullaahi Jaamac of Jigjiga, to employ the *dhaanto* as a means of attracting the youthful ear.[17] By speaking in their own language, as it were, he was able to deliver his serious message in the midst of a dance, and to retain the attention of most of those present. Ironically, the text of his dhaanto-sermon called for youths to abandon the *dhaanto* and turn their activities toward God. Sheekh Caaqib has used the *dhaanto* for other religious poetry, including a prayer for rain (*roobdoon*).[18]

The miniature poem has also been used in recent times by lorry drivers and passengers on lorries to lighten the tedium of tiresome journeys.[19] Indeed, this practice was important in the spatial dispersion of the miniature poem, especially the *belwo*. Finally, at religious festivals and national holiday gatherings, one could hear genres from this family.

But at such social meetings, then as now, many other genres could be heard.

History, structure, and usage, then, serve to unite these four genres (including the *belwo* which is covered in the next chapter) into one larger group, distinct from the rest of Somali poetry. As we shall see in Chapter 4, the modern poem could be said to have begun historically as the fifth miniature poem, for in its early stages it too shared the above characteristics.

—

The Poetry of the Miniature Family

We have attempted to show that the four genres classified as the Family of Miniature Genres belong together in a single unit. One argument used to determine this was to compare their structures. But another reason exists for examining these structures, one perhaps more important for us since the modern poem is our chief concern. The *heello* might be said to have begun as the fifth miniature poem, or mega-miniature poem, as we have called it. The following discussion deals with the structure of the miniature poem, both from the point of view of form and content. The dialect in which such poetry is composed, as well as the device of alliterating the entire poem with only one sound, are the same as other traditional pastoralist poetry. The remaining characteristics of the miniature poem have been broken down and discussed in greater detail. We begin our discussion where the poem begins—with the introductory formula.

Several genres in Somali poetry are introduced by a series of rhythmic syllables which serve as an introduction to the poem following them. The miniature poem is introduced by this formula:

> Heelloy, heellelloy,
> Heelloy, heellelloy,

or by its longer version:

> Heelloy, heellelloy,
> Heelloy, heellelloy,
> Heellelli kalaynu leenahayeey.

O heello, O heellello,

O heello, O heellello,

[And] we sing[20] [yet] another heellello.

This formula, the short version of which is more common with the miniature poem, serves at least three functions. First, it summons the attention of an audience to the poet, who then goes on to sing his poem. Second, it focuses the listeners' attention on the poet's verse so that the first line of the poem itself is not missed. Otherwise, the point may be lost, for in some cases the first line represents fifty percent of the entire poem. The third purpose might be described as a sort of signature tune.[21] It must be pointed out that the use of this formula extends to other genres, notably the *hees-cayaareed*, "dance-song." Furthermore, the *wiglo* and *belwo* have their own introductory formulae which they may employ even though they often use the "heelloy" formula. If this formula does not announce the specific genre to come, as does the one used with the gabay, it at least announces the general type of poem to follow. "Heelloy, heellelloy" heralds a light poem, often to be used with the dance, more often still with a theme centered around love.

Like many features of Somali poetry, the origin of this formula is lost in the haze of the past. Its meaning is also gone; unlike the early introductory formula of the *belwo* (see below, p. 59), its etymology cannot be determined. The oldest mention of the term known to my informant is found in a poem composed by Yoonis Tuug (Yoonis, "the Thief"),whose great grandchildren are alive today.[22] This would make the formula at least four generations old, but it is probably even older.

Poetic devices used in the miniature poem do not differ drastically from several other genres of Somali poetry. The method of alliteration (see p. 23, note 31), for instance, is the same as with most traditional poetry. Furthermore, the imagery of the miniature poem, like most genres, is closely tied to the pastoralist way of life. A few modern images inevitably creep into the more recent poems. This is not difficult to understand; what is unusual about the modern poem, as we shall later see, is that modern images are not more common with it. The proportion is about the same as with the miniature poem.

Another device of poetic diction common to most genres is the hidden message.[23]

Lovers send word to each other of secret rendezvous in poetic codes. Thieves tell each other what to steal through concealed messages in poems. The colonial administration, as well as the Somali government, are criticized in the verse of the modern poem, as we shall later see. One form of this concealed diction was examined in the last section, where the poetic challenge was presented in the form of a riddle.

Two devices, however, are unique to the miniature poem: concise language and panegyric naming. The size of the miniature poem understandably influences its language, necessitating the most concise method of expressing a complete thought. The panegyric naming of women, although it occurs in a few other genres, is most fully developed in the miniature family.

Alliteration needs no further elucidation, but the other devices outlined above require exemplification.

The images illustrated in the poems below occur frequently in the poems I collected. Understandably, not as many *wiglo*, *dhaanto*, and *hirwo* are remembered as *belwo*. For this reason, I was able to collect many more *belwo* than poems of the other three genres.

During the long dry season in Somalia water is so scarce that domesticated animals often die. Even men have been known to die of thirst during this harsh time of year. The earth becomes so parched that in some places it resembles a vast ocean of potato chips. Only a few trees offer solace and shade from the scorching, glaring sun, and the northern plain visibly supports only the yellow grass of *jiilaal*, the dry season.

When rain finally falls, it is not just a necessary substance for the renewal of life on the desert. It is a symbol for that life. Indeed, it becomes the mother of all positive symbols in Somali poetry as metaphoric extension expands its semantic sphere. Rain is "the source of all virtue,"[24] victory in strife, happiness, and many other things as well. Without rain there is no milk, for the camels literally dry up. Milk is also a symbol for life,[25] for it satisfies hunger as well as thirst.[26] When the poet of the following *wiglo* sings of milk, he is talking about much more than its physical substance:

> Hadday Dhudi caano ii dhibtooy,
> Intaan dhamo sow ma dhaafeen?

> If Dhudi[27] gives me milk, and
> I drink [thereof], how can I leave her?

She has given him much more than milk; she has given him life itself.

When poets sing of their love, they more commonly equate it with illness. Love is a sickness, a malady not as serious as death, but still an affliction. This poet speaks of illness in his *wiglo*, but the Somali audience knows he speaks of love:

> Markaan bukay way bariidin jirtee,
> Badbaado u geeya, Beer-Nugul.

> When I was ill, she used to wish me well;
> [Now] take [my] blessing[28] on to her, [to] Gentle-Heart.[29]

The poet is saying that his lover always returned his love, even before she fell in love with him. He loved her (was ill) for a while before she learned to love him (fell ill and came in need of his blessing).

The tree is one of several images in Somali poetry which has more than one possible interpretation. Sometimes it is a metaphor for a woman's beauty, for it is tall and straight, like young Somali women. It can also be a symbol for Somali customary law (*xeer*), for it is in the shade of a tree that elders meet to hold court. At still other times, the tree is used in an individualistic manner and must be interpreted in the context of the poem, as in the following *wiglo*:

> Adduunyadu waa ul geed sudhan e,
> Abaal ma uu dhigatay aakhiro eey.

> The world is a dead branch[30] hanging on a tree:
> Have you put anything for yourself in the next world?

In this poem, the tree is a precarious foundation for the world. At any moment the wind or some other disaster could topple the world into oblivion. The poet asks the listener if he is prepared for death.

Along with specific objects, Somalis use situations as images, and they often choose a situation from the nomadic way of life, as in the following *hirwo*:

Sidii reer degoon,

Dab Loo shidin,

Xalaan dilaalyooday eey.

I—[who am] like the family which has just encamped

And for whom a fire has not [yet] been lit—

Felt the cold of last night.

When a family group (*reer*) finishes the move of the camp from one site to another (*geeddi*), everyone is hungry, cold, and exhausted. This poet compares himself to a camp (or family head of that camp) at the end of a move. To be without his lover is to be cold and at the end of his nerves.

In many poems, domesticated animals are used as images. But wild animals are also popular, especially the lion. In the following *dhaanto*, the roar of the lion symbolizes the grief of longing for one's beloved:

Naa, libaax laba jeenni dhiig darayoo,

Hooy, bad-weyn ka jibaadayaan ahayee.

O woman, I am the lion who puts his front paws into blood,

And roars [as loudly as] the ocean [in storm].[31]

The ocean is an area some Somalis know quite well, for many have been sailors in the world's merchant marines. Somalis have sailed the seas for longer than anyone can remember.[32] Accordingly, the ship is also used as an image in poetry, as in this *wiglo*:

Sidii markab maanyo soo maray eey,

Wax baa iiga muuqday meel-dheer ey.

Like a ship passing over the sea,

Someone appeared to me in a far distant place .

The sailor-poet who was visiting a distant land caught a passing vision of his love, like a ship passing from afar.

There are other nonnomadic images in Somali poems, some quite new to the Somali scene. Three have been chosen here to illustrate how imported or foreign machines have made their way into the imagery of the miniature poem.

Light is an image for truth, wisdom, and, more recently, education. In the following *hirwo*, light from automobile lamps is used to symbolize the wisdom of a woman who illuminates the path in the midst of darkness:

> Fatoorad La fuulay fiidkii yoo,
> Faynuus fanka Loo sudhaad tahay.

> A car being driven in the early evening
> With a lamp hanging from its front, are you.

Unlike the lorry, which was almost immediately useful to Somalis, their first contact with an airplane was during a bombing raid. The Sayid Maxamed Cabdille Xasan was finally driven away from his fort at Taleex in northern Somalia when airplanes were called in by the British from Aden to bomb it. One can understand the concern expressed in the following *dhaanto*:

> Dayuurad duushaa La sheegaa yee,
> Allow, dalka roobka noo mari yeey!

> It is said that airplanes [actually] fly;
> O God, send rain for us [in our] land!

The poet cries for rain, here a symbol of deliverance from the drought or horror of flying machines.

Finally, the motorcycle, perhaps the last of the three machines to reach Somalia, has also become an image in the miniature poem, as in this *dhaanto*:

Sidii dhugdhugley, dhul dheer mari baa,
Dhawaaqayga Loo dhegaystaa.

Like a motorcycle, travelling far away,
My clamor can be heard.

In the Somali bush, far from the large cities of the world where many sounds mingle, one can hear for miles around. An approaching motorcycle or trade truck can be heard far in advance of its arrival. The poet compares the sound of a motorcycle to his cries of grief that can be heard for many miles.

Imagery in the miniature poem is usually universally understood in Somalia (like rain and milk) or can be determined from context (like the tree in the poem on p. 35 above). Sometimes, however, an image can carry a double or hidden meaning. This device is common enough in Somali poetry to be treated separately.

The hidden message as a device in Somali oral literature is not unique to the miniature family. Indeed, it is not unique to the poetry, for it can be found in folktales as well. As the name of this device implies, what is involved is the passing of a message from one person (or group) to another in such a way as to prevent a third party from understanding or suspecting. To accomplish this the poet must employ images which seem to imply one point to the third party but which pass the oral message on to the person for whom it is intended. This is no easy task, and the less universal or unified the metaphors are in the poem, the more suspect is the poet. The hidden message is used in a variety of situations and for a number of reasons. Lovers "speak" to each other using this device. Sometimes the third party is a husband, as we shall see in the example below; sometimes he is a girl's father. But often it is merely the community in general from whose gossip the lovers wish to conceal their feelings. The hidden mes-sage has also been employed to conceal political messages. Poets often address the entire Somali nation. The third party was sometimes the colonial administration and sometimes the independent Somali government in Muqdisho. It is obviously more difficult to compose hidden messages against the Somali government, for the third party, like the second, is Somali and therefore understands the system from which the imagery is taken. But there is yet another function of the hidden message which might be described as the aesthetic enjoyment of the Somali audience. Poems with hidden messages are often recited inside folk narratives. Whether or not such tales are true or apocryphal is really irrelevant, for their purpose is to entertain. We shall illustrate such a story below.[33]

It is said that a man once loved a woman who was already married. One night he arranged for a rendezvous with her. Waiting for a long time at the appointed place, the man became restless when she failed to appear. So he went to a place nearby her compound and chanted this wiglo to her:

Caweeya, Cawooy, Caweeya, Bullooy,
Ciddliinu cawaysiin dheeraay ey.

O Caweeya, [my] Cawo, O Caweeya, [my] Bullo,[34]
Oh, how long is the rest period[35] of your people!

Hearing her beloved chant this message, she chanted another *wiglo* to him, pretending to sing to her cow [a very clever act to the Somali audience, for it is with poems addressed to domesticated animals that panegyric naming also occurs]. The woman was actually addressing herself.

Dabeeti libaaxle Dhiin-Gorayow,
Ninkii dhaqay dhayda Loo badiyay.
O Dhiin-Gorayo[36] which has the tail of a lion,
[Your] plentiful fresh milk is for the man who raised [you].

The man who raised the cow, the woman's husband, had returned unexpectedly to the compound and now overheard both *wiglo*. Suspecting the truth, the husband countered with yet a third *wiglo*:

War belaayo rag baan u baaliday oo,
Birtay nimay gaadhdhay baan ma lahee!

O man, I am experienced in the conflicts of noble men;
There is no treatment for the man whom my steel reaches!

The woman's lover then departed from her compound and perhaps
from her life.

The following *wiglo* was used to arrange a rendezvous:

Naa haddaan docda soo harraatiyo,
'Doddoo' dhehoo dabar la soo bood.

O woman, [tonight] when I kick the side [of your hut],
You [must] say 'doddoo' and jump up with a *dabar*.

The woman sleeps in an area near the front of the *aqal*, or portable nomadic hut. It is here where the fire is kept and where the poet plans to kick. Camels often kick the *aqal* at night, for it is located inside the camel corral. The animals are brought inside at night to protect them from wild beasts. *Doddoo* (or *dudduz*) is a nonsense word used to make a camel be still. A *dabar* is a hobbling rope or leather strap used to bind together the front legs of a domesticated animal to prevent his running away. The poet plans to act like a camel, kicking the front of the aqal. When the woman hears this, she is to slip out of *aqal* on the pretense of having to do a domestic chore, hopefully unsuspected by her husband, who will go back to sleep. The hidden message thus delivers the maximum amount of information with the minimum number of morphemes, since those involved can fill in between the lines and make inferences as to the true meaning of the verse. This use of concise language is, in a broader sense, common to all miniature poems and is a general characteristic of their diction. In longer poems poets are capable of developing a theme to a much greater extent. The diction of the genres in the miniature family is influenced by the size of the poem, for a complete thought must be expressed in only a few words. What B. W. Andrzejewski says of the *belwo* seems to me to apply to all the genres in this family:[37]

. . . in two lines, or even one, the poet had to work out a complete and
rounded utterance which would please a discriminating public used to the

appreciation of poetry and delighting in the deciphering of the poet's message.

In some cases the poet is able to lengthen his poem by what he implies rather than by what he says in the text. In the following hirwo this device can be clearly observed:

> Hadduu cirku cuurcuuraa yoo,
> Caashaay ma calaama roob baa ye?

> When the sky is overcast:
> O Caasha, is [this] a sign of rain?

Clouds sometimes bring rain and sometimes blot out the sun. The poet here employs both meanings and implies: O Caasha, does this mean that you love me? (rain); or, O Caasha, are you (the sun) cut off from me? Sometimes the connection between the lines of a miniature poem is not clearly observable upon first hearing them. One is forced to connect them by thinking beyond the words of the verse, thus lengthening the poem in a sense. The above poem, like those on pp. 35 and 37, is of this sort.

The use of concise language is perhaps most dramatically demonstrated with the poetic challenge, including the form in which a riddle is presented. We have seen a poem of this type (and its answer) on pp. 29-30, and shall consider more of them in Chapter 3 (see pp. 57-58). In the case of the challenge or riddle, the vague language must be understood and answered in yet another poem. The best answer to a challenge is, moreover, delivered with the same alliteration.

Another device which shares at least one thing in common with concise language is that of panegyric naming (praise-names). In this case, praising women by inventing elaborate names expands the implications of the poem beyond the mere words of the text. Such a technique occurs in other genres of traditional poetry, but this device is most fully developed for the praise of women in the miniature family.[38]

Panegyric naming is also employed for purposes other than elevating the female. Camels and other domesticated animals are given elaborate names in other genres. Infants are also endowed with praise names by mothers who prefer to keep these special names for their children secret in some cases.

Still another genre in which panegyric names occur is the modern poem, and here, as with the miniature poem, they are used to praise women. This device in the modern poem was clearly inherited from the Family of Miniature Genres.

There are two main functions of praise-names for women. First, they praise some attribute the poet wishes to bestow upon his love. Second, they conceal the identity of the poet's lover, so that angry kinsmen are not given cause for pursuing the poet. In reality the poet does not always have a specific woman in mind every time he composes a poem. Some panegyric names are merely chosen for their alliterative sounds; but others, as the one in the following *dhaanto*, are chosen because they bear a relationship to the imagery of the poem:

> Intaan Dahabooy, Ku daawan lahaa,
> Miyuu dayixii daruur galay?

> O Dahabo, [once] when I would have enjoyed the sight of you,
> Did the moon [not] go behind[39] a cloud?

Dahabo is a panegyric name which means "the Golden One,"^ a color often assumed by the moon, especially when it is near the horizon. The poet implies by the second line: "Are you (Dahabo) taken from my sight (perhaps by your family)?" Dahabo, like many panegyric names, is also a girl's name in society. It, like many regular Somali names, functions as a panegyric name as well, but many praise names are found only in verse. The following is a list of examples taken from the *wiglo*, *dhaanto*, and *hirwo* in my collection:

1. *Beer-Nugul*. 'The Tender/Sensitive One' (i.e., She-Whose-Bosom-Is-Tender/Sensitive).
2. *Caweeya*. 'She-Who-Was-Born-in-the-Calm-of-the-Rest-Period].' This is the part of the late evening before the animals are milked and everyone goes to bed.
3. *Cawo*. 'The Lucky One.'
4. *Bullo*. 'She-Who-Is-of-the-Color-of-the-Best-of-Horses.' Horses are the most prized of all animals among the traditional Somalis. Indeed, the Sayid

Maxamed Cabdille Xasan even entombed one of his favorite horses at Taleex when it died. They are prized even above the camel, which is considered the wealth of the nomad, while sheep and goats are considered subsistence. The color referred to is chocolate (or red, as Somalis see it), the skin color most praised in Somali aesthetics.

5. *Dhudi.* 'The-Tall-and-Slender-Tree.' This is a metaphor for beauty; tallness and straightness of body are considered very beautiful.

6. *Indha-Yar* . 'Little-Eyes.'

7. *Rubbo.* 'The Coin.' From the Indian coin (*rupee*), the first currency used by the British in the Somaliland Protectorate

8. *Geelo.* 'The Wealthy One.' From the Somali word *geel*, "camel." Camels are considered wealth by the nomads.

9. *Hani.* 'The-One-Who-Deserves-Praise.'

10. *Macaan.* 'The Sweet One.'

11. *Qaaxa-Yar.* 'The-One-with-the-Small-Neck.'

12. *Qoor-Dheer.* 'The-One-with-the-Long-Neck.'

13. *Liqanyo* (or *Laqanyo*). 'The-One-Who-Saturates-Those-about-Her.'

14. *Asli.* 'The Original One,' or 'The-One-of-Ancient-Descent.' (From Arabic *asl*, "origin/root/source/cause/lineage.")

15. *Maandeeq.* 'The-One-Who-Satisfies-the-Mind.'

The list goes on, and we shall encounter many more panegyric names with the belwo and heello.

Although there is no radical difference between the themes of the *belwo* and those of her sister genres, the present discussion is confined to the first three genres, as the *belwo* is treated separately in the next chapter. All but one of the themes in the poems I was able to collect have been given as examples of the characteristics of structure in our discussion thus far. Rather than repeat these examples, we have placed their page numbers in brackets after the themes as they are presented. The following survey covers my entire collection, but the page references refer only to the poems used as examples in this book.

Of the fifty poems I was able to collect in the genres of *wiglo*, *dhaanto*, and *hirwo*, twenty-nine of them (over half) are on the topic of love (p. 34, p. 35 [top], p. 36 [middle],

p. 36 [bottom], p. 37 [top], p. 40 [middle], p. 42), including laments of lovesick poets (p. 36 [middle], p. 38, p. 39 [top]. The use of love as the most common theme in the genre was to be inherited by the modern poem, and it is necessary to point out that the rest of the themes in our collection do not necessarily illustrate a balanced survey of the miniature family. We are fairly safe, however, in declaring that love is the most common theme.

Of the remaining poems, six are concerned with the theme of the dance and five deal with military themes in one way or another (p. 30 [bottom], p. 31 [two poems]). Three are reproofs (pp. 39-40, and three are philosophical (p. 39 [middle]). Four themes have one example each: a plea to God (p. 37 [bottom]), a poetic challenge (p. 29), and its answer (p. 30 [top]), and a poem in praise of two villages.

Between the years 1943 and 1945, when the *belwo* first appeared in the society of the town dweller in northern Somalia, it was this background from the pastoralist, then, that it inherited, these artistic characteristics that it received with which to operate. But what has been presented as background here only helps to answer questions concerning the structure which the *belwo* was to acquire. Why did the *belwo* appear when it did and what exactly were the characteristics of its structure that differed from the usual features of the miniature poem? Before these questions can be approached, we must first examine the historical background, including the changes in the social and political scene in the British Somaliland Protectorate in the early 1940s.

NOTES

1. The Somali scholar Muuse X. I. Galaal includes the *baalbaal* (or *dheel*) in this family. Limited research on this genre prevents any further comment on this from me, but one thing is certain. The four genres studied in this book are the most important ones, and they are recognized by the majority of those I interviewed to be in this family.

2. Conclusions in this part of the book were drawn for the most part from interviews with Somali poets and scholars. (See Preface.)

3. For the text of a long *dhaanto*, see Andrzejewski 1970. It might be pointed out that the religious use of the *dhaanto* is not common and is marginal to the main trend of the genre. In the source mentioned above, the poem is composed on the "string of pearls" principle, i. e., each line (or stanza) is a unit connected by a sequence of alliterations based on the letters of the Arabic alphabet.

4. For a general discussion on how genres are differentiated in Somali poetry, see Andrzejewski and Lewis 1964, p. 46.

5. It is interesting to note that, although I was not aware of it at the time I carried out my experiment, B. W. Andrzejewski had done the same experiment about fifteen years earlier with another informant and had reached the same conclusions.

6. It should be pointed out that a special genre also exists for the dance. Entitled *hees-cayaareed*, "dance-song," it is perhaps more commonly used with the dance than is the miniature poem.

7. See Andrzejewski and Muuse X. I. Galaal 1963.

8. In order to save space, and because it is the same each time, the introductory formula has been omitted before the poems in this book. See pp. 32-33 for a full description of the introductory formula.

9. Line division in this book is based on the musical delivery of the poem. In the poem on p. 30, for example, lines 2, 4, 6, and 8 share an identical musical delivery, relative to their differing syllable counts. Likewise, lines 3, 5, and 7 are relatively the same. Only the first half of the first line is different when sung by some Somalis. Other Somalis will sing the first line as 3, 5, and 7. With the miniature poem, the problem of line division was easy to solve, for this rule holds with all the miniature poetry, whatever the genre or melody. With the *heello*, however,

line division, also based on the musical delivery, is more complicated, for each poem has its own melody. In this case, each poem was treated separately, since no overall pattern exists.

10. *Dabka.* "The weapons"; literally, "the fire."

11. Such labor was usually paid with one animal per year's work, plus an allowance for the daily sustenance of the bachelor.

12. See Andrzejewski and Lewis 1964, p. 49.

13. *Jidle.* Name of a Somali clan.

14. Rain is a Somali symbol for life, prosperity, and success. This line implies: "O God, give us the victory."

15. I. E., [or of a woman]. Men are not permitted to lie with their wives when they are mobilized for battle.

16. See Chapter 3, pp. 58-59.

17. A short biographical sketch of this Sheikh is given in Andrzejewski 1969.

18. See Andrzejewski 1969.

19. See Andrzejewski 1967, p. 12.

20. *Leenahay.* "Sing/chant"; literally, "say/possess."

21. We now know that the introductory formula also sets the characteristic prosody for the genre.

22. It should be pointed out that Yoonis's nickname need not necessarily mean that he was a thief. He may have got this name from behavior in his childhood when many nicknames are given.

23. See Andrzejewski and Muuse X. I. Galaal 1966.

24. Muuse X. I. Galaal 1968, p. 14.

25. Ibid.

26. Indeed during some parts of the year milk alone comprises the diet of many camel herders.

27. *Dhudi.* Panegyric name. See p. 43, number 5.

28. *Badbaado.* "Blessing"; literally "safety."

29. *Beer Nugul.* Panegyric name. See p. 42, number 1.

30. *Ul.* "Dead branch"; literally "stick."

31. Note that there are two possible translations of this line, the more likely of which appears in the text. The other possible interpretation might read as follows: "And roars [from the coast of] the ocean."

32. There are many communities of Somalis, mostly made up of sailors, in several areas of the world. Cardiff in Wales, for example, supports a population of approximately 3,000 Somali immigrants.

33. It should be pointed out that I had to paraphrase this story, because it was not collected in its authentic context. The poetry, being more conservative in form than the prose, has not, however, been paraphrased. I understand that the usual method of delivery is for the reciter to tell the story with the poems appearing in the body of the recitation, as I have done here.

34. Panegyric names. See p. 42, numbers 2, 3, and 4.

35. *Cawaysiinka.* "The rest period." The period of time in the evening when the animals have been rounded up, but before they are milked.

36. *Dhiin-Gorayo.* Panegyric name. *Dhiin* is the reddish purple color of a cow. *Gorayo* is an ostrich. The feeling for this color is the same as for the panegyric name *Bullo* (see p. 42, number 4). The ostrich is prized for its soft feathers, which at one time were sought on the world market. The use here refers to the softness of the hair of the person to whom the panegyric name is directed.

37. See Andrzejewski 1967, p. 7.

38. Most notably in the *gabay* of Cilmi Bowndheri (see Mohamed Farah Abdillahi and Andrzejewski, 1967).

39. *Gal.* "Go behind"; literally "enter."

3

THE EMERGENCE OF THE *BELWO*

The Historical Background

As a distinct and separate genre the *belwo* first appeared in Somali society in the town of Boorame between the years 1943 and 1945. It spread rapidly, and by 1954 it had completely permeated the British Somaliland Protectorate. Margaret Laurence remarks in her book, *A Tree for Poverty*, that the "belwo and gabei appear to be the most popular types [of genres] at the present time."[1]

Unlike its sister genres, the *belwo* first appeared in the society of the town dweller, though the form and content of the new genre remained almost identical to the other miniature poems. In fact the *belwo* could be considered as a cultural link between the pastoralist and the town dweller, and it was inside urban life that the new elite of Somalia arose and developed. Also unlike its sister genres, the *belwo* did not remain frozen in its structure but began to change soon after its emergence.

But why did the *belwo* change when other genres in the Family of Miniature Genres remained stable? Before this question can be answered, the social and political setting of the Protectorate during these periods must be considered. The period discussed below, 1943-55, parallels both the period of the *belwo* and the first period of the *heello*.

Before 1941 the British had done little to develop their Somaliland Protectorate. In this year, however, they regained control of the area by defeating the Italians, who had conquered it in August of the previous year. British administration in the past had been carried out from Berbera, and Somalis had little contact with their colonial rulers. Their daily lives were much the same as they had been before colonialism. There were reasons for this in both the British and Somali camps.

First, British interest in Somaliland had been minimal. Worried about foreign powers which might endanger her interests in East Africa and India, Britain wanted Somalia for its strategic position. The British were especially worried about the French. Also, Somali livestock was needed to feed Britain's important refuelling station in Aden.[2]

The Somali livestock rearing, which was more than sufficient to feed Aden, needed no development. Furthermore, the British were unwilling to put more money into the Protectorate after the long war with the Dervishes of the so-called Mad Mullah, in which they had "spent so much on military operations so completely out of proportion to their interests in Somaliland."[3]

Second, the Somali population was unwilling to accept British interference in its traditional way of life and was extremely suspicious of any colonial activity during the uneasy peace just after the Dervish War. Twice the administration attempted to establish education, and twice it was rebuffed with riots, both times in the town of Burco. The first riot occurred in the early 1920s, when, having been refused funds from the government in London, the administration attempted to collect a tax in order to finance its education plans. This resulted in the death of the British district commissioner in Burco. Again in the mid 1930s riots over education claimed the lives of three Somalis.[4] Having been exposed to foreign educators before by the priests of the Catholic mission in Berbera (closed by the administration in 1910), the Moslem Somalis were extremely suspicious of any attempts at reintroducing education into their country. No further efforts were made until after the British Military Administration was established in 1941.

In 1940, the state of northern Somalia, indeed of all Somalia, began to change rapidly, and this change was not to be quelled by traditional society as it had been in the 20s and 30s. Beginning in such areas as colonial administration and education, the big change in Somalia was to spread rapidly through the urban societies of the North. It was in this new atmosphere of change that the *belwo* began its period of change, culminating, as we shall later see, in the first period of the *heello*.

In August the Italians drove the British off the Horn and occupied the Protectorate. Seven months later the reverse occurred, and with British reoccupation, "the old care and maintenance policy of the past [was] abandoned in favor of more progressive policies."[5] To begin this new era the administrative capital was moved from Berbera to Hargeysa. No longer were the colonial rulers to be spectators in Somaliland; now they were to take an active role in Somali internal affairs, and for the first time were to establish the agencies which would carry the Protectorate to independence in 1960.

Experiments with radio broadcasting began shortly after reoccupation in 1941, and Radio Kudu was established in 1943 with a 100 watt transmitter.[6] In the following year a mobile cinema, operated by the Department of Education headed by C. R. V. Bell, was carrying films to the towns of the North, and the radio transmitter was strengthened to 600 watts. Receiving centers equipped with loudspeakers were established in several places which were to become popular gathering sites. In the evening crowds of Somalis assembled at these centers, listening to the news broadcast in Somali (edited from B. B. C. releases), spreading the local news of the day and enjoying the facilities for games and pastimes especially provided for them. Somalis began to hear their colonial overlords speak of "freedom and the right of all peoples to choose the form of government under which they were to live."[7] The "peoples," of course, were those in Hitler-dominated Europe. They also began to hear new forms of art, particularly songs which would exert a heavy influence on the musical setting of the *heello*. Moreover, the radio, at this time new to Somalia, was to become one of the major devices for the spatial dispersion of modern poetry. Later, the combination of radio, modern poetry, and the feeling of freedom to choose one's own form of government gave impetus to the drive toward independence.

The radio station, renamed Radio Hargeysa in 1944, gradually increased its transmission power from 1 kilowatt in 1945 to 5 in 1957; in 1955 it installed receiving equipment for foreign (B. B. C.) broadcasts which were relayed by the station. With the invention of the transistor, radios spread to Somali-owned tea shops and private individuals. The radio was used by the administration to spread propaganda for its activities.

Among these activities was the renewed attempt to establish education. The work of C. R. V. Bell in this field had not been in vain, for World War II had its effect on the Somalis and "there was now appreciably less hostility to secular progress and social change."[8] In 1945 seven elementary schools were operating. By 1950 two intermediate schools had been established, and in 1952 a nurses' school for girls in Hargeysa as well as a vocational training center in Boorame were founded. In the following year a girls' school in Burco and a secondary school in Sheekh were set up. This was followed in 1954 by the establishment of a standing committee on education and the appointment of a Somali education officer.[9] Progress had not been completely smooth. Somali as well as expatriate teachers had been stoned in public,[10] but the progress was not to be halted again as it had been in the 20s and 30s.

Other activities which brought the Somalis and the British into closer contact occurred in the field of agriculture. Development here was greatly needed, for the war had made the import of foodstuffs difficult. By 1950 experiments in new crops and fertilizers had been carried out, and a number of small state plantations were operating. Grazing control schemes, to be of great use to future Somalia, had also been put into effect.[11] Programs of this nature violate traditional Somali nomadic beliefs, and attempts to carry out such schemes in later years after independence were met with opposition.

As one might imagine, increased political activity also resulted from the war. Political clubs had existed in the Protectorate since 1933,[12] and by 1946 many of them had joined with the Somali National Society, an organization founded by Somalis to encourage modern education and progress. The resulting organization, called the Somali National League, was the first real political party in the Protectorate.

Like other changes of this period, political activity did not progress without incident. Despite riots in Hargeysa in 1947, the administration did not oppose political development.[13] Indeed, it had encouraged such development in the South during the war from fear of the large Italian population in that part of the country.[14]

Together with party development came the beginnings of self rule. In 1945 and 1946 township committees and town planning boards were set up in several places. In July of 1946, the Protectorate Advisory Council, presided over by Governor Sir Gerald Fisher, convened for its first meeting in Hargeysa to discuss the progress of the Protectorate.[15]

Not to be omitted from the political development of this period were the border changes which saw the Horn gradually regain her prewar political boundaries. With the defeat of Italy in 1941, the British Military Administration had gained control of all the territory inhabited by Somalis, with the exception of French Somaliland. In 1948 the Ogaadeen, the main area of Ethiopia where Somalis live, was turned over to the Ethiopian government. A part of this area (the Hawd and Reserved Area), where the Somali clans under British protection migrated seasonally, was retained by the Protectorate government, now returned to civil authority under the governor, Sir Gerald Reece. In 1950 the former Italian colony was handed over to Italy as a United Nations trusteeship. The border change which most affected the political life of the Protectorate, as well as the artistic development there, occurred in 1955, when the Hawd and Reserved Area were given to Ethiopia. This date is a convenient and not at all arbitrary one for marking the beginning of the second period of the *heello* in Somalia. But this is to jump too far in advance.

By the time the British had turned over its control of the Hawd and Reserved Area to Ethiopia in January of 1955, northern Somalia had changed greatly. Somali nomadic life was much the same as it had been throughout the colonial period; but for the new elite and townspeople of Somalia, things were different. As Touval states:[16]

> But for the sedentary part of the population, their way of life
> as well as their social and political concepts [had] changed
> because of the development of commerce and industry, the
> growth of government bureaucracy, and the spread of a cash
> economy. Social dislocations resulting from such change [had]
> been a stimulant to political activity.

And to this can be added, "had been a stimulant to artistic activity." It was upon this new and greatly changed scene in the life of northern Somalia that modern poetry appeared and developed.

The *Belwo* is Born

Let us now turn to the beginning of the *belwo*, the immediate predecessor of the *heello*, and to its inventor. It may be remembered that one of the characteristics of the miniature poem was its use particularly in times of stress. It is not surprising, then, that the *belwo* appeared in the early 1940s.

The *belwo* (also called *balwo*) was the invention of a Somali poet named Cabdi Deeqsi, who was in the subsection Reer Nuur of the Gadabuursi branch of the Dir Clan Family.[17] This subsection lives in and around the town of Boorame, west of Hargeysa in northwestern Somalia.

Cabdi Deeqsi was born in a section of the Boorame area named Jaarraa-Horato, where he spent most of his youth. Unlike the overwhelming majority of Somali poets, he was never a camel boy in the Somali bush, living in the traditional manner; rather Cabdi Deeqsi was a town dweller from the beginning. Early in his manhood he went to Jabuuti in French Somaliland where he learned something about lorry mechanics as a helper/apprentice. Returning to Boorame in about 1941, he was employed as a lorry driver/mechanic by a wealthy merchant named Xaaji Xirsi. By now Cabdi had passed his thirtieth birthday and had acquired the nickname Sinimo, "Cinema." He was a first rate teller of stories and jokes, and because of his habit of acting out his stories, the nickname seemed to fit him very well. His outgoing personality made him very popular, especially among the youth.

Cabdi's trade route took him from Seylac and Jabuuti to Boorame and Hargeysa and sometimes even as far away as Dirir Dhabe in Ethiopia. One day, sometime between 1943 and 1945, his lorry broke down in the bush. Somali oral tradition debates the whereabouts of this incident. Some say it occurred in a place called Habaas, others say in Ban Balcad; while still others claim the place was Selel, on the plain of Geryaad, thirty miles south of Seylac. Wherever it was, Cabdi could not determine what was wrong with the lorry and was unable to repair it. Finally, after much frustrating work, he sat down, and, as the Somali poet Xasan Sheekh Muumin states, "These words escaped from his mouth:"

> Belwooy, belwooy, hoy belwooy,
> Waxa i baleeyay mooyaane.
>
> Belwooy, belwooy, hoy belwooy,[18]
> I am unaware of what caused me to suffer.

The following variation is also sometimes quoted as the first *belwo* by some Somalis:

> Balwooy, hoy balwooy,
> Waxa i balweeyay mooyaane,
> Waxa i balweeyay baabuur e.
>
> Balwooy, hoy balwooy,
> I am unaware of what caused me to suffer;
> What caused me to suffer was a lorry.

When Cabdi returned to Boorame after having his lorry towed back to Seylac, he recited his short poem in public. It was an immediate success which, no doubt, inspired him to compose other *belwo*.[19] Other poets followed suit and began to compose in the new genre, and it soon spread rapidly.

Poetic ability is a major device for raising one's status among Somalis, and poems always gain prestige for their composers, at least from some segment of the population. So it was for Cabdi who, like so many poets of past Somali history, quickly became a social magnet. People would come to his house in the evening to sit and listen to him sing his poems to the rhythm of a drum made from an empty petrol tin. Very soon a corps of supporters was established and people from other towns began to come to Boorame to hear Cabdi's poetry. With more and more reinforcement and prestige as well as financial support from his supporters, Cabdi soon resigned from his work with Xaaji Xirsi in order to devote all his time to the belwo.

As had happened in the past, a small company of artists was formed around Cabdi, including a girl named Khadiija Ciya Dharaar who was soon nicknamed Khadiija "Belwo." Among Cabdi's supporters, Khadiija and three others are best remembered, for their names appear in the texts of *belwo*. They are: Xaaji Axmed Naalleeye, the interpreter for a Mr. Lawrence, the British district commissioner of the Boorame area during this period; a man called Beergeel, who was the agent of Cali Ibraahin Nuur, a merchant in Aden; and a man called Barre, who was the district commissioner's driver. Many Somalis remember the following *belwo* which has become one of the most famous of all Cabdi's poems:

> Belwooy, belwooy, hoy belwooy,
> Haddii quruxdaada Layga qarshooy,
> Khadiija Belwooy, qac baan odhan.

> Belwooy, belwooy, hoy belwooy,
> O woman, if your beauty were hidden from me,
> O Khadiija Belwo, I [would] break [in two].

Khadiija herself composed the other two *belwo* in which the names of these supporters appear:

> Balwooy, hoy balwooy,
> Waxa i balweeyay mooyaane,

Barre iyo boyga Loorens iyo,
Waxa i balweeyay Beergeel.

Balwooy, hoy balwooy,
I am unaware of what caused me to suffer;
Barre, the Servant of Lawrence, and
Beergeel are those who caused me to suffer.

And:

Balwooy, hoy balwooy,
Wuxuu Ingiriis ka xoogsaday,
Iyo xoolihii,
Ma ka saaray Xaajigii ?

Balwooy, hoy balwooy,
What he earned from the English,
And [his] wealth:
Have I [not] taken it [all] from the Xaaji [Axmed]?

By 1946 the members of the company who were least bound to duties in Boorame began to tour other towns in the North.[20] Hargeysa was their first stop. There public performances were held in which Cabdi would sing his *belwo*, and the troupe, especially the women, would dance.[21] These performances brought prestige and money to the company. In order to entice contributions from the crowd, Khadiija would sing one of her compositions:

Balwooy, hoy balwooy,
Balwadii barannoo,
Ku baas-noqonnay e,
Bakhshiishna ma ka helaynaa?

Balwooy, hoy balwooy,
We have learned the *belwo*

56

And we have mastered it:

Shall we [not] receive a reward for it?

Touring continued, and in 1948 the company went to Jigjiga. By 1950, however, it had fallen apart, and Cabdi left the Protectorate to live once again in Jabuuti. Except for short visits to Boorame, he remained in Jabuuti until his death in that city on 19 March 1967. Khadiija left the Protectorate in 1952 to marry a Saudi Arabian. Until she died in 1962, she lived in and around Mecca.

Even before Cabdi left the Protectorate, his genre had been adopted by artists and poets in Hargeysa. This was to prove very important for its development, for as pointed out earlier, Hargeysa had become the center of the political and social change which was gradually growing stronger in the Protectorate at this time. The spirit in which this adoption took place can be seen in the following *belwo*, one of the first to come from a Hargeysa poet:

Belwooy, belwooy, hoy belwooy,

Waxa i baleeyay Boorame eey.

Belwooy, belwooy, hoy belwooy,

What caused me to suffer was Boorame.

True to Somali tradition, this parody was accepted by the poets of Boorame as a poetic challenge.[22] Immediately answers were forthcoming, such as:

Belwooy, belwooy, hoy belwooy,

Waxa i baleeyay beer-geeleey.

Belwooy, belwooy, hoy belwooy,

What caused me to suffer was [the one who eats] the liver of camels.[23]

And :

Belwooy, belwooy, hoy belwooy
Belwadii baxsatoo bari bay qabatee,
Baabuur ma ku baadi doonnahayeey?
Belwooy, belwooy, hoy belwooy,
The *belwo* escaped and went to the East;[24]
Shall we search for it in a lorry?[25]

Hargeysa offered an even more important contribution to the dispersion of the *belwo*: the radio. *Belwo* were a regular part of radio programming almost from the beginning of broadcasting in Somalia and offered a convenient filler between programs because they were short.[26] Although opposed by more religious Somalis, the *belwo* received a somewhat formal acceptance among the new elite, as one can witness by its use on the wireless station. No doubt this helped the *belwo* to spread and be accepted more rapidly by the urban populations of the North. But the radio, as we shall see in Chapter 7, played a larger role with the *heello*.

It was pointed out earlier that social changes during this period, especially in the field of education, were not accomplished without some difficulty from the more conservative elements in Somali society. The opposition, however, was unsuccessful in halting the progress of development begun and encouraged by the British administration.

Paralleling this resistance to social change was a resistance to the *belwo*. The miniature poem had been, indeed still is today, opposed by many religious leaders and the more conservative elders of Somali clans. The *dhaanto* and *hirwo* had been formally challenged by sheikhs since their creation in earlier times, for they had been linked with mixed, public dancing. A well-known Somali proverb illustrates this opposition:

Sacabka haddaan xeeladi ku jirin,
Maxaa habeenkii Loo tumaa?

If there is no trick in dancing and singing,
Then why do they do it [only] at night?

"They" are Somali youth, and the trick referred to in the proverb implies such irreligious practices as illicit sexual behavior.[27]

At best the *belwo* was considered to be composed only by the young and frivolous. Older Somalis considered its composition as an unskilled craft.[28] But stronger opposition than verbal protest is attested in the early days of the *belwo*. The religious leaders and elders of Boorame at one point refused to allow the fathers of Cabdi Sinimo and Khadiija Belwo to enter the mosque they usually attended for prayer. In so doing these elders hoped to put pressure on the fathers of the young singers so that their "immoral" poetry could be stopped. Despite such opposition, however, the *belwo* was not to be halted. It continued to spread and develop.

It might be pointed out that religious opposition to the miniature and modern poems still exists in Somalia today, especially when ambiguous lines with sexual overtones make up part of the poem. Protest letters against modern poetry have been received at the offices of the broadcasting stations of Radio Muqdisho and Radio Hargeysa.

The Poetry of the *Belwo*

Most of the poetry of the *belwo* has already been covered in the preceding chapter, for the *belwo* is a miniature poem. Topics such as the hidden message, concise language, and panegyric naming apply to the *belwo* as well as the *wiglo, dhaanto,* and *hirwo* and shall not be repeated here. The imagery and themes of the *belwo* given below are presented to illustrate the genre. One feature, however, did at first differ from the miniature poem: the introductory formula. The function of the introductory formula of the *belwo* is the same as for the miniature poem in general (see above, pp. 32-33). The text, however, is different. This formula, *Belwooy, (belwooy), hoy belwooy,* was used only with the *belwo,* although the general formula was later employed in its stead. Unlike the general formula, the meaning of the term used in the *belwo's* formula is known. Borrowed from the Arabic *bala÷,* "affliction/trouble/trial," the word has a meaning in Somali which could be translated as "Woe is me!" Some Somalis I interviewed claimed that the *belwo's* formula was discarded because of its mournful overtones. "Woe is me," they said, is not always appropriate to introduce poems about love.[29]

As the overwhelming majority of *belwo* are concerned with the theme of love, so the overwhelming number of images in the *belwo* are traditional. Although the genre was a new work of art from Cabdi Sinimo's experience, "a work of art is not simply the embodiment of experience but the latest work of art in a series of such works; it is . . . a poem 'determined' so far as it is determined at all, by literary tradition and convention."[30] Some images, however, were new. Following is a resume of the images used in the poems in my collection.

It was many a poet indeed who viewed the condition of love negatively. The following poets saw it as a disease:

> Cishqigu maaha cuud La dhaqdee,
> Waa cudur ka bilaabma curuqyada.

> Love is not incense to be used sparingly;
> 'Tis a disease which begins in the joints.

Or an illness:

> Anigoo buka baahidaada iyo,
> Ku baal-maray beerku may gozay?

> Whilst I was ill with the need of you,
> I passed you by; did [my] liver break?[31]

Some poets saw love as a special sort of insanity, as in this *belwo*:

> Maankiyo maddaxaa i kala maqanoo,
> Idinna waygu maadsanaysaan.

> My mind and my head are apart,
> And all of you make fun of me!

Somali poets also agreed about what happened to a man when this dread disease of love came over him. One common ailment was the lack of balance, as in this poem:

> Labiyo toban jeer baa Lay lumiyoo,
> Liicliicay luggooyadaan qabo.

> Twelve times I have been led astray.[32]
> I stagger [off balance because of] the trouble I endure.

And of keeping one's foot firmly on the ground, as in this *belwo*:

> Cirkoo igu ciiray, caban maayee,
> Culayska i saaran ciirciiroo,
> Caguu qaban waaye, ciidda dhulkoo,
> Cawo-darnaan baan ku ciirsaday.

> If the sky leaned on me, I would not [make] complaint:
> I have swayed side to side from the weight put on me;
> And my feet failed to rest firmly on the sand of the earth.
> I have leaned on bad luck.

And in this one:

> Sidaan u dhammaaba, Lay dhufayoo,
> Cirkiyo dhulka, meel dhexdooda ah oon,
> Dhannaba jirin baan dhacdhacayaa.

> My whole self has been lifted up
> Somewhere into a place 'twixt sky and earth,
> Which is not of either; I stagger and I sway.

Another common malady poets of the *belwo* agreed upon was the sleeplessness of the man in love, as exhibited in this verse:

Ma seexdoo hurdadaan ka selelaayoo,
I saaqdayoo way i sidataa.

I [can] not sleep and am awak'd from rest;
She touched me deep' and carries me [away].

It is common to find references to various types of plant life in Somali poetry, and here the *belwo* is no exception. The tree, for example, is a common image. In the *belwo* the tree functions in the same way as it does in the miniature poem in general (see above, p. 35). The following *belwo* exhibits the use of the tree in this genre:

Sidii baxrasaaf ku yaalla bustaan,
Ayuun baad hadba ii bidhdhaantaa.

Like a eucalyptus tree growing in a garden,
You always appear to me from a distant place.

The contrast between the dry and wet seasons on the Horn of Africa is quite significant. When the rains come, the apparently dead bush comes suddenly to life and clumps of yellow grass turn green. This change in the bush is used to symbolize the beauty of women:

Cagaarka ka baxay, caleen-weyniyo,
Cosobaan cidi daaqin baad tahay.

The growing buds and leaves mature,
The fresh and ungrazed grass are you.

And with the rain come the flowers of the desert, another source of metaphor for beauty among the *belwo* poets:

Haddaad ubax tahay, mid aad u urtoo,
Udgoon badan baad ahaan layd.

Were you a blossom: one that smelled so [sweet],
You'd be [a bloom] that had abundant scents.

In some *belwo* one can find images which refer to traditional social practices. The following poem alludes to brideprice, which is a payment made by the groom's kinsmen to the family of his bride-to-be:

Sooryiyo kama bixinin geel sidig oo,
Haddii aan seexdo Laygu simi maayoo,
Samirku waxba iima soo sido.

I have not paid either brideprice[33] or *sidig* camels.[34]
If I sleep, [then her kinsmen] will not pause.[35]
For me patience will not be rewarding!

One might suspect that, because the imagery in Somali poetry can be so easily classified, variation in this poetry is greatly limited. This is not the case; but in facing the problem of variation, the key lies not in the addition of new imagery but in how the poet uses the imagery available to him. The manipulation of the set stock of images, rather than the addition of new ones, is how variation in this poetry is accomplished. New images were not, however, banned from the *belwo*. A few made their way into the new genre, as did the tractor in the following poem:

Billaahi cagafyahay caawaan Ku baryayey,
Cagtaadan ballaadhan e culusiyo,
Codkaagu maxay daweeyaan?

O tractor [mine], tonight I beg of you, in the name of God!
This wide and heavy tire of yours,
And your [chugging] voice: what use are they to me?!

Here the poet expresses impatience with his vehicle which he finds too slow to take him to his lover.

And finally, Somalis had been exposed to writing from Arabia as well as from the British and the Italians, so the origin of images dealing with this topic cannot be easily determined. The use of writing as an image can be seen in this verse:

> Haddii aan qor is adhi,
> Qaraamka i galay,
> Kitaab Lagu qoro,
> Ma qaadeen.

> If I say to myself: "Write [about]
> The love which entered me,"
> The book which could be written
> Would not contain it all.

And in this one:

> Baddoo qad ah iyo dhirtoo qalimmo ah,
> Caleenta qoyan oo qardaas Laga dhigo,
> Haddii Lagu qoro qaraamka i galay,
> Malaa ways qalliqi lahaayeen.

> [If all] the sea were ink, and [all] the trees were pens,
> [If all] the leaves so green were changed to paper [thin] ,
> If thus the love which entered me were writ' with [all these things],
> Perhaps there would be [just] enough [to write my thoughts of love for
>   thee].

The overwhelmingly theme of the *belwo* is love,[36] but it is "mainly physical love, whereas a [traditional] gabei on the theme of love will place value on a woman's wit and thrift as well as her beauty."[37] Indeed, the feelings expressed in the *belwo* are those of individuals. The needs and desires of their clans had no place here. Love in the *belwo* was treated as it was in the other genres of miniature poetry.

Poets in love used the *belwo* to praise the girls they fancied, as in this poem:

Markaan Ku ag-maro, Ilwaad-Quruxeey,
Sidii ubaxaad udgoontahayee.

When I pass near to you, O You-Who-Are-Pleasing-to-the-Eyes,
You smell sweet like a blossom.

To praise their lovers, poets often referred to them as the perfect creation of God:

Qudhdhaydu ma jaclayn inaan Ku qasbee,
Qummaatigan Eebbe Kuu qoray iyo,
Waxay qaaday qaararkaa baxay.
Myself I did not want to make you [love me].
But the perfect way in which God sculpted you
And your matured limbs overwhelmed me.

And here:

Wuxuu qoray ruuxna Kaama qaado,
Oo qawadi maayo, qaybta i taal.

What He has shaped, no one will take from you;
I am not vexed with the share placed [here for] me.[38]

Many *belwo*, however, are composed as laments over unsuccessful love, like this one:

Cishqigu waa toddoba haddii La tirshoo,
Mid aan tegin taabka Lay saar.

If counted, there are seven kinds of love,
And one which will not go away was cast into my hands.

A common complaint of the broken-hearted poet is that no one sympathizes with him:

> Dhibtayda dadkaa ka dhuumanayow,
> Dhirtoo maqashaa i dhaafteenoo,
> Dhagaxyaa damqan laa dhibaatada.

> O you people who hid from my problem:[39]
> While the trees lend an ear, you passed me by;
> [Even] stones would sympathize with my plight.

Sometimes the source of the poet's ill fortune was another man:

> Nasiib-darridaa i nacasaysee,
> Noolaada adigiyo ninkaagu ba!

> Bad luck has made a fool of me;
> Long life to you and your husband!

But sometimes the poet struck back when he was rejected. Waiting for a girl to return his love was too much for the following poet. By the time she fell in love with him, he had become bitter:

> Markaan bukay waadigii bed-qabee,
> Bagay adigu na bestaa tahay.

> While I was ill, your state was good,
> Hurrah! Now you are seriously ill.

It is not difficult to understand the objections some religious leaders and more conservative Somalis had for the belwo when one examines *belwo* of the following sort:

> Anigu naag ma qabo,
> Oo ma qaadi karo,

> Ee ninkii mid qaba,
> Yaan ka qayb geli!

> I have no wife,
> And cannot take one.
> The man who has one:
> I'll share with him!

And:

> Aniyo Qamar,
> Yaa is ka qooqayna ee,
> Ninkii qabayow,
> Ha qoonsan!

> Qamar and I
> Are merely playing.
> O man who is married to her:
> Don't be suspicious!

Some of these illicit remarks were more subtle, as in this poem :

> Waxaanad helaynin,
> Ee aad handataa,
> Hahey! Hagardaamo weeyaan!

> What you will not find,
> And [yet] you strive to get:
> Hahey![40] 'Tis very distressing!

The implication of this poem concerns the enjoyment of a woman, not her love.[41]

The poetic challenge (see above, p. 29-30) was also employed with the *belwo*. Two challenges delivered to Cabdi Sinimo by unknown poets and answered by him serve as excellent examples of this theme as employed in the *belwo*. One poet challenged Cabdi with this:

> Waxaan La helaynin,
> Ha Laga hadho!

> What cannot be found:
> Let it be forgot!

And Cabdi replied with this:

> Sideen uga hadhaa,
> Anoon helin?

> How can I forget
> What I have not found?

What Cabdi had not yet found, of course, was love. Another poet delivered this to Cabdi:

> Hohey, hadal Lama dhammayn karo!

> Hohey,[42] speech can ne'er be completed!

And Cabdi countered with this:

> Hohey, hadal waa dhammaadaa yoo,
> Kolkaad dhimato ba, dhag weeyee!

> Hohey, speech will [surely] be completed:
> When you die, 'tis through!

Moslem religious belief worked its way into some *belwo*, like the following one:[43]

Wixii Ku helaa,
Ka hadal ma leh.

There is no cause to talk about
The things which happen to you.

Here the poet expressed belief in predestination. This poem was accepted as a challenge by another poet, and although the Islamic belief was not contradicted, the other poet approached the question with a different attitude:[44]

Wixii Ku helaa,
Ka hadal yeeshee,
Ilaahii Ku halqay,
Yaad ku hiiftaa!

There's cause to talk about
The things which happen to you.
['Twas] God created you—
You cast the blame on Him.

More modern philosophical themes are also expressed in the *belwo*, as can be seen in this poem:

Hohey, Lacageey wax kala haadshaay,
Ninkii haya way u hadashaa,
Hub bay noqotaa hannaan wacan.

Hohey, O Money, O You-Who-Grade-Men,
It speaks for the man who has it.
It becomes a valuable weapon.

As will be seen in the next chapter, the *belwo* was not originally used with the dance. But when it eventually was, the theme of dancing made its way into the text of the poem, as in this *belwo*:

> Kuwii lugo-qabayba lama loollee,
> Maxaa Ku luraaya laangadhe?

> We never dance with those who have [sound] legs,
> What's both'ring you, O crippled one?[45]

And in this one:

> Waan liitaa is loodin kari waayee,
> Liciifaye sow lug bay jaban.

> Ah, I am weak and can turn to no [side].
> I become tired and my leg is broken.

Although there are a few *belwo* which do not fall into the above mentioned categories, these are the major themes of the *belwo* in my collection.

NOTES

1. Laurence 1954, p. 6.
2. Lewis 1965, pp. 40, 41, 44, 46, 85; Touval 1963, p. 32.
3. Lewis 1965, p. 102.
4. Ibid., p. 103.
5. Ibid., p. 132.
6. For a detailed account of the development of radio broadcasting in Somalia, see Suleiman Mohamoud Adam, 1968.
7. Touval 1963, p. 78.
8. Lewis 1965, p. 132.
9. Ibid., pp. 148-49.
10. Related to me in 1968 by Maxmuud Axmed Cali, a pioneer in education in the British Somaliland Protectorate. Somalis call Maxmuud "The Father of Somali Education in the North."
11. Lewis 1965, p. 133.
12. Ibid., p. 114, and Touval 1963, p. 65.
13. For the background of these riots, see Lewis 1965, p.135.
14. Ibid., p. 122.
15. Ibid., p. 134.
16. Touval 1963, p. 82.
17. Conclusions in this part of the book were drawn for the most part from interviews with Somali poets and scholars. (See Preface.)
18. *Belwooy, belwooy, hoy belwooy.* Introductory formula. See p. 59 for explanation and meaning.
19. Cabdi had a unique method of gaining inspiration for composing his poetry. He had one long hair in the middle of the rest of his hair. This long hair he protected from the barber when he went to have his hair cut. When he wished to compose, Cabdi would stroke and pull on this hair. (From a conversation with Cabdullaahi Qarshe on 4 June, 1969.)
20. It should be pointed out here that such semiprofessional activity was not common in traditional Somalia. Real professionalism in Somali poetry was to await the coming of the radio. (See Chanter 8.)

21. Khadiija "Belwo" was especially talented in a dance called "Xarrigaad" or "Taxriig," which Somalis say came from South Arabia. During this dance glasses are sometimes balanced on the shoulders or breasts of the dancer.

22. For a detailed description of the Somali tradition of poetic challenge, see Andrzejewski and Muuse X. I. Galaal 1963.

23. The population of Boorame is involved in agriculture more than their neighbors and eat less camel meat than their brothers in Hargeysa. Thus the people of Hargeysa have been given the nickname *beergeel*, "[the ones who eat] the liver of camels," by the people of Boorame. Because liver is rarely eaten in the bush, this term might also be a panegyric name for the people of Hargeysa, meaning "Those-Who-Are-as-Tough-in-the-Mind-and-Body-as-a-Camel."

24. "To the East," i. e., Hargeysa, which is to the east of Boorame.

25. Note the sarcasm in this line, the original *belwo* having been composed as a result of Cabdi Sinimo's broken down lorry.

26. Suleiman 1968, p. 7.

27. For a poetic attack on the miniature poem, see Andrzejewski and Lewis 1964, pp. 151-52.

28. Laurence 1954, p. 7.

29. See Cabdullaahi Qarshe's explanation of why this formula was changed in the Foreword to the 1996 Edition, p. xii.

30. Wellek and Warren 1949, p. 72.

31. I. E., "Was my heart broken?" The liver is one of the seats of emotion in Somali poetry.

32. I. E., Twelve love affairs, or being rejected by his love twelve times.

33. *Sooryo.* According to the informant from whom this *belwo* was collected, Maxamed Jaamac Galaal, *sooryo* is the first payment of brideprice to the girl's clan. The term *sooryo* is used more often in urban communities; the bush community uses the term *gabaati*. The final payment (and term for brideprice in general) is called *yarad* by both communities. *Sooryo* differs from *gabaati* in that it normally consists of money, whereas *gabaati* usually consists of livestock. *Yarad* shares a similar difference, although Maxamed reported that it is losing its hold on townspeople.

34. *Geel sidig.* Part of the brideprice mentioned in the poem. A *geel sidig* is highly prized as brideprice. Under this system one calf is shared by two she-camels. When for some reason a she-camel's young dies (note that it is sometimes killed

during a drought in order to create the *geel sidig* situation), the she-camel is coerced into suckling another she-camel's baby. This produces more milk for human consumption and ensures that at least one of the baby camels will survive. There are several ways of persuading a she-camel to accept a baby which is not her own. One of them is to put the skinned hide of her own baby (*maqarsaar*) on another baby camel so that the smell of her own baby is evident. Another method is a "shock treatment" (*tolmo*) by partly stopping the she-camel's nostrils and frightening her with suffocation. After a while, the nostrils are freed and the she-camel is so releaved with her liberation that she accepts the strange baby and allows it to suckle her.

35. I. E., "If I waste any more time, her clan will take someone else's brideprice and I will lose her altogether."

36. Of the 79 *belwo* collected during my researches, 52 are on the subject of love, while only 27 deal with other topics.

37. Laurence 1954, p. 8.

38. "Share," i. e., the girl he loves.

39. His problem is that he is in love.

40. *Hahey*! Exclamation of excitement.

41. It is somewhat ironic that the composer of these last three *belwo*, a man called Shey-Waal, eventually became a sufi.

42. *Hohey*! Variation of *hahey*. See note 40 above. This expression is usually used in sorrow.

43. Note that the lines have been transposed in the English version for ease of translation.

44. The first two lines have been transposed in the English version for ease of translation.

45. I. E., "I will dance with you even if you are crippled."

4

THE HEELLO: PERIOD ONE

The Metamorphosis: *Belwo* to *Heello* A

The most obvious difference between the *belwo* and its sister genres has already been discussed. The *belwo* originated in the society of the town dweller and not in that of the pastoralist; indeed, we have proposed to call the *belwo* a cultural link between these two groups. But the cultural setting was not the only difference. The first change which caused the *belwo* to deviate from the other short genres in structure, and certainly from most genres in northern Somali poetry, was the addition of the (petrol tin) drum.[1] The drum had been used consistently in traditional northern poetry only by women. Rarely had men used any accompaniment aside from hand clapping to the recitation of poetry. This early innovation no doubt assisted the other changes which were to follow, including the later addition of more and more musical instruments.

Another practice associated with the early days of the *belwo* was the type of social gatherings held for its recitation. Social gatherings of young people around miniature poetry were not new in Somalia, and we have seen them used for dancing at such occasions as weddings where both men and women participated. Somalis of both sexes did not, however, enter a house in the evening, away from the watchful eyes of members of the older generation, in order to recite and listen to poetry on the subject of love. This restriction was ignored by Cabdi Sinimo and his early followers.

Perhaps the most radical early deviation and example of permissiveness associated with the *belwo* was its recitation by both sexes. It thus represented the beginning of new relationship between men and women. This move toward social equality was to be reflected more and more often in modern poetry, even working its way into the text of later *heello*.[2] Khadiija Ciya Dharaar "Belwo" has already been mentioned. This woman composed *belwo* herself, an accomplishment yet to be equalled by any woman in the periods of the *heello*. Other women who participated in the early movement to spread the *belwo* were Maryan Ciya Dharaar, Khadiija's sister, and two other women from Boorame, Cawa Shir-Doon and Barako.

Of all women in the early period of modern poetry, perhaps the most important, though not as well known as Khadiija Belwo, was Khadiija Cabdullaahi Dalays. It was she who weathered the widespread criticism of women in modern poetry, and because of her resistance to the pressure of tradition, probably more than any other woman she established the "right" of women to recite the modern poem. Dalays began to sing at first for political rallies in 1951 and joined Radio Muqdisho in 1952. Many artists and poets associated with the radio stations today have a high regard for her and consider her a pioneer in this field.[3]

Radio Hargeysa was not to be outdone by Radio Muqdisho, and on 19 August 1953, a woman named Shamis Abokor, nicknamed "Guduudo Carwo," sang a *heello*.[4] Guduudo Carwo faced the criticism as Dalays had before her and became the first female artist on the radio in the North.

By the time the *belwo* had spread to Hargeysa, musical instruments other than the drum found their way into the delivery of the new poem. The tambourine (*daf*), probably imported from Arabia but used also in Seylac, and the lute (*cuud*), known to have come from Aden, were early additions. Also an early addition was the flute (*biibiile*), which was probably contributed by a man named Raw who originally came from the Indian subcontinent. As time passed the violin and guitar came to be used.

In 1955 Radio Muqdisho, then under the direction of Axmed Maxamed Allora, acquired a full orchestra from the remnants of a military band. An Italian military musician was loaned to the radio station for six months to instruct the members.[5] By the time the two foreign-ruled Somalilands joined in independence in 1960, and the *heello* had six years of development behind it, the accompaniment of modern poetry had substantially developed. The latest addition to the orchestra is an organ. The fact that musical accompaniment to modern poetry in Somalia is a foreign influence is easily supportable. Not only was musical accompaniment new, but the saxophone and snare drum are hardly products of the nomadic way of life.

The first form of the *heello* developed almost immediately after the *belwo* spread to Hargeysa and is what we have termed the mega-miniature poem. In several ways the new form fell well within the definition of a miniature poem. The *heello* A was a "tacking on" of many *belwo* to make one long poem. Each stanza, then, was a separate *belwo*, composed by an individual poet who was not influenced by the other stanzas (*belwo*) of the poem, for the combining of the stanzas had been done after their composition. For this reason, the *heello* A was not a unified composition in its theme, though each *belwo* usually dealt with the subject of love. Furthermore, the influences of length in miniature poetry were exerted on the imagery of the *heello* A. The mega-miniature poem contained a sequence of unconnected images, while in the *heello* B, soon to develop from the earlier form, there was often a masterly blending of images and symbolism, a superstructure of connected images making up a unified conceptual framework of imagery behind the lines of the poem (see below, pp. 195-206). Again for the same reasons, the alliteration, though unified in each stanza, was not uniform throughout the entire poem, each stanza alliterating with a different sound. What the new form represented in effect was the structural link between the *belwo* and the developed heello of later times.

Changing its name to *heello* because of the use of the general introductory formula for miniature poetry, the lamenting *belwo* formula was abandoned.[6] At first only the formula changed, as can be seen in the following poem:

> Heelloy heellelloy, heelloy heellelloy,
> Waddada bariyeey, Ku weheshadayeey,
> Warkiyo hayga gozin waraaqaa.

> Heelloy heellelloy, heelloy heellelloy,
> O road [that travels] to the East, I kept you company;
> Do not cut me off from news and letters [from my love].

Gradually the *heello* A increased in length until as many as fifteen or twenty *belwo* were employed in the same poem.[7] This practice of stringing *belwo* together was strengthened by two factors. First, the new poetry was used in the dance, where a two or three line poem was too short to be practical. Second, the *belwo* had acquired a commercial value. The radio stations in Somalia began to use the *belwo* early, because it was useful as a filler between programs and was popular at the time.[8] It was the practice of Radio Hargeysa to pay a fee for the use of a poem on the air; the fee increased with the length (i. e., time on the air) of the poem. Obviously the longer a poem, the more money it would bring.

The payment of fees for poems used on the radio influenced the *heello* A even more importantly, because it introduced the convention of line repeats. As a systematic device, line repeating had not been so common in Somali poetry, except in work songs. In classical poetry, when line repeating occurred in any one poem, this did not mean that it would recur the next time the same poem was delivered, even by the same man. In the *heello*, however, line repeating became a systematic device. Example 3 below illustrates this device as well as the joining of *belwo* to form a *heello* A. This *heello* was obtained from a tape from Radio Muqdisho, but stanzas I-IV and IX were also collected separately as *belwo*. The differing alliteration of each stanza (i. e., *belwo*) is clearly visible.

Example 3:
I.   1   Aaa, adigaa hudhudyow hawada lalaayee,
     2   Haweeya hadal mayga gaadhsiin e,
         (*repeat, ll. 1-2*)

II. 5   Aaa, Maryama Muxubooy madheedka Wareey,
     6   Midhihii ka bislaaday baad tahay eey,
         (*repeat, ll. 5-6*)

III. 9   Aaa, sidii cir ku hooray meel cosobloo,
     10 Cadceeddii u soo baxdaad tahay eey,
         (*repeat, ll. 9-10*)

IV. 13 Aaa, Gaaroodoo roobleh geedihii ka baxiyo,
     14 Guudkeeda maLa mooday gammaan faras,
         (*repeat, ll. 13-14*)

V.   17 Aaa, sidii aan godob qabo hurdada ma gamzee,
     18 Maxaa Layga gooynayaan galay ee
         (*repeat, ll. 17-18*)

VI. 21 Aaa, xabaal nin galaa xaq weeyaan ee,
     22 Illayn xubi baan xagnabaw dhicin e,
         (*repeat, ll. 21-22*)

VII. 25 Aaa, barbaartii horiyo banaad sidii yeey,
     26 Ha baadhbaadhin beri samaadkii,
         (*repeat, ll. 25-26*)

VIII. 29 Aaa, magaalada geed ku yaal Muxubooy,
      30 Ayaad midabkiisa leedahay eey,
          (*repeat, ll. 29-30*)

IX. 33   Aaa, sidii doonni dufsatay duufaaneey,

34   Cidlaan hadba sii dabayshanayaa yee.

(*repeat, ll. 33-34*)

I.   1   Ah, hoopoe bird hey! You are flying [around in] the air;

2   Will you carry a message [of love] to Haweeyo[9] for me ?

(*repeat, ll. 1-2*)

II. 5   Ah, O Beloved Maryan, the berry bush[10] of *War* :[11]

6   You are its ripened fruit.

(*repeat, ll. 5-6*)

III. 9   Ah, like the heavens dropping rain in a place where fresh grass [grows],

10   And the sun, which rises on it, are you.

(*repeat, ll. 9-10*)

IV. 13   Ah, the Gaaroodi Plain[12] [is she], where rain [abounds] and green grass grows;

14   Does it [not] seem that her [luxuriant] hair[13] is like that of the young horse?[14]

(*repeat, ll. 13-14*)

V.   17   Ah, like a guilty man, I do not sleep well:

18   What have I done to be persecuted?

(*repeat, ll. 17-18*)

VI. 21   Ah, entering the grave is right for man;

22   Indeed love does not fall to any side.

(*repeat, ll. 21-22*)

VII. 25   Ah, like the young men and girls of olden times,

26   Do not postpone the good times 'till tomorrow.

(*repeat, ll. 25-26*)

VIII. 29   Ah, O Beloved, the tree in the village:

30   You possess its [most beautiful] color.

(*repeat, ll. 29-30*)

IX. 33   Ah, like a ship carried [off by] a storm

34   To a desolate place, each time I am blown [off my course by her love].

Carrying the method of poem lengthening one step further can be observed in Example 4. Here—and only in stanzas II and III—the use of a refrain at the end of each stanza has developed. Later in many *heello* the refrain is to be sung by a chorus of male, female, or mixed voices, but again, many refrains are to be sung by the soloist alone. The theme in Example 4, a lament over a lost love, is also much more united. The informant from whom this *heello* was collected believed stanzas II and III to have been composed by the same poet. Their alliteration ("C" in both stanzas), setting them apart from the other two stanzas, lends credence to this possibility. Certainly the four stanzas (*belwo*) were more carefully chosen for their content than were those of Example 3.

Example 4:

I.   1   Heelloy heellelloy,
         (*repeat 3 times*)

     5   Hir aan ii dhowayn,

     6   Ma halabsaday ey,
         (*repeat, ll. 5-6, twice*)

II. 11 Caqliga waxa gartee,

     12 Culun ma lihi ye,
         (*repeat, ll. 11-12*)

     15 Ceel yaa igu rida,

     16 Cidhiidhiyahay,
         (*repeat, ll. 15-16, twice*)

III. 21 Ceebooboo nolol,

     22 U caban maayee,
         (*repeat, ll. 21-22*)

     25 Ceel yaa igu rida,

     26 Cidhiidhiyahay,
         (*repeat, ll. 25-26, twice*)

IV. 31 Heddaa idin kala,

     32 Kaxayn mooyee,
         (*repeat, ll. 31-32*)

35   Ifkaydin isku waayi,

36   Ku maan wadiney,

    (repeat, ll. 35-36, twice)

I.   1   Heelloy heellelloy,

    (repeat 3 times)

    6   Did I grasp at

    5   A distant horizon, which was not to be close to me ?

    (repeat, ll. 5-6, twice)

II.   11-12   I do not have intelligence, neither the knowledge for understanding things.

    (repeat, ll. 11-12)

    15   Who will [then] drop me into a [deep] well?

    16   Oh, misfortune!

    (repeat, ll. 15-16, twice)

III.   21-22   I have become [so] disgraced and do not complain to life.

    (repeat, ll. 21-22)

    25   Who will [then] drop me into a [deep] well?

    26   Oh, misfortune!

    (repeat, ll. 25-26, twice)

IV.   31-32   Unless death drives you [both far] apart,

    (repeat, ll. 31-32)

    35-36   I don't think this world will fail to find you two together.

    (repeat ll.35-36, twice)

After some time with the *heello* A, a new impetus entered the scene. Cabdi Sinimo and Khadiija Belwo had left the Protectorate and the growing genre was known throughout the area. The new push behind the *heello* came from a group of young Somali poets who added even more variation to the *heello* so that it changed yet again.

The Modern Poem: *Heello* A to *Heello* B

Because of its name and its difference in size compared to the *belwo*, the *heello* A belongs to the first period of the modern poem. However, it had not yet evolved into its present shape. This general form (which shall be referred to in this chapter as the heello, Form B) was to continue side by side with the A form until the latter eventually disappeared.[15] But what gave this new impetus? For the answer to this question we must look to the new poets who came onto the scene, the most important of whom was Cabdullaahi Qarshe.

After Cabdi Sinimo, the most influential man in the development of modern poetry in Somalia is Cabdullaahi Qarshe. Cabdullaahi is known in Somalia as "The Father of Somali Music," and it is he who introduced the lute (*cuud*) to the accompaniment of the *heello*. Furthermore, he was intimately involved in the early development of the *heello* B. Cabdullaahi is still popular as a poet in Somalia today, and has recently received a bronze medal from the government for his poetry.

If we are to understand fully the modern poem, we must first consider Cabdullaahi's background. He was born in the Somali expatriate community in Moshi, (then) Tanganyika, in 1924. Like Cabdi Sinimo, Cabdullaahi did not spend his early years in the traditional manner as a camel boy. In 1931 he went to Aden where he was sent to school by his family.

It was in Aden that Cabdullaahi first heard radio broadcasts and went to the cinema. English, Hindi, and Arabic music and songs could be heard on the radio, but this was not the case for Somali, for there were no Somali songs of this sort at the time. "I wanted music to be for Somali as for the other languages," said Cabdullaahi, and he made a purchase which was to accomplish this goal, although not until 1948; he bought a lute. Hiding it from his family for fear of condemnation, he did not learn to play it well until an Arab named Bakri taught him in Berbera some years later.

In 1945 Cabdullaahi went to Hargeysa, where he became a clerk for the British Military Administration. It was at this time that the *belwo* was first spreading in northern Somalia, and he was greatly influenced, this time by an indigenous art form. Three years later he composed his first—and one of *the* first—*heello* B.

To date Cabdullaahi has continued to play a role in the development of modern poetry. He was part of the Walaalo Hargeysa, "the Brothers of Hargeysa," an important group of artists and poets founded in 1955 (see below, pp. 101-02), and continues to compose poems and melodies. He is a man of considerable prestige today and is still associated with Radio Muqdisho.

In 1948 Cabdullaahi Qarshe composed his first *heello,* "Ka Kacaay." The *heello* A, as we have seen was a collection of *belwo* with different composers; its diction was limited by its miniature size. Being composed by one man, Cabdullaahi's poem (see Example 5 below) was much more unified in theme than the *heello* A. The *heello* B which were to follow "Ka Kacaay" were also to be composed by one poet. Where more than one poet was involved they worked together on the composition (see Example 6 below). Thus, one long unified modern poem had evolved.

Contributing to the unification of the *heello* B was its uniform alliteration. Many early *heello* B had differing alliteration, usually one alliterative phoneme per stanza, but traditional Somali euphony gradually overtook mixed alliterations until this practice disappeared almost completely, although this transition was not to be accomplished fully until later.

As Cabdullaahi's title "The Father of Somali Music" implies, Somalis believe it was he who brought melody to modern poetry, though in fact others were involved. Heretofore only the genre could be recognized by the tune to which it was recited. Hearing a Somali whistle a tune, for example, an observer might conclude that he was hearing a *belwo* or a *wiglo.* With the *heello* B this system changed radically. Hearing the tune of a *heello* B, the observer could now identify the specific poem. No longer was he to recognize only the genre. Moreover, a *heello* B now required two creative processes: the composition of the poem and the composition of the melody to which the poem was to be sung. Many times Cabdullaahi was to collaborate with other poets; he would compose the melody to fit the poem. Example 7 illustrates just such a joint effort, with the words by Ismaaciil Sheekh Axmed and the melody by Cabdullaahi Qarshe.

Cabdullaahi's poem brought about an even more important marriage for the prestige of modern poetry, and this between the *heello* and the theme of politics. Although a few *belwo* had political themes, that genre was principally preoccupied with love. With the composition of "Ka Kacaay," the subject matter of modern poetry was, within the Somali value system, raised to the level of classical poetry, and the *heello* B became the mouthpiece for the drive toward independence. The ultrapatriotic lines of "Dhulkayaga" (Example 7) illustrate how politics permeated the new poetry. This poem became so popular and gained so much prestige that a stylized version of its melody became the signature tune of Radio Muqdisho.

With the lengthening of the *heello* in its B form, and with the addition of politics as a theme, the diction of modern poetry became more sophisticated. Politics brought a host of new images into the *heello*, the great majority of which came from traditional poetry. The hyena, for instance, an animal disliked by Somalis, had been used to represent the enemy in traditional poems. The *heello* B employed this image for the colonialist. Place names were to be used in the *heello* B as they had been in traditional poetry (see Example 6 below). We shall see in the following chapter that the diction of modern poetry became more and more sophisticated as time passed; indeed the diction of the *heello* in the 1960s was to rival traditional poems and raise the value of modern poetry to such an extent that the *heello* would replace the *gabay* in urban and elite societies.

Example 5:

I.	1	Ka kacaay, ka kacaay,
	2	Ka kacaay, ka kacaay,
	3	Kol horaynu jabnee,
	4	Ka kacaay, ka kacaay,
		(*repeat, ll. 1-4*)
II.	9	Ka kacaay, ka kacaay,
	10	Ka kacaay, ka kacaay,
	11	Kooralay La gubyee,
	12	Ka kacaay, ka kacaay,
		(*repeat, ll. 9-12*)
III.	17	Ka kacaay, ka kacaay,
	18	Ka kacaay, ka kacaay,
	19	Kun faceen La dilyee,
	20	Ka kacaay, ka kacaay,
		(*repeat, ll. 17-20*)
IV.	25	Ka kacaay, ka kacaay,
	26	Ka kacaay, ka kacaay,
	27	Kufrigu badayee,
	28	Ka kacaay, ka kacaay,
		(*repeat, ll. 25-28*)

V.   33   Ka kacaay, ka kacaay,

     34   Ka kacaay, ka kacaay,

     35   Kiiniisado La dhisyoo,

     36   Ka kacaay, ka kacaay,
          (repeat, ll. 33-36)

VI. 41   Ka kacaay, ka kacaay,

     42   Ka kacaay, ka kacaay,

     43   Kama-Kamaz yimidee,

     44   Ka kacaay, ka kacaay,
          (repeat, ll. 41-44)

VII. 49   Ka kacaay, ka kacaay,

     50   Ka kacaay, ka kacaay,

     51   Kiiniyuu gubayee,

     52   Ka kacaay, ka kacaay,
          (repeat, ll. 49-52)

VIII. 57 Ka kacaay, ka kacaay,

     58   Ka kacaay, ka kacaay,

     59   Kilaab afaraa,

     60   Inoo kulantee,

     61   Illaaha ka weyn,

     62   Ayaa kicin,
          (repeat, ll. 59-62)

     67   Ka kacaay, ka kacaay,

     68   Ka kacaay, ka kacaay,

IX. 69   Ka kacaay, ka kacaay,

     70   Kacaay, ka kacaay,

     71   Kol uun baa La dhintaayee,

     72   Ka kacaay, ka kacaay.
          (repeat, ll. 69-72)

I.   1   Wake up! Arise![16]

     2   Wake up! Arise!

     3   We were destroyed earlier.

	4	Wake up! Arise!
		(*repeat, ll. 1-4*)
II.	9	Wake up! Arise!
	10	Wake up! Arise!
	11	Kooralay[17] was burned.
	12	Wake up! Arise!
		(*repeat, ll. 9-12*)
III.	17	Wake up! Arise!
	18	Wake up! Arise!
	19	A thousand of our generation were killed.[18]
	20	Wake up! Arise!
		(*repeat, ll. 17-20*)
IV	25	Wake up! Arise!
	26	Wake up! Arise!
	27	The infidels increased [in number].
	28	Wake up! Arise!
		(*repeat, ll. 25-28*)
V.	33	Wake up! Arise!
	34	Wake up! Arise!
	35	Christian churches were built.[19]
	36	Wake up! Arise!
		(*repeat, ll. 33-36*)
VI.	41	Wake up! Arise!
	42	Wake up! Arise!
	43	Kama-kamaz[20] came [to govern us].
	44	Wake up! Arise!
		(*repeat, ll. 41-44*)
VII.	49	Wake up! Arise!
	50	Wake up! Arise!
	51	He burned Kenya.[21]
	52	Wake up! Arise!
		(*repeat, ll. 49-52*)
VIII.	57	Wake up! Arise!
	58	Wake up! Arise!

59   The four who are dogs[22]

60   Met [to discuss] our [case].[23]

61   God, who is greater,

62   Will cause them to depart.

     (*repeat, ll. 59-62*)

67   Wake up! Arise!

68   Wake up! Arise!

IX.   69   Wake up! Arise!

70   Wake up! Arise!

71   One [can] only die once![24]

72   Wake up! Arise!

     (*repeat, ll. 69-72*)

Example 6:

I.   1   Hadhuub nin sitoo hashiisa irmaan,

     2   Ha maalin La leeyahay baan ahay,

       3   Ka kacaay, ka kacaay, ka kacaay, ka kacaay,

II.   4   Dagaal nimuu haysto meel halisoo,

     5   Hubkiisu hangool yahay baan ahay,

       6   Ka kacaay, ka kacaay, ka kacaay, ka kacaay,

III.   7   Wixii ku habboon nin haybsanayoo,

     8   Bahdii ka hor-joogto baan ahay,

       9   Ka kacaay, ka kacaay, ka kacaay, ka kacaay,

IV.   10   Habaas nin dhex jiifta oo ku haftoo,

     11   Hayaanka ka soo hadhay baan ahay,

       12   Ka kacaay, ka kacaay, ka kacaay, ka kacaay,

V.   13   Nimuu hadalkiisu hadhqoodaalkiyo,

     14   Haweenkaba dhaafin baan ahay,

       15   Ka kacaay, ka kacaay, ka kacaay, ka kacaay,

VI.   16   Hobyiyo Herer iyo Hawaasta galbeed,

     17   Hadmay isu hiillin doonaan,

       18   Ka kacaay, ka kacaay, ka kacaay, ka kacaay.

I.   1-2   I am a man who carries a milk vessel and who is forbidden to milk his own she-camel.[25]

        3   Wake up! Arise! Wake up! Arise![26]

II.   4-5   I am a man who is in battle in a dangerous place, and whose [only] weapon is a *hangool*.[27]

        6   Wake up! Arise! Wake up! Arise!

III.   7-8   I am a man who is considering what is best for himself, and whose [own] brothers[28] reject him.

        9   Wake up! Arise! Wake up! Arise!

IV.   10-11   I am a man who sleeps in the middle of dust which is drowning him, and who strayed behind [his companions] on a journey and became lost.

        12   Wake up! Arise! Wake up! Arise!

V.   13-14   I am a man whose speech goes no farther than to women or to the shade of [his own] house.

        15   Wake up! Arise! Wake up! Arise!

VI.   16-17   When shall [the people] of Hobyo,[29] Harar,[30] and west of Hawaas[31] assist each other [in their struggle for independence]?

        18   Wake up! Arise! Wake up! Arise!

Example 7:

I.   M: 1   Dhulkayaga, dhulkayaga,

          2   Dhulkayaga, dhulkayaga,

          3   Wow dhimanaynaa, dhulkayaga,

        C: 4   Dhulkayaga, dhulkayaga,

            5   Dhulkayaga, dhulkayaga,

            6   Wow dhimanaynaa, dhulkayaga,

II.   M: 7   Dhallin iyo dhallaan, waayeelka dhursugay,

          8   Dhallin iyo dhallaan, waayeelka dhursugay,

          9   Wow wada dhannoo, wow wada dhannoo,

          10   Wow dhimanaynaa, dhulkayaga,

        C: 11   Dhulkayaga, etc.

III.   M: 14   Dhiig inaan ku shubo, aan dhagar ku galo,

          15   Dhiig inaan ku shubo, aan dhagar ku galo,

		16	Waan ku dhaarsannaa, waan ku dhaarsannaa,
		17	Wow dhimanaynaa, dhulkayaga,
	C:	18	Dhulkayaga, etc.
IV.	M:	21	Wow dhalannayoo, waanu dhiirrannee,
		22	Wow dhalannayoo, waanu dhiirrannee,
		23	Dhibiyo xumman, dhibiyo xumman,
		24	Waa ka dhowraynaa, dhulkayaga,
	C:	25	Dhulkayaga, etc.
V.	M:	28	Kaan ku dhaadani, wuu dhoohanyoo,
		29	Kaan ku dhaadani, wuu dhoohanyoo,
		30	Waa dhega lazyee, waa dhega lazyee,
		31	Wow dhimanaynaa, dhulkayaga,
	C:	32	Dhulkayaga, etc.

I.	M:	1	Our country, our country,
		2	Our country, our country,
		3	We will die for our country.
	C:	4	Our country, our country,
		5	Our country, our country,
		6	We will die for our country.
II.	M:	7	The youth and the children, the elders who waited a long time.
		8	The youth and the children, the elders who waited a long time.
		9	We are all united for it; we are all united for it.
		10	We will die for our country.
	C:	11	Our country, etc.
III.	M:	14	That we [would] spill blood; that we [would] kill for it,
		15	That we [would] spill blood; that we [would] kill for it,
		16	[This] we swear to; [this] we swear to.
		17	We will die for our country.
	C:	18	Our country, etc.
IV.	M:	21	We were born for it; we are brave.
		22	We were born for it; we are brave.
		23	Difficulty and hardship, difficulty and hardship:

24   We protect our country against them.

C: 25 Our country, etc.

V.   M: 28   One who is not proud of it is ignorant.

29   One who is not proud of it is ignorant.

30   He is deaf; he is deaf.

31   We will die for our country.

C: 32   Our country, etc.

As one reads through Example 7, it becomes clear that the *belwo* had come quite a way since Cabdi Sinimo's truck broke down. The composition of belwo was not to disappear entirely,[32] but poets of the new form were to turn the greater part of their attention to the *heello*.

NOTES

1. Conclusions in this part of the book were drawn for the most part from interviews with Somali poets and scholars. (See Preface.)

2. The theme of the equality of women was also used as the basis of two complete plays in the modern Somali theater. The first, *Shabeel Naagood,* "The Woman [Stalking] Leopard," by Xasan Sheekh Muumin, has been transcribed and translated by B. W. Andrzejewski (1974). The second, *Yaxaas Dhega-Dhuub,* "A Crocodile with Pointed/Elongated Ears," was composed as a reaction to the first. See also the poems on pp. 7-11 and pp. 155-60.

3. Suleiman 1968, pp. 22-24.

4. As reported in *War Somali Sidihi,* no. 19, 26 September, 1953.

5. Suleiman 1968, pp. 14-15.

6. See p, 59.

7. Laurence 1954, p. 7.

8. Suleiman 1968, pp. 7, 14.

9. *Haweeyo.* Panegyric name. It means "The Best One of All."

10. *Madheedh.* A berry bush either *cordia gharaf* or *cordia ovalis.*

11. *War.* Name of a Somali settlement in the Hawd in Ethiopia.

12. The *Gaaroodi* Plain. A plain south of Burco in northern Somalia.

13. *Guud.* "Hair"; literally "top."

14. Somalis value the horse above all animals, even the camel. This line is a compliment to the beauty of the girl's hair. For a poem praising the qualities of a horse, see Andrzejewski and Lewis 1964, pp. 66-70.

15. It will be remembered that nomenclature was the biggest problem in my research. What I have called "*heello* A and B," Andrzejewski and Lewis 1964, call "*heello*" and "modern *hees.*" I have pointed out that Somalis themselves use two terms for the modern poem, *heello* and *hees* (see pp. xix-xx). This usage is further complicated, because the term *hees* is used for several other genres and the term *heello* is almost always used when the modern poem is under discussion by Somalis. Andrzejewski and Lewis's terminology, then, presents a problem because it is somewhat oversimplified; the problem of attaching appropriate names to the different stages in the development of modern poetry is complex. Considering the ambiguity of the

Somali nomenclature, I have chosen not to mix the two terms, but to choose the one describing a poetic genre. Thereafter, its stages have been called Form A and Form B. Perhaps the problem can be clarified by the following chart:

Colloquial Somali	Andrzejewski and Lewis, 1964	Usage in this book
belwo, balwo	*belwo*	*belwo*
belwo or *heello* (early)	*heello*	*heello*, Form A
heello or *hees* (later)	modern *hees*	*heello*, Form B

16. Two translations of the Somali phrase *Ka kacaay* ("stand up/get out of it/arise") have been employed in order to cover the semantic sphere of the phrase.

17. *Kooralay.* Place name. Probably a fictitious place since no references can be found to it in any gazetteer of Somalia or on any map. Furthermore, the governor, Sir Gerald Reece, about whom this poem was composed, did not burn any town in Somalia or Kenya. The word was probably chosen for its alliteration.

18. Note that this poetic hyperbole does not refer to any massacre in the history of the British Somaliland Protectorate.

19. Sir Gerald Reece never attempted to encourage proselytizing of Christianity in Somalia. This line in the poem is a poetic hyperbole.

20. *Kama-kamaz.* Somali nickname or Sir Gerald Reece. The nickname refers to the stammer or stutter characteristic of Sir Gerald's speech. It might also be mentioned that many Somalis have told me that Reece was the most popular governor to serve in the Protectorate. This poem was composed in the year he took office, and his popularity grew only after he left Somalia.

21. Sir Gerald Reece had been in charge of the Northern Frontier District of Kenya where Somalis live before he went to Somalia. This line is also a poetic hyperbole.

22. I. E., The four powers which divided up Somalia: France, Italy, Britain, and Ethiopia.

23. I. E., To divide Somalia.

24. I. E., The Somalis are ready to die for their country's independence and unification.

25. Milk is a common image in Somali poetry for wealth and prosperity.

26. See note 16 above.

27. *Hangool.* A stick about a yard long with a two-teethed, forked end and a hooked end. It is used for uprooting (with the forked end) thorn bushes and carrying them (with the hooked end) to a place where a fence or a corral is to be constructed. The hangool is a common wedding present to a man.

28. "Brothers." Literally "Bah" brothers, which are from the same father and mother; i. e., one's closest kin. By metaphoric extension, this line could also refer to all the Somalis.

29. *Hobyo.* City on the coast of Somalia in the region of Mudug.

30. *Harar* or *Adari.* Town in Ethiopia just south of *Dirir Dhabe* (*Dira Dawa*).

31. *Hawaas.* Town in Ethiopia on the train route between Addis Ababa and Jabuuti. This is the last Somali town before one enters Oromo country.

32. The latest *belwo* I collected were composed in 1968.

5

THE *HEELLO*: PERIOD TWO

The Historical Background

Political events on the Horn of Africa in January 1955 produced a new chapter in the history of Somalia. This was the time when modern political awareness was to mature among many Somali clans. Furthermore, it marked the beginning of a more concerted and serious drive toward independence that was to terminate with the accomplishment of that goal in 1960. And why was a major political crisis to return to Somalia for the third time in the twentieth century? As before, the answer lies with forces which were beyond the control of the Somali people.

More than a catalyst, the border shift agreed to between the British and Ethiopians in November 1954 disrupted the status quo of fourteen years of peace since the termination of the battles of World War II that had been fought in East Africa. Deeper rumbles of the desire for freedom from colonial administration also began to be felt in London. Indeed, Somalia now took her place in the independence movement, which was sweeping the entire continent of Africa.

To a people for whom poetry is a potent means of political expression (among its other functions), one would expect such a border crisis to be reflected in the oral art. This was indeed the case, and along with politics, modern poetry entered the new chapter of Somali history.

The events which led to the final border shift in Somalia before its independence undoubtedly lent fire to the already growing political awakening and drive for independence. A large part of Somalia had been united under the Italian fascist government in East Africa. Joined to the Italian Somaliland colony were the Ogaadeen section of Ethiopia and, after August 1940, the British Somaliland Protectorate. This unity of administration was maintained by the British when Italian East Africa fell in 1941. From then until November 1954, the gradual return of the Horn to her pre-Ethio-Italian War and pre-World War II boundaries (see pp. 52-53) had caused little unrest.[1] All this changed, however, in January of 1955, when the Ethio-British Agreement was made public. The

British and Ethiopians had left the council table in November 1954, having agreed that a section of the Protectorate called the Hawd and Reserved Area would revert to Ethiopian control.[2] This area, although occupied by clans nominally under British protection, had been controlled by Ethiopia from 1897 to 1935. With the return of this territory to Ethiopia, however, the political situation reached a boiling point as interest in national political events moved from the urban elite to the nomadic population of the interior.[3]

Why this, the last border change the British were to bring about on the Horn, should be of such paramount importance is probably connected with rights to the rich grazing land of the Hawd. The intellectuals of the elite might well complain of unfair treatment and foul international law, but the nomad was rarely affected to such a great extent by colonial activity, even heightened as it was since 1941. With the potential loss of important grazing land, however, the great majority of the Protectorate's population was affected. Even though the government of Ethiopia assured the British that grazing rights would remain in Protectorate Somali hands, those nomads using the Hawd were suspicious lest the border be closed in the heat of a political argument and their herds suffer inevitable famine from the loss of necessary pastures. Modern politics had, as it were, reached grass roots level. I. M. Lewis describes the situation as follows:[4]

> At the end of 1954, however, an event occurred which changed the whole course of political life and led eventually to full independence. This precipitant was the final liquidation of British administration in the Hawd and Reserved Areas and the complete surrender of these vital grazing lands to Ethiopian control.

Somali reaction in the Protectorate was swift and bitter.

The outcry in the Protectorate when the Ethio-British agreement was made public was "both immediate and widespread."[5] Riots and large demonstrations occurred throughout the Protectorate to protest against this agreement.[6] Somalis had become accustomed to the changes brought about by Italian colonial expansion into Ethiopia and by British rule over the entire Horn. The boundary shift now represented more than a return to a sad condition; it was a new outrage. The complete unity of the various political factions in northern Somalia, in opposition to this territorial transfer, was demonstrated in the formation of the National United Front. Originally an organization composed of representatives of all the political parties of the Protectorate, the N. U. F. organized a delegation, headed by Michael Mariano, to go to London and New York. Their intentions were twofold.

In London the N. U. F. delegation pleaded for the return of the Hawd and for the independence of the Protectorate. In New York, at the United Nations, the delegation opened a complicated debate on international law, especially involving questions relating to the status of a protector and a Protectorate population.

Although the arguments put forth by the Somali delegation had little effect in convincing the British or the U. N. to return the Hawd to them, the quest for independence was not in vain. If the gravity of the situation could be witnessed by several armed clashes at the new border, the British response could be seen as one of unquestionable diplomatic retreat. Two things support this argument. First, in the following year a Mr. Dodds-Parker, the Parliamentary Under-Secretary for Foreign Affairs, visited Addis Ababa in an attempt to purchase the Hawd and Reserved Area from Ethiopia. He was received with hostility by the Ethiopian officials and the plan failed.[7] Second, in May of the same year, the Under-Secretary of State in the Colonial Office, Lord Lloyd, announced before political leaders in Hargeysa the intention of the British Government to grant Somalia a speedy independence.[8] What had begun as a black cloud over Somalia had clearly ended with a silver lining. The irony of the loss of the Hawd was that it led to more rapid independence for northern Somalia.

If the loss of the Hawd is remembered in Somalia as the political event of 1955, then the composition of a particular poem must also be remembered as the artistic event of 1955. Several Somalis with whom I have spoken remember the poem "Jowhariyo Luula" as the first *heello*, though several poems by Cabdullaahi Qarshe and others predate it. This claim, although erroneous, does point to an important fact about the development of the *heello*. "Jowhariyo Luula" is remembered as being somehow different from all the poems that preceded it, and as the beginning of a new period of this genre.

"Jowhariyo Luula" is a Form B *heello*, and did not have the same alliteration throughout. It did have united alliteration in each stanza, however. There were, as we shall see presently, many poems like it during this period. Why, then, did it usher in the second period of the *heello*? The answer lies in its theme rather than in its structure.

97

"Jowhariyo Luula" was not the only poem composed about the loss of the Hawd, but it was the first. Its timing is of major importance in understanding its role as the first poem of period two.

Since no form of art develops independently from the culture that creates it, so no art form appears independently of the historical period in which it occurs. The importance of "Jowhariyo Luula" lies in its being composed during this political crisis, and it became a sort of "*Marseillaise*" to the general public. With this poem the *heello* was no longer to be questioned as an important genre of political expression for the new elite. After its composition many new, serious political poems were to appear to which the urban population reacted in a manner formerly reserved for classical poetry.

With the loss of the Hawd and Reserved Area, then, and with the composition of this poem, the new genre was firmly established as the voice of the elite. The modern poem as a political device (opposed to the classical genres) became the tongue of those who demanded and began the drive for independence. Following is a transcription and translation of this poem.[9]

Example 8:

I.	1	Illayn jaahil, jin iyo xoog ma lahoo,
	2	Intaan jiifay, wax ma Lay jaray oo,
	3	Jabayoo, jilbis jeebka Lay geliyoo,
	4	Jidhkaygii is galay, jidhiidhicadii,
	5	Jidboodayoo, dood jid-dheer u maroo,
	6	Jirdahaan magansaday, ima ay jalinoo,
	7	Afkay iga soo jufeeyeen,
	8	Jowhariyo Luulaay,
	9	Jiidhka igu yaalleey,
	10	Alla, ma joogee,
	11	Jeex dhan bay maqaneey,
II.	12	Jiidaal ma tawana, naf jeellaniyoo,
	13	Jeerooy hesho sheyga ay jaceshahay,
	14	Aroor walba, way jarmaaddaayoo,
	15	Jidiinkaa i engegay jirkoo dazay oo,
	16	Anoon jidibkayga, soofayn oon,
	17	Jahaad gelin, jaalahay ka hadhoo,

	18	Jibaadkaygu laabta ma uu jiro,
		19 Jowhariyo Luulaay, etc.
III.	23	Bankii Fedes, beerihii Jigjigaad,
	24	Beelihii degganaa ka baydaade oo,
	25	Libaax bulbul laa boqnaha-jaray oo,
	26	Barwaaqadii guuldarraa beddeshoo,
	27	Ku baadshay dhurwaa, biyaha kululoo,
	28	Boorame Layga mari xaggaa bariyoo,
	29	Bad iyo xeebi baadi ii noqotoo,
	30	Basaase indhihii bilan jiray,
		31 Jowhariyo Luulaay, etc.
IV.	35	Aaa, kol ay Sawaaxili tahay,
	36	Soodaan iyo kolay Sawaaxili tahay,
	37	Dadkii silci jiray harow socoyoo,
	38	Siday doonayeen La wada siiyee,
	39	Miyaynaan la sinnayn dadkaa sugayoo,
	40	Saagaanku ku ool sideenaayoon,
	41	Sagaal Lagu dhalin Soomaalida eey,
		42 Jowhariyo Luulaay, etc.
V.	46	Aaa, kii La maydhin dhalaal ma lah oo,
	47	Dharka ba kii La maydhin dhalaal ma lah oo,
	48	Dhagahha burburaa dhismaha ma qabtee,
	49	Dhabbaha La maraa dhulkaw ma ekee,
	50	Dheehii baa iga daatay dhabanada eey,
		51 Jowhariyo Luulaay, etc.

I.	1	To be sure, an ignorant man has no strength.
	2	Whilst I slept, was a portion of my flesh [not] sliced from me?
	3	I was shattered; someone put a snake in my pocket, and
	4	My flesh shrank in a shiver, and
	5	I swooned. I travelled a great distance to dispute [my case].[10]
	6	The tree trunks[11] behind which I sought protection gave me no solace.[12]

	7	They struck me on the mouth, [humiliated me] with the butt of a spear.[13]
	8	O Jowhara and Luula,[14]
	9	Who are the flesh [of my body]—[15]
	10	O God, I am not completely here,
	11	[For] part of me is missing.[16]
II.	12	The soul which craves for what it lacks[17] is never without constant strain
	13	Until it finds that which it desires;
	14	Each morning it sets out [to search for it].
	15	My throat is parched whilst heavy showers fall.
	16	So long as I fail to sharpen my axe and
	17	Shrink from Holy War, I remain retarded, behind my friends, and
	18	My shouting is not sincere.[18]
	19	O Jowhara and Luula, etc.
III.	24	The [people of] the hamlets which were settled have fled
	23	From the Plains of Fedes and the farms of Jigjiga.[19]
	25	The maned lion has hamstrung them.[20]
	26	Defeat supplanted prosperity
	27	And I [had to] chase hyenas away with hot water.[21]
	28	Boorame has [now] become the East.[22]
	29	And the ocean and shore are lost from me.
	30	The eyes which once sparkled have all dried up.
	31	O Jowhara and Luula, etc.
IV.	35	Ah, the Swahilis—
	36	Even the Sudanese and the Swahilis,
	37	Who were tormented, have progressed.
	38	They were granted all that they wished.
	39	Are we not equal to those people who reached [their goal]?[23]
	40	And who possess full manhood, like us?[24]
	41	And have we not been born in nine months, O ye Somalis?[25]
	42	O Jowhara and Luula, etc.
V.	46	Ah, that which is unwashed has no shine—
	47	Clothes which are unwashed have no shine.

48   A crumbling stone [can]not be used for building;

49   The path upon which one treads does not resemble other land.

50   [Like an old cup], the enamel has been chipped away from my face.

    51   O Jowhara and Luula, etc.

Another important event in the mid 1950s, important both for politics and the development of modern poetry, was the formation of the Walaalo Hargeysa, "The Brothers of Hargeysa." It has been pointed out earlier (see above, p. 50) that Hargeysa had become the center of both art and politics in the Protectorate, and it is not surprising that the Walaalo began there.[26] The purpose of the new group was to organize and perform Somali plays. Many of the plays contained poetry and often *heello*, such as Example 9. This of course meant that political implications and intrigue were to surround the group from the beginning. But one thing must be made clear. The Walaalo Hargeysa are important for their part in popularizing the drive for independence and for composing many varied poems. They are remembered because of their potency of verse and not for acts of terror or violence which they in no way perpetrated.

The theater in Somalia at the writing of this book has developed a long way from the early plays of the Walaalo Hargeysa. Today the great majority of Somali plays are full of *heello* and other verse. The theater in Somalia has certainly been one of the motivating influences upon the composition of modern poetry. The following poem, composed by Xuseyn Aw Faarax (words) and Cabdullaahi Qarshe (music), was the only poem to appear in the Walaalo production of *Soomaalidii Hore iyo Soomaalidii Dambe*, "*Somalis of Yesterday and Today*" (1955). Its topic, the loss of the Hawd and Reserved Area, again demonstrates the importance of the political crisis and also serves as a good example of the early poetry inspired by the Walaalo Hargeysa.

Example 9:

    I.   1   Inta arligiyo, adiga tahay,

            2   Asaanay laabi, laba ahaanaynin,

                3   Agtayda ha marin, ishayduna ye,

                4   Ayaanay Ku arkine, ha ii iman,

II.   5   Awaare intaan, ka oodnahay,

        6   Asaanan Afmeer, degayn ambadee,

           7   Agtayda ha marin, ishayduna ye,

           8   Ayaanay Ku arkine, ha ii iman,

III. 9   Intay ergedeennu maqantahay,

      10   Asaan abxinayo Amxaaradee,

          11   Agtayda ha marin, ishayduna ye,

          12   Ayaanay Ku arkine, ha ii iman,

IV. 13   Inta arligiyo adiga tahay,

      14   Asaanay laabi, laba ahaanaynin,

          15   Amaana Alla, ayaad intaa tahay,

          16   Ayaankeennu waa anoo hela.

I.   1   While [the dispute] is between you and [our] country,

       2   And when [our] heart [can]not be halved,

          3   Do not pass near me, and my eye

          4   Will not see you; do not come to me.[27]

II.   5   As long as I am prohibited from entering Awaare,[28]

       6   And [can]not encamp in Afmeer,[29] I am lost, [so]

          7   Do not pass near me, and my eye

          8   Will not see you; do not come to me.

III. 9   While our envoys are away,[30] and

      10   I am pleading for peace with the Amharas,

          11   Do not pass near me, and my eye

          12   Will not see you; do not come to me.

IV. 13   While [the dispute] is between you and [our] country,

      14   And when [our] heart [can]not be halved,

          15   The Peace of God be upon you at that time;[31]

          16   Our fate is to recover [the lost territories] for ourselves .

The Walaalo Hargeysa were to prove their importance as an inspiration for the composition of modern poetry, for the second period of the *heello* is marked by a rapid rise in its prestige, at least among urban populations and the new elite. More and more skilled poets were naturally attracted to modern verse because of this, and many of their poems are still remembered.

The Poetry of the Second Period

The overall structure of the majority of poems during this period is very similar. Stanzas were short and much line repeating was used, so that the length of the *heello* was often taken up by this device. With the addition of politics and various themes which could be classed under it, many new, albeit simple and straightforward, images came to be used. Although hidden messages in the imagery of many *heello* were unrecognizable by colonial administrators, they were clear to the general public. When the poet Xuseyn Aw Faarax addressed his love as "Wiilo" in the following poem, Somalis understood that the girl represented the Protectorate. They also understood "Warsame" to represent the British administration. "Wiilo" was composed in 1956 by Xuseyn Aw Faarax and was set to music by Cabdullaahi Qarshe. It was an immediate success and spread throughout the Protectorate.

Example 10:

I.	1		Wiilooy waxaan ahay wadaad lugloo,
	2		Wiilooy welinimo ku soo degay,
		3	Wiilooy adna weer cad soo xidha ey,
		4	Wiilooy adna weer cad soo xidha ey,
II.	5		Wiilooy waalidkaa war Kuuma hayee,
	6		Wiilooy wacadkii ha beenayn,
		7	Wiilooy adna weer cad soo xidha ey,
		8	Wiilooy adna weer cad soo xidha ey,
III.	9		Wiilooy Warsamaa Ku weheshanaayee,
	10		Wiilooy ha is cunsiin waraabaha,
		11	Wiilooy adna weer cad soo xidha ey,
		12	Wiilooy adna weer cad soo xidha ey,
IV.	13		Wiilooy fule waran ma qaabilo,
	14		Wiilooy wadnahaagu yuu baqan,
		15	Wiilooy adna weer cad soo xidha ey,
		16	Wiilooy adna weer cad soo xidha ey,
V.	17		Wiilooy waxaan Kaa wacdiyaayeey,
	18		Wiilooy wadhi inay ku raacdaayeey,

19   Wiilooy adna weer cad soo xidha ey, .

20   Wiilooy adna weer cad soo xidha ey,

I.   1   O Wiilo,[32] I am a wadaad[33] without [the use of] a leg.[34]

     2   O Wiilo, I appeared [in this world] with special powers.[35]

       3   O Wiilo, wear a white mourning cloth.[36]

       4   O Wiilo, wear a white mourning cloth.

II.   5   O Wiilo, your father has no news for you,[37] but

     6   Wiilo, do not break the promise.[38]

       7   O Wiilo, wear a white mourning cloth.

       8   O Wiilo, wear a white mourning cloth.

III.   9   O Wiilo, Warsame[39] keeps you company.[40]

     10   O Wiilo, do not allow the hyena to eat you.[41]

       11   O Wiilo, wear a white mourning cloth.

       12   O Wiilo, wear a white mourning cloth.

IV.   13   O Wiilo, a coward does not face the spear.

     14   O Wiilo, your heart [must] not be afraid.

       15   O Wiilo, wear a white mourning cloth.

       16   O Wiilo, wear a white mourning cloth.

V.   17   O Wiilo, what I warn you about is[42]

     18   O Wiilo, that shame accompanies you.

       19   O Wiilo, wear a white mourning cloth.

       20   O Wiilo, wear a white mourning cloth.

We have said that rain is an important positive image in Somali poetry because of the nomad's need for water on the semi-desert of the Horn. When the poet Cali Sugulle complains of suffering drought during the rainy season, then, the audience knows that something is wrong. A common image in the *heello,* the drought in the midst of a rainy season in the following poem, signifies that the poet has been rejected by his love. He expects happiness in a certain situation (rainy season) and finds only sorrow (drought). This poem, composed in 1957, also illustrates the new license the poet could take with his verse. No longer restricted to a bound melody, freedom could be taken with the structure of the poem and the melody could be composed to match the lines later. The third and fourth lines of each stanza in Example 11 yield the following pattern:[43]

> A,   A,
> A,   B.

where B either completes the phrase grammatically or semantically.

A similar method can be observed in "Jowhariyo Luula," where the beginning of the fourth and fifth stanzas yields the following pattern:

> B
> A,   B.

Here, A completes the flow of thought involved in the phrase (see above, pp. 98-101). We shall observe this device in a later poem (see below, pp. 128-33).

Example 11:

I.	1	Ma helin hengeshiina maan furinoo,
	2	Ma helin hengeshiina maan furinoo,
	3	May hoorin, may hoorin,
	4	May hoorin, weli hogoshii Dayreedey,
		(*repeat ll. 3-4*)
II.	7	Hohey sow mar qudh ah ma haakah idhoo,
	8	Hohey sow mar qudh ah ma haakah idhoo,
	9	Hadal aan, hadal aan,
	10	Hadal aan ku jeclaysto kama helo eey,
		(*repeat ll. 9-10*)
III.	13	Is hiifay markaan hor-joogsadoo,
	14	Is hiifay markaan hor-joogsadoo,
	15	Hawl iyo, hawl iyo,
	16	Hawl iyo hagar-daamo korodhsadayey,
		(*repeat ll. 15-16*)
IV.	19	Heddii Alla gooynayaa hoyatee,
	20	Heddii Alla gooynayaa hoyatee,
	21	Sow tan, sow tan,

22   Sow tan halis ahee Lay helayey,

     (*repeat ll. 21-22*)

V.   25   Hooggaygii gacantaan ku haystaayoo,

26   Hooggaygii gacantaan ku haystaayoo,

27   Hadhkaa, hadhkaa,

28   Hadhkaagay naftaydu hoddaayeey,

     (*repeat ll. 27-28*)

VI. 31   Aduun baa Nabsiga hor-dhaca ku dhamee,

32   Aduun baa Nabsiga hor-dhaca ku dhamee,

33   Ma hiinhiin, ma hiinhiin,

34   Ma hiinhiinsaday huubadiisii ey,

     (*repeat ll. 33-34*)

I.   1   I did not find her; I have not cast aside my mourning.

2   I did not find her; I have not cast aside my mourning.

3   It has not [yet] rained! It has not [yet] rained!

4   Still the cloud has not rained during the Dayr.[44]

     (*repeat ll. 3-4*)

II.   7   Hohey,[45] did I not once say "Haakah?"[46]

8   Hohey, did I not once say "Haakah?"

9   [Kind] words, [kind] words,

10   [Kind] words [to encourage] my love [for her], I failed to receive.

     (*repeat ll. 9-10*)

III. 13   I blamed myself whenever I stood before her.

14   I blamed myself whenever I stood before her.

15   Difficulty, difficulty,

16   I increased my difficulty and distress.

     (*repeat ll. 15-16*)

IV. 19   The soul taken by God goes home.[47]

20   The soul taken by God goes home.

21   Here, here,

22   Here I am in danger and something happened to me.

     (*repeat ll. 21-22*)

V. 25 I hold my calamity in my hand.[48]

26 I hold my calamity in my hand.

27 Your shadow, your shadow,

28 My soul betrays you shadow.

(*repeat ll. 27-28*)

VI. 31 At first, only you drank the Nabsi.[49]

32 At first, only you drank the Nabsi.

33 Did I drink? Did I drink?

34 Did I drink the last dregs of it [myself]?[50]

(*repeat ll. 33-34*)

Also becoming much more common during this period was the style of unifying the alliteration of the poem throughout the whole of the verse following the model of Somali classical poetry. Indeed, by the end of this period in 1960, I was able to find only one poem which lacked uniform alliteration. We have seen that in "Jowhariyo Luula" the alliteration was still not unified. In it, as in Example 12, composed in 1958, each stanza made up an alliterative unit, but unlike the *heello* A, the theme of the poem was unified.

Example 12:

I. 1 Aaa, qod baad tahay, meel qabow ka baxoo,

2 Qajeel ubaxiina wada qariyoo,

3 Qacdaan Ku arkaan is qoonsadayoo,

4 Bal qabsoo waa baan Kuu qandhanayahay ey

(*repeat l. 4, three times*)

II. 8 Aaa, geedkii ka magoola, meel gebi ya ba,

9 Malaggu geela waa ku madhin jiray,

10 Mowdkaygii dhunkaal ma muudsaday ey,

(*repeat l. 10, three times*)

III. 14 Aaa, hed mooyee, habaar ba Looma dhintee,

15 Haaddu na subaxdii hortay ma kacdee,

16 Aniyo hilbahaygii kala hoyannee,

17 Labaysu hilowdaa hayga hadhdhee,

18   Hammooy beene sow tan Lay helayey,

    (*repeat l. 18, three times*)

IV. 22   Aaa, haddii aan muusanaabay, aanu i maqlayn,

23   Asaanan midigtayda maanta ku hayn,

24   Wax ii mar war roon, anigoo mar sugoo,

25   Mowlaha Rabbigay la magansada ey,

    (*repeat l. 25, three times*)

I.   1   Ah, you are the straight branch of a tree,[51] which grows in a cool place,

2   Often completely covered with flowers.[52]

3   The moment I saw you, I felt something strange [inside] myself;

4   Take my word for it,[53] at times I tremble for you.

    (*repeat l. 4, three times*)

II. 8-9   Ah, the Death Angel used to destroy camels by the tree which sprouted in a place by a precipice.[54]

10   Did I [not] suck the poison[55] of my death?

    (*repeat l. 10, three times*)

III. 14   Unless the appointed time for death [comes], one does not die from a curse;

15   No bird of prey wakes before me in the morning;[56]

16   My flesh is becoming separated from me;[57]

17   Let me abandon the [feeling of] sincerity which two people [can] have for each other.

18   O false hope, [grief] has found me here.

    (*repeat l. 18, three times*)

IV. 22   If I cry out for help, [and] he does not listen to me,

23   And I do not have him in my right hand today,[58]

24   [Then] the best advice[59] for me now is that I [should] wait for a while,

25   And seek protection from the Lord, my God.

    (*repeat l. 25, three times*)

Anticolonial themes, such as those in "Jowhariyo Luula," "Inta Arligiyo," and "Wiilo" were common during the second period of the *heello*. The theme of love, as we have seen in Examples 11 and 12, though now sharing its place with politics, was no less common. Panegyric naming remained a frequent device, as illustrated in Example 13, composed in 1958 by Cali Sugulle.

Example 13:

   I.   1   Hibooy amba waan Ku haybinayaa yee,

           2   Inaabti ma ii han-weyntahay ee,

                (repeat ll. 1-2)

   II.   5   Hubaal aawadaa cishqigan i hayaa,

           6   Heddeeyoo jar baan u halis ahay e,

                (repeat ll. 5-6)

   III. 9   Harraad nin qabo biyaha ma huree,

          10   Maxaa soo hor-maray hagaaggii yeey,

                (repeat ll. 9-10)

   IV. 13   Hilbiyo kala qalan illayn hadal eey,

          14   Haasaawaha waynu wada haynee,

          15   Heshiinnee maxayna kala helay eey?

                (repeat ll. 13-15)

   I.   1   O Hibo,[60] I am searching for you;[61]

           2   O cousin,[62] do you love me?[63]

                (repeat ll. 1-2)

   II.   5   To be sure, I have love for you;

           6   My time is up and I am in danger of falling over a cliff.

                (repeat ll. 5-6)

   III. 9   The man who thirsts [can] not dispense with water;

          10   What has come to stand in the way of [our] happiness?[64]

                (repeat ll. 9-10)

   IV. 13   Indeed meat and speech are two different things;[65]

          14   [Once] we spoke [freely] to each other.

          15   We agreed together; what happened between us?[66]

                (repeat ll. 13-15)

Another theme becoming more and more common at this time was that of patriotism. Enhancing the ever growing feelings of nationalism, the patriotic poem laid emphasis on praising the country rather than condemning the administration. Although mention was sometimes made of such political subjects as the separated parts of Greater Somalia, the main emphasis in the patriotic poem was to praise the Somalis as a whole. No longer could one discover mention of clans or sub-clans of the Somali nation. So-called tribalism is notable in modern poetry for its absence rather than its presence.

The following patriotic poem, another collaboration between Xuseyn Aw Faarax (words) and Cabdullaahi Qarshe (music) was composed in 1955 and revised in 1957. When I left Somalia in 1969, it was still one of the most popular patriotic poems in the country.

Example 14:

I.	M:	1	Qolaba calankeedu waa caynoo,
		2	Qolaba calankeedu waa caynoo,
		3	Innaga keenu waa cirkoo kale ey,
		4	Aan caadna lahayne, caashaqa ey,
	C:	5	Qolaba calankeedu waa caynoo,
		6	Innaga keenu waa cirkoo kale ey,
		7	Aan caadna lahayne, caashaqa ey,
II.	M:	8	Xiddigyahay caddi, waadna ciidamisee,
		9	Xiddigyahay caddi, waadna ciidamisee,
		10	Carrada keligaa adow curadee.
	C:	11	Cadceedda sideeda caan noqo ey,
		12	Qolaba calankeedu, etc.
III.	M:	15	Cashadaad dhalataa caloosheena,
		16	Cashadaad dhalataa caloosheena,
		17	Sidii culaygii cidaad marisee,
	C:	18	Allow ha ku celin, cawooy dhaha ey,
		19	Qolaba calankeedu, etc.
IV.	M	22	Shanteenaa cuduudood cadkii ka maqnaa,
		23	Shanteenaa cuduudood cadkii ka maqnaa,
		24	Adow celiyana caawimayey,

C: 25   Waa calaf cisigaysku keen simayee,

     26   Qolaba calankeedu, etc.

I.   M: 1   Every nation has her own flag;

     2   Every nation has her own flag;

     3   Ours is like the heavens[67]

     4   Without any clouds;[68] [Somalis] love it!

    C: 5   Every nation has her own flag;

     6   Ours is like the heavens

     7   Without any clouds; [Somalis] love it!

II.   M: 8   O white star, you give us strength.

     9   O white star, you give us strength.

     10   Only you are the firstborn of the country.

    C: 11   Become famous like the sun.

     12   Every nation, etc.

III.   M: 15   On the day you were born,[69] our stomach[70]

     16   On the day you were born, our stomach

     17   You cleaned, as with the firebrand[71] and cleansing fibre.[72]

    C: 18   O God, do not take [the star from us];[73] [O Somalis], say "Good Luck" [to it].

     19   Every nation, etc.

IV.   M: 22   The flesh of our five upper arms[74] was missing.

     23   The flesh of our five upper arms was missing.

     24   It is you who [can] return it to us and help us;

    C: 25   It is destiny that made us all equal in honor.

     26   Every nation, etc.

We will see how the timing of modern poetry, including "Jowhariyo Luula," contributed to its success; indeed, timing is probably a major reason for its success (see below, pp. 216-19). Such was also true of the poetry of the third period of the *heello*, though perhaps not so dramatically. With the coming of independence in 1960, new themes came into being and the structure of the *heello* gradually changed into a longer, more complicated poem.

NOTES

1. Lewis 1965, p. 151.

2. For the complete background to this meeting and the territory involved, see Drysdale 1964, Chapter VII: "The Haud Fiasco," pp. 74-87; and Lewis 1965, pp. 129-31. For further background on why this decision was made, see Lewis 1965, pp. 50-60, which describes the reasons behind the ceding of this territory to Ethiopia for the first time in history.

3. Touval 1963, p. 103.

4. Lewis 1965, p. 150.

5. Ibid., p. 151.

6. See the photograph facing p. 242 of Lewis 1961.

7. Drysdale 1964, p. 82.

8. Ibid. , p. 83.

9. Note that the text of stanzas IV and V and their differing alliterations indicate that they were added after 1955, when the main body of the poem was composed. Allusion to the Swahilis being granted all that they wished refers to the Kenyan independence in 1964.

10. Possibly a reference to the N. U. F. delegation to London and New York.

11. Possibly a reference to the treaties signed between the Somalis and the British. "The tree trunks [treaties] . . . gave me no solace [failed to protect me]."

12. *Jal.* "To give solace"; literally, "to give food (usually sweet) to an ill or dying person."

13. The Somali spear (*waran*), like other spears, has a blade (*bir*) and a staff (*samay*), but in addition it has a small blade (*jufo*) at the bottom end of it. To stab a man with the *jufo* quite literally is to add insult to injury. Again, the enemy referred to is the British; the insult is to fail to live up to their treaty obligations, while the injury is the giving away of land under their protection.

14. *Jowhara* and *Luula.* Panegyric names. *Jowhara* means "precious jewelry" while *Luula* means "pearls." These two women to whom the poem is ostensibly addressed represent the Hawd and Reserved Areas.

15. I. E., who are of the same clan as me. This phrase is often used as a compliment to a lover, because one's own clan is the most important group to which one belongs.

16. Obvious reference to the loss of the territories.

17. The verb *jeellan* literally means to "suffer from a deficiency of salt."

18. This line reads literally, "My shouting is not from [my] bosom/chest."

19. The Plains of Fedes and the farms of Jigjiga are inside the Hawd and Reserved Area.

20. The maned lion is a reference to the Lion of Judah, one of the titles of Emperor Haile Sellassie I of Ethiopia.

21. The poet was driven away from his prosperous area (lines 23-24) by the maned lion (line 25) into a famine stricken area where the hyenas were so hungry that they would boldly enter homesteads and would have to be chased away with hot water. Somali women usually keep a pan of boiling water on the compound fire inside the thorn fence for this purpose.

22. This is a reference to the naming of directions and places with the pivotal point at Boorame, where the poem is being composed. Hargeysa was the first town of the east (*bari*) and Boorame, Camuud, Jigjiga, and other towns west of Hargeysa were in the west (*galbeed*). With the border shift, however, the poet says that Boorame must now be considered a part of the east.

23. There are two possible translations of this line, the most likely of which is given in the main body of the poem. The other possible translation reads as follows: "Are we not equal to those people who waited [patiently for their rights]," etc. The problem arises in the progressive past tense of the weak verb, when the two verbs involved are pronounced exactly alike.

24. This line reads literally, "And who possess testicles, like us ?"

25. I. E., "are we not fully human and honorable like them?"

26. A similar group of artists called *Hay Sheegsheegin*, "Do Not Talk About Me," was formed in the South, but limited research prevents any comment about them. Their purpose undoubtedly parallelled the *Walaalo Hargeysa* as did their activities.

27. The poet is addressing the British.

28. *Awaare* is a town about forty miles south of Hargeysa. It was included in the area ceded to Ethiopia.

29. *Afmeer*. A town in the Hawd between the boundary of the Somali Democratic Republic and Awaare.

30. I. E., to London and New York (?).

31. I. E., the Somali people.

32. *Wiilo.* Panegyric name. From the Somali , "boy," it means "The-Girl-Who-Is-as-Honorable-Strong-Intelligent-as-a-Man."

33. *Wadaad.* Man of God. For a complete definition of a *wadaad,* see Lewis 1961, pp. 27f., 199, 213f., and 259f. Note that the poet himself is not a wadaad, but he needed a word beginning with a "W" for the sake of alliteration.

34. I. E., handicapped. The particular handicap is that the poet lives under colonial rule. Also, Cabdullaahi, who sang this poem in public, is himself crippled in one leg. Although he did not compose the poem, it seems likely that Xuseyn Aw Faarax composed it for him. Several Somalis have explained this line to me thus because of Cabdullaahi's handicap.

35. *Welinimo.* "Special powers." From the Somali *weli*, "saint." For a description of *welinimo*, see Lewis 1955/56.

36. Somalis wear white as a mourning cloth. The girl is instructed to put on a mourning cloth to mourn for her country, which is under foreign rule.

37. The poet perhaps means that no progress has been made toward independence, but line 6 implies that the struggle must go on.

38. The poet perhaps means the promise to struggle for independence.

39. *Warsame.* Somali male name, i. e. the British administration. The names of paired lovers in Somali poetry are often made to alliterate by poets.

40. I. E., "Wherever you go, the British are watching you."

41. *Waraabe.* "Hyena," i. e., the British.

42. *Ka wacdi.* "To warn about"; literally, "to preach against something so that the person will avoid or cease from doing that thing."

43. Note that this poem on the theme of love has vague images implying some hidden political message unknown to my informant.

44. *Dayr.* The secondary rainy season in Somalia which occurs during the autumn.

45. *Hohey.* See page 73, note 41.

46. *Haakah.* Exclamation word of general satisfaction, usually of the senses.

47. I. E., to the other world. This line reads literally, "The soul which God is going to cut goes home."

48. I. E., I caused my problems myself.

49. *Nabsi.* A Somali belief related to the Moslem belief in fate. The word has many overtones, but in general it is a great and powerful balancing force. If a man is

happy today, he will be sad tomorrow; if there is rain this season, there will be drought during the next; if a man is wealthy as a young man, he will be poor when he grows old. *Nabsi* is sometimes used with a meaning approximating "avenging fate" (see line 70 of the poem on pp. 120-29 of Andrzejewski and Lewis 1964). *Nabsi* is probably a Cushitic belief and not of Islamic origin, though it does not conflict with Moslem theology. Compare the use of this belief in the poems on pp. 120-22, line 33, and pp. 163-65, lines 24-43; and in the story of the Soothsayer (number 23) on pp. 49-61 of Muuse X. I. Galaal and Andrzejewski 1956, which is also translated into English in Andrzejewski 1963, pp. 149-63.

50. I. E., now I am suffering. This line implies that at first the girl loved the poet who rejected her. Now the situation is reversed.

51. *Qod.* "Straight branch of a tree." This metaphor implies that the man is handsome and straight of body like a tree branch.

52. Flowers are the result of rain. This image can be classified under rain as a positive symbol. The man is a bringer of prosperity or is living in prosperity.

53. *Bal qabso.* "Take my word for it"; literally, "just take it [for the truth]." This idiom is fairly new in Somali and is not widely used by older people.

54. One hazard of stock rearing in Somalia is the danger of cliffs. Camels will lean over a cliff in order to reach the tasty leaves of the acacia tree and sometimes lose their balance and fall.

55. *Dhunkaal.* "Poison," i. e., the love for the man. Love, often seen as an illness, is here symbolized as poison.

56. I. E., love keeps her from sleeping soundly.

57. I. E., love keeps her from eating properly, and she is becoming thin.

58. To have something in one's right hand. This is an Islamic image meaning to hold something securely. The left hand is considered ritually unclean.

59. *War.* "Advice"; literally, "news/rumors."

60. *Hibo.* Panegyric name. It means "the Gifted/Talented One."

61. *Haybi.* "To search"; literally "to search for one's clan" or "to search for one's position in the clan." The poet means here either that he is always keeping track of Hibo by watching her clan's movements, or that by learning her genealogy, he can determine if she can be married to him.

62. *Ina abti.* "Cousin"; literally, "the daughter of one's mother's sister." This kind of cousin is marriageable to a young man who is rarely refused to be allowed to marry her. *Ina abti* is also applied to one's father's sister's daughter, but marriage through this line is rare.

63. *Han-weynyahay.* "To love"; literally, "to have great pride/regard for something/to mean much to."

64. *Hagaagga.* "Happiness"; literally, "goodness/virtue;" i. e., the good thing (love) between us.

65. This line is taken from a Somali proverb: *Hadal iyo hilbaha kala qalan.* "Speech and meat are two different things." i. e., "subject has become clear."

66. I. E., they have parted against the wishes of the poet.

67. A description of the Somali flag will clarify the images in this poem. The Somali flag is a white, five pointed star on a blue field. The five points on the star symbolize the five parts of Greater Somalia: the former British Somaliland Protectorate, the former Italian Somaliland, the former French Somaliland, the Northern Frontier District in Kenya, and the areas in Ethiopia where Somalis live. Only the British and Italian parts ever united into an independent government.

68. I. E., nothing is blotting out the sun, an image for wisdom.

69. I. E., on independence day, 1 July 1960.

70. "Stomach." One of the seats of emotion in Somali poetry. The poet implies here that on independence day, all the unpleasant emotions of living under colonialism were wiped clean.

71. *Culayga.* "Firebrand." A piece of wood which has been burned and charred. It is used to coat the inside of a milk vessel (*dhiil*) in order to sterilize it.

72. *Cidaad.* "Cleansing fiber." A group of bound reeds used to clean (most of) the char out of the milk vessel when the sterilization process is finished. It is also used for wiping the ghee from one's hand after a meal and is believed to be an insect repellent. For this reason it is stored inside the hut (*aqal*).

73. This line reads literally: "O God, do not make [the Star] return [to where it came from]."

74. "Five upper arms." The five territories in which the Somalis live (see note 67 above). The upper arm is an image of strength.

6

THE *HEELLO*: PERIOD THREE

The Historical Background

In 1960 the newly independent state of Somalia saw the beginning of many changes which were the result of a number of factors. The republic had gained control of its own political destiny (as much as any newly independent state could in 1960), and there was the question of integrating the inherited British and Italian systems of education, economics, civil service, police and army, and law. The new elite, now the ruling class of Somalia, began to define its role, especially the female members of that elite. Apart from other changes, what is important for this study is that the change extended into and was reflected by the modern poem.

Most of the poetry I was able to collect in Somalia is from the third period, part of the duration of which I spent in the country. It becomes easier, therefore, to relate the (sometimes very topical) *heello* of this period to the unfolding history of the country. Furthermore, the most mature poetry was composed during this time. Lewis (1965) has followed the history of Somalia through 1963, but little has been written about it since then.[1]

Because the *heello* may yet change, one hesitates to claim that it fully matured during its third period; suffice it to say instead that modern poetry became much more refined at this time. Change in it was manifested in two ways. First, new themes became possible (e. g., pro- and antigovernment themes), while others became popular since they reflected current social debates (e. g., the role of women). Furthermore, the use of the poem expanded and completely new poems emerged (see the poem about football on pp. 160-62). Second, the structure of the *heello* changed yet again, and together with the new themes added to the growing prestige of modern poetry. We shall first consider the new political situation wherein the *heello* found itself and then examine in detail the poetry of the third period.

On 26 June 1960, the former British Somaliland Protectorate gained her independence. Four days later, on 1 July, this part of Somalia joined with the former United

Nations Trusteeship Territory of Somalia under Italian Administration to form the Somali Republic. Festive activities and celebrations of all kinds erupted in the new republic. One would be very hard pressed indeed to find a Somali who opposed the coming of independence to any part of this country. The unity of the two territories, however, is another question entirely. This joining of the two former colonies, although unanimously supported by a resolution in the legislative council of the British Protectorate on 6 April 1960, had been previously opposed by Maxamed Xaaji Ibraahiin Cigaal,[2] then leader of the majority party and "Leader of Government Business."[3] The relative acceptance of this unity was to be postponed until Cigaal became Prime Minister of the Republic in July of 1967.

The following two poems illustrate these tense feelings about the unity of the two territories quite well. Example 15, composed by Cali Sugulle in 1968, looks back to this "marriage" and praises it as a time when disaster left the Somali people and victory was gained. The poem, chanted in canticle form by a male and female chorus, is entitled "Kuwa Libintii Gaadhoo" ("Those Who Reached the Victory").

Example 16, composed in late 1960 or early 1961, was never presented over the radio. For Somalis to compose poetry that criticized the colonial administration, and to hide their criticism in metaphor, is one thing. When the administration was made up of Somalis themselves, it was no longer as easy to criticize with hidden messages. The poet might well claim that his poem was composed in objection to the traditional system of marriage when one often had little choice in choosing a spouse. The following stanzas, using different images but essentially stating the same thesis, could then be said to support the first stanza. Government officials, however, saw the poem in a different light. To them, all the stanzas supported an unstated thesis: that the marriage of British and Italian Somalilands had been a mistake. The poem was banned so early that no melody for it was remembered by my informant.

Example 15:

I.   F: 1   Kuwa libintii gaadhoo,

           2   Aan La loodin karayn,

             (repeat ll. 1-2)

    M: 5   Laydhsadaan nahee,

             (repeat ll. 1-5)

         11   Goormaan ladnaannayey?

F: 12   Lixdankii,

M: 13   Luggooyadii na daysayey?

F: 14   Lixiyo labaatankii Juun,

M: 15   Aaa, goormaan lulannayey?

F: 16   Lixdii saac,

M: 17   Goormaan liibaannayey?

F: 18   Kowdii Luliyo laba midowdayey.
              (*repeat ll. 11-18*)

II.   27   Kuwa cadowgii laayoo,

          28   Isticmaarkii lumiyoon,
                (*repeat ll. 27-28*)

M: 31   Liidan baan nahayey,
                (*repeat ll. 27-31*)

          37   Goormaan ladnaannayey? , etc.

III. F: 53   Kuwa yeeshay laxaad oo,

          54   La sinnaaday adduunkoon,
                (*repeat ll. 53-54*)

M: 57   Liicin baan nahay ey,
                (*repeat ll. 53-57*)

          63   Goormaan ladnaannayey?, etc.

IV. F: 79   Kuwa laan sare noqdoo,

          80   Labadii ka maqanyiin,
                (*repeat ll. 79-80*)

M: 83   La sugayaan nahayey,
                (*repeat ll. 79-83*)

          89   Goormaan ladnaannaayey?, etc.

I.   F: 1   Those who reached the victory,

            2   Who cannot be bent, and
                  (*repeat ll. 1-2*)

M: 5   Who walk in the cool breeze, are we.
                  (*repeat ll. 1-5*)

            11   When did we recover our health?

F:		12	In 1960.[4]
M:		13	When did disaster leave us?[5]
F:		14	On the twenty-sixth of June.[6]
M:		15	Ah, when did we churn [our milk]?[7]
F:		16	At twelve midnight.[8]
M:		17	When did we gain victory?
F:		18	On the first of July when the two united.[9]

(repeat ll. 11-18)

II.   27   Those who killed the enemy,

           28   Who caused colonialism to become lost, and

(repeat ll. 27-28)

M: 31   Who are not weak, are we.

(repeat ll. 27-31)

           37   When did we recover, etc.

III.   F: 53   Those who acquired strength,

           54   Who became equal with the world, and

(repeat ll. 53-54)

M: 57   Who did not lean off balance, are we.

(repeat ll. 53-57)

           63   When did we recover, etc.

IV.   F: 79   Those who became the top branch,

           80   From whom the two[10] are missing, and

(repeat ll. 79-80)

M: 83   For whom people have waited, are we.

(repeat ll. 79-83)

           89   When did we recover, etc.

Example 16:

I.   1   Haweeyoo geyaanoo, gacal igula taliyaa,

     2   Haweeyoo geyaanoo, gacal igula taliyaa,

     3   Garbo ii hillaacdoon, sii daayay gacantee,

     4   Garbo ii hillaacdoon, sii daayay gacantee,

          5   Anigaysu geystoo, galabsaday xumaantee,

          6   Wixii ila garaadow, gobannimo ha tuurina,

	7	Anigaysu geystoo, galabsaday xumaantee,
	8	Wixii ila garaadow, gobannimo ha tuurina,
II.	9	Adoo guri barwaaqo ah, geel dhalay ku haysta,
	10	Adoo guri barwaaqo ah, geel dhalay ku haysta,
	11	Geeddi Lama lallaboo, abaar Looma guuree,
	12	Geeddi Lama lallaboo, abaar Looma guuree,
	13	Anigaysu geystoo, etc.
III.	17	Adigoo golmoonoo, gaajo ay ku hayso,
	18	Adigoo golmoonoo, gaajo ay ku hayso,
	19	Gorofkaaga xoorka leh, Layskama gembiyo e,
	20	Gorofkaaga xoorka leh, Layskama gembiyo e,
	21	Anigaysu geystoo, etc.
IV.	25	Intaan gudin afaystaan, laabatada is gooyoo,
	26	Intaan gudin afaystaan, laabatada is gooyoo,
	27	Caqligayga guuroo, garab maray wanaaggee,
	28	Caqligayga guuroo, garab maray wanaaggee,
	29	Anigaysu geystoo, etc.
V.	33	Nabsigaan guntaday baa, goobtaa i joojoo,
	34	Nabsigaan guntaday baa, goobtaa i joojoo,
	35	Ninna garawsan maayoo way goonni xaajadu,
	36	Ninna garawsan maayoo way goonni xaajadu,
	37	Anigaysu geystoo, etc.

I.	1	When [my] kinsmen advised me [to wed] Haweeyo,[11] who is marriageable to me,
	2	When [my] kinsmen advised me [to wed] Haweeyo, who is marriageable to me,
	3	Lightning flashed for me by a precipice and I stretched out [my] hand [toward it].
	4	Lightning flashed for me by a precipice and I stretched out [my] hand [toward it].
	5	'Tis I who brought [this] evil upon myself;
	6	All ye who think as I do, don't cast aside [your] freedom.[12]

7   'Tis I who brought [this] evil upon myself;

8   All ye who think as I do, don't cast aside [your] freedom.

II.   9   While you keep camels which have just given birth in a prosperous camp,

10   While you keep camels which have just given birth in a prosperous camp,

11   [You should] not arrange a move[13] and travel into a drought.[14]

12   [You should] not arrange a move and travel into a drought.

13   'Tis I who brought, etc.

III.   17   You who are lean[15] and whom hunger grips,

18   You who are lean and whom hunger grips,

19   Should not o'erturn your frothing[16] milk vessel.

20   Should not o'erturn your frothing milk vessel.

21   'Tis I who brought, etc.

IV.   25   When I sharpened the axe, I cut my own joint;

26   When I sharpened the axe, I cut my own joint;

27   My senses left me—I have missed the good things [of life].

28   My senses left me—I have missed the good things [of life].

29   'Tis I who brought, etc.

V.   33   The Nabsi[17] which I tied for myself halted me in that place;

34   The Nabsi which I tied for myself halted me in that place;

35   I will take counsel from no one, for the matter is special to me.[18]

36   I will take counsel from no one, for the matter is special to me.

37   'Tis I who brought, etc.

The uniting of the two territories, as we have stated, led to numerous difficulties because of the clash between the two colonial administrative heritages. One of the areas in which the difficulty was so great that it appeared almost insurmountable was education. English had been used in northern schools and Italian in the South. Frustrated students and teachers, together with others who had strong nationalistic feelings about rendering Somali to a written form, provided the theme of countless debates and poems that has become one of the pillars of the platforms of many political parties. Every government since independence promised to have the language written, but they all ran into social and religious pressures to postpone the decision. Finally, in 1972, the Barre regime introduced a Somali alphabet based on Latin script.[19] Prior to this time, however, several poems were composed on this issue, like the following one, composed in 1960 by Cali Sugulle. It was popular in Somalia for about six years and could be heard frequently on the radio.[20]

Example 17:

I. M: 1 Asaaggeen horow maraan arkayaa,

         2 Ilays calanyow iftiiminaya,

         3 Asaaggeen horow maraan arkayaa,

         4 Ilays calanyow iftiiminaya,

    F: 5 Ammankaag iyo yaab, argaggax,

         6 Abboowe macaanow hooy,

         7 Ii sheeg maxaa Kuu daran,

         8 Abboowe macaanow hee,

    M: 9 Waan asqaysanahee,

         10 Ku aaway, abbaayo macaaneey hooy,

    F: 11 Ii sheeg maxaa Kuu daran,

         12 Abboowe macaanow hee,

    M: 13 Af qalaad aqoontu, miyaa?

    F: 14 Maya, maya!

    M: 15 Ma ahee af qalaad aqoontu, miyaa?

    F: 16 Maya, maya!

         17 Ma ahee waa intuu qofba Eebbe geshaa,

         18 Ayay nala tahay annagee,

         19 Waa intuu qofba Eebbe geshaa,

         20 Ayay nala tahay annagee,

         21 Ma ogtahay, dib Looma abuuro dadkee,

    M: 22 Ma ogtahay aqoonta ammaah Laysuma siiyee?

    F: 23 Ma ogtahay aqoonta abaal Laysuma tartee?

         24 Ma ogtahay aqoonta ammaah Laysuma siiyee?

    F: 25 Ma ogtahay aqoonta abaal Laysuma tartee?

    M: 26 Ma ogtahay aqoonta miyaa La iibsan karaa?

    F: 27 Maya, maya!

M: 28   Ma ogtahay aqoonta miyaa La soo ergistaa?

F: 29   Maya, maya!

T: 30   Ma ahee waa intuu qofba Eebbe geshaa,

      31   Ayay nala tahay annagee,

      32   Waa intuu qofba Eebbe geshaa,

      33   Ayay nala tahay annagee,

      34   Ma ogtahay dib Looma abuuro dadkee?

II. F: 35   Oggoli oo wax barashadu waa ii egtahay,

          36   Af shisheeye ayaynu addoon u nahee,

          37   Oggoli oo wax barashadu waa ii egtahay,

          38   Af shisheeye ayaynu addoon u nahee,

          39   Waan asqaysanahee,

          40   Ku aaway abboowe macaanow hooy,

     M: 41   Ii sheeg maxaa Kuu daran,

          42   Abbaayo macaaney hooy,
               (*repeat ll. 39-42*)

     F: 47   Af qalad aqoontu, miyaa?, etc.
               (*with roles reversed*)

III. M: 69   Itaalkii baa Lays ammaahinayaa,

          70   Iskeen ma u wada adeegnaayeey,

          71   Itaalkii baa Lays ammaahinayaa,

          72   Iskeen ma u wada adeegnaayeey,

     F: 73   Ammankaag iyo yaab, argaggax, etc.
               (*as stanza I*)

IV. F: 103   Aboor baa dundumo ilkaha ku dhisee,

         104   Aqbalka na qof kalaa arrinshoo ururshee,

         105   Aboor baa dundumo ilkaha ku dhisee,

         106   Aqbalka na qof kalaa arrinshoo ururshee,

         107   Waan asqaysanahee, etc.
               (*as stanza II*)

I.   M: 1   I see our equals [in the world] making progress;

          2   Oh, [my] glowing flag!

          3   I see our equals [in the world] making progress;

124

	4	Oh, [my] glowing flag!
F:	5	Astonishment, surprise and shock.
	6	O [my] sweet brother,
	7	Tell me what troubles you;
	8	[Tell me], O my sweet brother.
M:	9	I am maddeningly confused [because I am taught too many foreign languages at the same time].
	10	[Now tell], where are you, [my] sweet sister?[21]
F:	11	Tell me what troubles you;
	12	[Tell me], O my sweet brother.
M:	13	Does education mean [learning] a foreign language?
F:	14	No, no!
M:	15	It does not. And does education [truly] mean [learning] a foreign language?
F:	16	No, not at all!
	17	It does not. [True education] is what God bestows on [each] person.
	18	This is our opinion.
	19	It is what God bestows on [each] person.
	20	This is our opinion.
	21	Do you think that people [can] be created again [and made into what they are not]?
M:	22	Don't you know that knowledge [can]not be given on loan?
F:	23	Don't you know that knowledge [can]not be given as a gift?
	24	Don't you know that knowledge [can]not be given on loan?
F:	25	Don't you know that knowledge[can]not be given as a gift?
	26	Do you think that knowledge can be bought?
	27	No, no!
	28	Do you think that knowledge [can] be borrowed?
	29	No, not at all!
	30	It can not. [True education] is what God bestows on [each] person.
	31	This is our opinion.

32 It is what God bestows on [each] person.

33 This is our opinion.

34 Do you think that people [can] be created again [and made into what they are not]?

II. F: 35 Oh, how I agree that education is essential for us,

36 But we are slaves to foreign languages.

37 Oh, how I agree that education is essential for us,

38 But we are slaves to foreign languages.

39 I am maddeningly confused [because I am taught too many foreign languages at the same time].

40 Where are you, O my sweet brother?

M: 41 Tell me what troubles you;

42 [Tell me], O my sweet sister.

43 I am maddeningly confused [because I am taught too many foreign languages at the same time].

44 Where are you, O my sweet brother?

45 Tell me what troubles you;

46 [Tell me], O my sweet sister.

F: 47 Does education mean [learning], etc.

(with roles reversed)

III. M: 69 People lend each other strength, but

70 Should we [not also] do something for selves?

71 People lend each other strength, but

72 Should we [not also] do something for selves?

F: 73 Astonishment, surprise and shock, etc.

(as stanza I)

IV. F: 103 The [tiny] termite builds the [huge] ant hill with [his own] teeth.

104 This agreement[22] has been engineered by others.[23]

105 The [tiny] termite builds the [huge] ant hill with [his own] teeth.

106 This agreement has been engineered by others.

107 I am maddeningly confused, etc.

(as stanza II)

Aside from the writing of Somali the other difficulties of integration between the two sections of the republic quickly led to a feeling of regionalism (North versus South). Coupled with what became known as "tribalism" at this time, regionalism threatened not only the stability of the new government but the republic itself.

What Somalis came to call "tribalism" might be better termed "clanism" because it was the various clans in the part of the nation within the republic's boundaries that vied for power in the new state. From a practical standpoint, however, Somali clanism functioned very nearly the same way as ethnic strife in other multiethnic African states. Nepotism has been one of the major manifestations of Somali clanism and the balance of clans represented in the Council of Ministers and in the government as a whole was, until the coup in 1969, parallel with the relative size and power of the clans in the republic. Overt action by the government to reduce the strength of clanism, such as the law making it illegal for political parties to bear clan names, had little effect on actually ridding the country of clan-based activity.[24] Lewis states the case as follows:[25]

> However precipitate and incomplete it may have appeared at the time, the union of the former British Somaliland and [Italian] Somalia had at once a profound effect on Somali politics. . . . The marriage of the two territories entailed significant, and in some cases, quite drastic changes in the political status of the various clans and lineages within the state. . . . Despite the patriotic fervour which acclaimed the formation of the Republic, the most all pervasive element in politics remained the loyalty of the individual to his kin and clan.

Clan strife was to plague the government until October 1969, when the successful coup took place, when it was suppressed for a while but again became a problem the longer Siyad Barre remained in power. Regionalism was based upon several factors. The inheritance of different colonial systems of government and languages of learning hindered communication. The shift of relative size—and therefore power—among the clans when the two territories joined was a major element. Furthermore, the center of politics for northern Somalis moved out of the North entirely as the importance of Muqdisho increased. Hargeysa, once the most important city in British Somaliland, now lost its position and became at most a regional capital. Unrest in the North gradually grew, being constantly reinforced by the problems of integration. Finally in December 1961, matters came to a head and a coup d'etat was executed in Hargeysa when a group of British-trained, junior officers arrested their southern superiors who had assumed command of the army units in the North. Claiming that they were acting against tribalism and corruption in the army and in the government, the junior officers announced that they had named General Dazuud, commander-in-chief of the army, as head of state. Although documents concerning this coup were never made public—if indeed any documents concerning it exist at all—it is doubtful that General Dazuud knew anything about the coup until it had occurred. Despite the announcement that the southerner, General Dazuud, was to be made head of state, trouble began on the following day when rumors spread to the effect that the object of the coup was not to take over the entire government but only that of the North. Faced with the prospect of splitting the republic, Somali nationalism lifted its angry head as private soldiers and noncommissioned officers arrested all the lieutenants long before the government could react.[26]

The actual motive or motives of this aborted coup may never be made public, and the only clear statement about it that can be made is to repeat what each side asserted. The lieutenants claimed that they were reacting against "tribalism" and corruption and that their intention, as Somali patriots, was to seize the reigns of government in the entire country. The government in power at the time, however, claimed that regionalism was the motive, and that the lieutenants were splitting the new republic into its former two colonial divisions. Whatever the motives, Parliament later voted to pardon all the participants. The following poem, wherein the lieutenants are represented in the figure of the "honorable man" (see line 71) and northern Somalia is personified as a "weak woman" (see lines 13 and 50), first appeared in 1962. The fact that the poem was banned when its implications became known speaks for the skill with which the poet employed the hidden message.

Example 18:

I.	C:	1	Diiyooy hiddii,
		2	Oo hiddidiiyooy hiddii,
		3	Ax hiddidiiyooy hiddii,
			(repeat ll. 1-3)

II.   M: 7   Laacay oo hinqaday,

             8   Hir bay laacay oo hinqaday,

             9   Oo hilaac bay baxoo handaday,

             10   Hadda na waayeyoo, hakaday,

      C: 11   Waayey oo hakaday,

             12   Halyey waayey oo hakaday,

             13   Oo haween baan ahoo habraday,

             14   Hiil iyo mid na hoo ma galo,

                 15   Diiyooy hiddii, etc.

III. M: 21   Aawadaa ma ledo,

             22   Hurdada aawadaa ma ledo,

             23   Hummaagaagii bay hor-kacay,

             24   Hawshaadii ma soo hadh-galo,

      C: 25   Kula qaybsadaa,

             26   Hawshaan Kula qaybsadaa,

             27   Oo harraadkaan Kula qabaa,

             28   Oo anigu waan Kula hayaa,

             29   Ee adaan i hagaajinayn,

                 30   Diiyooy hiddii, etc.

IV. M: 36   Ya, hal baan lahaa,

             37   Way, adduunyo hal baan lahaa,

             38   Haaneedkii na wow hayaa,

             39   Ee maxaydin hayee, idin helay?

      C: 40   Ya, siduu i gozay,

             41   Halbowle siduu i gozay,

             42   Haabhaabtay waxaanan hayn,

             43   Hoogayoo bazayey, ma hadhay?

                 44   Diiyooy hiddii, etc.

V.   M: 50   Ma dhammaa La yidhi,

             51   Haween ma dhammaa La yidhi,

             52   Hablow anigaydin hanan,

             53   Ee hubaal hal ma siisannaa?

      C: 54   Hubsitow halyey,

		55	Hanadow hubsitow halyey,
		56	Hawraarsane hadal-gobeed,
		57	I hoo adigu na i hano,
		58	Diiyooy hiddii, etc.
VI.	M:	64	Halkay ahayd,
		65	Way, dhadhiini halkay ahayd,
		66	Dhabbadaa dhagax-dhagax u maray,
		67	Dhawaaq maad celisidaa?
	C:	68	Maylka u diglayn,
		69	Wiilka sidaa maylka u diglayn,
		70	Ee magaalada laba u dhixi,
		71	Miiganow miridh deyni maayo,
		72	Diiyooy hiddii, etc.
VII.	M:	78	Qawlow qadhqadhay,
		79	Roobka soo qawlow qadhqadhay,
		80	Qaawanaantayduu arkaa,
		81	Ee qudhdhayda xaggee dhigaa?
	C:	82	Yane waa Illaah,
		83	Kuu dhammeeye na waa Illaah,
		84	Kuu dhisaaye na aabbahaa,
		85	Ani Illaahay ii dhammee,
		86	Aabbahay baan ii dhisayn,
		87	Diiyooy hiddii, etc.
VIII.	M:	93	Ninle baa gudbane,
		94	Uustar-dheere ninlaa gudbane,
		95	Oo aroos nin helaa hadh gala,
		96	Ee Aroori anaa ku hadhay,
	C:	97	Nin sitow qummane,
		98	Uustar-dheere nin sitow qummane,
		99	Fiicanow fidhin laan gobeed,
		100	Diiyooy hiddii, etc.
IX.		106	Diiyooy hiddii, etc.

I.	C:	1	Diiyooy hiddii,
		2	Oo hiddidiiyooy hiddii,
		3	Ax hiddidiiyooy hiddii,[27]

(*repeat ll. 1-3*)

II.	M:	7	[Something] appeared and I peered at it;
		8	Distant shapes [of clouds] appeared to me on the horizon and I stared at them.
		9	And lightning[28] appeared to me, and I yearned for it.
		10	However, I failed to find it and I hesitated.[29]
	C:	11	I failed to find him and I hesitated;
		12	I failed to find a champion and I hesitated.
		13	I am a woman who dared not act;
		14	I [can]not support anyone, [can]not give aid.
		15	Diiyooy hiddii, etc.

III.	M:	21	For your sake I [can]not sleep;
		22	For your sake I [can]not [rest in] sleep,
		23	[For] your image rises before me.
		24	[Because of] the toil [you caused me], I [can]not rest.[30]
	C:	25	I share [all] with you;
		26	I share all the toil with you;
		27	And I share the thirst with you.
		28	And I sympathize with you.
		29	However, you are not treating me right.
		30	Diiyooy hiddii, etc.

IV	M:	36	*Ya,*[31] I owned only one she-camel;[32]
		37	*Way,*[33] of all [worldly] possessions, I owned only one she-camel.
		38	I still keep to the left side of the camel.[34]
		39	What troubles you? What befell you?[35]
	C:	40	*Ya,* as if it were cut;
		41	As if an artery of mine were cut.
		42	I searched hurriedly for the thing I did not have.[36]
		43	Alas! Alas! Was I [not] left out?
		44	Diiyooy hiddii, etc.

V.	M:	50	People say that they are not complete [like men];[37]
		51	People say that women are not complete [like men].
		52	O girls, I will take care of you.
		53	But shall we trade certainty for a she-camel?[38]
	C:	54	O [my] champion, who is armed,
		55	O protector, O champion, who is armed,
		56	All right, [your] speech [is that] of noble men.
		57	Take me and cherish me
		58	Diiyooy hiddii, etc.
VI.	M:	64	To the place where it was,
		65	*Way*, to the place where Dhadhiin[39] was,
		66	I walked on the road stone by stone.[40]
		67	Why did you not answer my cry?[41]
	C:	68	Walks tirelessly for miles—
		69	The boy who walks tirelessly like that for miles
		70	Takes only two [nights] to walk to the town;
		71	Oh man of honor, I will not leave him alone [even] for a minute.[42]
		72	Diiyooy hiddii, etc.
VII.	M:	78	O thunder; I shivered—
		79	O thundering rain[43] [coming] toward me; I shivered;
		80	He sees my nakedness;[44]
		81	Where shall I hide myself?
	C:	82	And it is God—
		83	[The one who can] do anything for you is God.
		84	The one who can arrange a wedding for you is your father.[45]
		85	God did everything for me;
		86	But my father did not arrange the wedding for me.[46]
		87	Diiyooy hiddii, etc.
VIII.	M:	93	The man who has it preserves it—
		94	The man who has the long rifle preserves it.[47]
		95	And the man who marries finds rest.[48]
		96	And I was left behind in Aroori.[49]
	C:	97	O you man, [who are] right—
		98	O you who carry the long rifle, [you are] right.[50]

99 O you clever man, [you are] a comb [made from] the branch of the
Gob Tree.[51]

100 Diiyooy hiddii, etc.

IX.   106 Diiyooy hiddii, etc.

Regionalism, if it does not still plague the country to some extent, was never a strong force in Somalia. When, as we stated, Cigaal became prime minister in 1967, the problem appeared to have been solved, for the North then felt that it had more of a share in the country's politics.[52] Whatever the case, Pan-Somalism has always played a stronger role in the country, a role which ironically enough has isolated Somalia from Pan-Africanist feelings of other newly emerging nation-states on the continent.

While the cry for independence in other very often multiethnic countries in Africa became the basis of a Pan-African movement on the continent, such a cry in Somalia has tended to isolate her from other African states. The reason for this is based upon the clan structure of the Horn. Unlike most African states, which are made up of several nations within their foreign-drawn boundaries, the independent state of Somalia contains only part of the Somali nation. The drawing of boundaries by foreign powers in the late nineteenth/early twentieth century led to the sectioning of the Somali nation into five major areas, two of which now make up the country. Faced with nationalist movements based on ethnic ties, other nations, unlike Somalia, would be split apart into separate political units. Conversely, Somalia's accomplishment of a Greater Somalia would mean the breaking off of large tracts of land from her immediate neighbors. Pan-Somalism, then, directly clashes with Pan-Africanism and is hard pressed to find support from any other African nation-state.

Despite this unique state of affairs on the international scene, Somalia has participated in the Pan-Africanist movement to some extent, albeit within her own boundaries. If these two movements clash in her foreign affairs, they certainly seem to go hand in hand on the domestic scene. The following pair of poems bears witness to this fact. The first poem (Example 19), composed in 1962 by Ismaaciil Sheekh Axmed, is but one of many *heello* supporting Pan-Somalism; and it should also be pointed out that the desire for unity among the five Somalilands is mentioned in many poems where it is not the major theme.

The second poem (Example 20) was composed by Cabdullaahi Qarshe shortly after the death of Patrice Lumumba in 1960. The popularity of this poem, (and it could still be heard on the radio in 1969), bears witness to strong Pan-Africanist feelings within the Somali Republic.

Example 19:[53]

I.   M: 1   Inta wiil dhiggeenniiyeey,

            2   Dhalankeenna necebyahayee,

            3   Aynnu dhiig qabownahayee,

              (repeat ll. 1-3)

      C: 7   Haddaan dhimashooy Ku diido,

            8   Haddaan dhalaashooy Ku sheegto,

            9   Haddaan dhaqashooy Ku raadsho,

            10   Haddaan dheregow Ku doono,

II.   M: 11   Intaan dhumucda weynahay ee,

            12   Nacab dhidhibbadaydii yee,

            13   Gowrac ugu dhakhsanayaan ee,

              (repeat ll. 11-13)

      C: 17   Haddaan dhimashooy, etc.

III. M: 21   Intaad ka dhimantahay ee,

            22   Magacaan ku dhaadanayooy,

            23   Waa noo dheg-xumo weyn ee,

              (repeat ll. 21-23)

      C: 27   Haddaan dhimashooy, etc.

IV. M: 31   Inta uu dhulkaygii yey,

            32   Qoqobuhu dhex-yaalan ee,

            33   En kala dhantaalnahay ee,

              (repeat ll. 31-33)

      C: 37   Haddaan dhimashooy, etc.

V: M: 41   Inta dayaxu dhicisyahay ey,

            42   Xidiggu na dhammeysyahay ey,

            43   Dhalanteedka ay tahay ey,

              (repeat ll. 41-43)

      C: 47   Haddaan dhimashooy, etc.

I. M: 1 While boys of our generation[54]

2 Hate our children,[55] and

3 Our blood runs cold,[56]

(repeat ll. 1-3)

C: 7 O Death, if I reject you!

8 O Clan Ties, if I claim you!

9 O Wealth, if I search for you!

10 O Prosperity, if I seek you![57]

[Then I am dishonorable.][58]

II. M: 11 While I am still strong and

12-13 My enemies make haste to slaughter my supporters,

(repeat ll. 11-13)

C: 17 O Death, etc.

III. M: 21 While you are [still] excluded,[59] and

22 I claim the name [of Somalia], and

23 It is a great shame to us,

(repeat ll. 21-23)

C: 27 Death, etc.

IV. M: 31-32 While there are boundaries[60] between [the parts of] my country, and

33 We are [still] divided,

(repeat ll. 31-33)

C: 37 O Death, etc.

V. M: 41 While the moon [of our national fulfillment] is [as small as] an infant born prematurely,

42 Even [though] the [five-pointed] star is complete[61] [on our flag],

43 [And while these things] are a mirage, [then],[62]

(repeat ll. 41-43)

C: 47 O Death, etc

Example 20:

I. 1 Lamumba ma noola, mana dhimaney,

2 Labadaa mid na haw maleynina ey,

3   Muuqii s oo La waayay mooyaaney,

4   Inuu maqanyahay ha moodina ey,

II.   5   Madax buu noo ahaa, mudnaan jirayey,

6   Miyey kaalintiisii madhantahay ey,

7   Lamumba ma noola, etc.

III.   11   Baddoo maqashaa ka murugootoo,

12   Maankiyo maskaxdaana wada roganee,

13   Lamumba ma noola, etc.

IV.   17   Madowgu giddi waa idinla meel oo,

18   Ogobey maanta waa mid ka gudhahey,

19   Lamumba ma noola, etc.

V.   23   Maangaabyada meel nagaga dhacay iyo,

24   Ma moogin godobta nagaga maqaney,

25   Lamumba ma noola, etc.

I.   1   Lumumba is neither living nor dead.

2   Do not imagine that [he is in] either of the two [conditions].

3   Although people have failed to find his person,

4   Do not imagine that he is absent.

II.   5   He was a leader to us who was honorable.

6   Is his position not empty [now]?

7   Lumumba is neither living, etc.

III.   11   The sea who hears [the news] grieves.

12   Our minds and brains are turned upside down.

13   Lumumba is neither living, etc.

IV.   17   All black people are on the same side with you.

18   Alas! Today he is the one [whose milk] has been cut off [from us],

19   Lumumba is neither living, etc.

V.   23-24   He was not ignorant of the unavenged injustice committed against us and of the stupid ones who have offended us.[63]

25   Lumumba is neither living, etc.

On the world scene Somalia emerged as a nonaligned country, like so many newly independent countries before and after it. From the beginning four countries, the

United States, the Soviet Union, Italy, and Egypt—and, to a lesser degree, mainland China and West Germany—have attempted to spread their influence on the Horn. At one time Somalia was receiving more dollars of foreign aid per capita than any other African state, but this statistic must not be overrated, for her population is under five million.

As far as the immediate future of Somalia is concerned, perhaps the most important aid given to her was that of equipment and training for the army. Turning down a moderate offer of Western military assistance valued at 6.5 million pounds, (then) Prime Minister Cabdi-Rashiid Cali Shar-Ma-Arke accepted nearly 11 million pounds of aid from the Soviet Union.[64] The presence of Russian arms in Somalia has sent the Emperor of Ethiopia to Moscow at least twice since 1960 and brought about a mutual assistance treaty between Ethiopia and Kenya.

The following poem, composed in 1967, long before the military coup, bears witness to the growing prestige of the Soviet Union as a result of her military aid. Its poet, Xuseyn Aw Faarax, one of the original Walaalo Hargeysa (see above pp. 101-02), is one of the most respected poets in the country. The poem is sung by a female chorus.

Example 21:

I. 1 Saaxiibbadaadu waa dar,

2 Kuu horseedoo,

3 Kuu sahan ahaadiyo,

4 Dar kaloo Ku sirayoo,

5 Sunta Kuu walaaqoo,

6 Adiga uun Ku sababee,

(*repeat ll. 1-6*)

13 Kala sooca labadoo,

14 Kala saaraay,

(*repeat ll. 13-14, three times*)

21 Ayay noo sinnaannin e,

22 Haynoo kala soke e yaan,

(*repeat ll. 21-22*)

II.   25   Saaxiibbadaadu waa dar,

26   Gacan Ku siiyoo,

27   Farxad Kugu salaamiyo,

28   Dar kaloo suuldaariyo,

29   Kuu dhiga sinsaara oo,

30   Seedaha Ku gooyee,

(repeat ll. 25-30)

37   Kala sooca labadoo, etc.

III.   49   Saaxiibbadaadu waa dar,

50   Kula socdoo,

51   Sama Kuu falaayiyo,

52   Dar kaloo Ku sudhayoo,

53   Seef Kuu afaystoo,

54   Surka Kaaga jaraayee,

(repeat ll. 49-54)

61   Kala sooca labadoo, etc.

I.   1   Some of your friends

2   Go on reconnaissance for you,

3   Seek out fresh grazing lands for you—

4   Others cheat you,

5   Stir poison for you,

6   And only cause you death.

(repeat ll. 1-6)

13   You must separate the two—

14   Differentiate between them.

(repeat ll. 13-14, three times)

21   They must not be made equal to us.

22   Let them be distinguished.

II.   25   Some of your friends

26   Help you,

27   Greet you with happiness—

28   Others trip you,

29   Knock you down with a hip-throw,

30   Hamstring you.

       (*repeat ll. 25-30*)

     37   You must separate the two, etc.

III.   49   Some of your friends

     50   Agree[65] with you,

     51   Do good for you—

     52   Others hang you,

     53   Sharpen a saber for you

     54   In order to cut off your neck.

       (*repeat ll. 49-54*)

     61   You must separate the two, etc.

As the poem implies, Somalia is not as neutral at present as she was in 1960. What preceded this state of affairs that began in great optimism and ended in complete defeat was a unique experiment in domestic politics.

Beginning as uniquely as it proceeded, the second political phase of Somali independence brought many changes to the Horn. On 10 June 1967, Parliament held elections for president. The incumbent, Aadan Cabdulla Cusmaan, was supported by the ruling party and was expected to win. After two ballots without results—and the balloting was being broadcast to the nation over the radio—Parliament recessed. It was during the recess that a program official at Radio Muqdisho placed a poem on the air which subsequently gained a new political significance. Composed earlier in the year by Axmed Suleebaan Bidde, "Leexo" was unique because it attained its most important implications after its composition (Example 22).

On the third ballot Dr. Cabdi-Rashiid Cali Shar-Ma-Arke was elected president and Aadan Cabdulla was defeated. It was the fate of the radio official to be arrested, for the new president did not take office until 1 July. Because the poem mentioned no names, however, nothing could be proved against him, and the most the government could do to him was to relieve him of his position at the radio station.[66]

Example 22:[67]

I.   1   Innakoo lammaane ah,

     2   Iyo laba naf-qaybsile,

3   Talo geed ku laashee,

4   Adigaa is lumiyo,

5   Isu loogay cadowgoo,

6   Libintaadii siiyee,

7   Waadiganse liitee,

8   Leexadu Ku sidatee,

9   Hadba laan cuskanayee,

    (repeat ll. 7-9)

    13   Liibaanteed adduunyada,

    14   Ruuxna laasan maayee,

    15   Maxaa luray naftaadii,

    (repeat ll. 13-15)

II. 19 Waa laac adduunyadu,

    20 Labadii walaalo ah,

    21 Midba maalin ladanyoo,

    22 Ruuxii u liil-galay,

    23 La ma loolo dhereggoo,

    24 Luggooyada ma geystee,

    25 Waadiganse laabtiyo,

    26 Lugaha is la waayaye,

    27 Meel sare lalanayee,

    (repeat ll. 25-27)

    31   Liibaanteed adduunyada, etc.

III. 37 Aniga ba lafiyo jiidh,

    38 Waa kii i laastaan,

    39 Liqi waayay oontee,

    40 Adigaa lis caanood,

    41 Iyo laad xareediyo,

    42 Laydhiyo hadh diidee,

    43 Waadigan sidii liig,

    44 Laasimay ugaadhee,

    45 Waaclada u leexdee,

    (repeat ll. 43-45)

    49   Liibaanteed adduunyada, etc.

IV. 55   Dhaaxaad ladnaan rays,

    56   Sidaad aar libaax tay,

    57   Tallaabada ladhaaysoo,

    58   Anna lahashadaadii,

    59   Ledi waayay ciil oo,

    60   Liidnimo i raacdee,

    61   Lallabaa habeenkiyo,

    62   Ma libdhaan jacayl oo,

    63   Waa labalegdoodaan,

      (*repeat ll. 61-63*)

      67   Liibaanteed adduunyada, etc.

V. 73   Innakoo lammaane ah, etc.

    (*as stanza I*)

I. 1   While we were [yet] together,

    2   Helping each other in every way,

    3   You cast good counsel away, to the top of a [high] tree;

    4   You caused yourself distress,

    5   And slaughtered yourself for your enemy,[68]

    6   Giving your victory to him.

    7   Now you are so weakened

    8   That the light breezes[69] bear you up,

    9   And from time to time, you grasp at a branch.

      (*repeat ll. 7-9*)

      13   For all the pleasures on this earth

      14   One cannot fully enjoy;

      15   [Tell me]: what causes you this distress?

      (*repeat ll. 13-15*)

II. 19   The world is [but] a mirage.[70]

    20-21   And for every two brothers, only one being happy each day,[71]

    22   The one who is fortunate

    23   Should not abuse his prosperity—

    24   Should not maltreat [his neighbor].

25-26   And in your case, however, [your] breast and feet were out of
accord.[72]

27   For you are drifting up, up [into the air].

(repeat ll. 25-27)

31   For all the pleasures, etc.

III.   37   [Look at me]: my flesh and [all] my bones

38   Were completely consumed by him[73]

39   I cannot even swallow food

40   The abundance[74] of milk,

41   [Pure] rainwater,

42   Fresh air and rest in the cool shade, you have rejected.

43   It is you who, like the male garanuug,[75]

44   Left the [other] game, and

45   Turned to a desolate place.

(repeat ll. 43-45)

49   For all the pleasures, etc.

IV.   55   So often in the prosperity of the rains—

56   As though you were a [proud] lion—

57   You walked about majestically,

58   Whilst I, because of your carousing

59   Had sleepless nights from impotent anger,

60   And [sometimes] behaved like a fool.

61   The [beacon] fire in the [dark] night

62   And love, never disappear;

63   They roll on [after you, unrestrained].

(repeat ll. 61-63)

67   For all the pleasures, etc.

V.   73   While we were [yet] together, etc.

(as stanza I)

With the election of a new president, another unique and rare event occurred on the
continent of Africa. On 1 July 1967, in an official ceremony, the old president stepped
down, relinquishing his power, and the new president assumed office. By the middle of
the month Maxamed Xaaji Ibraahiin Cigaal had been appointed prime minister, and his

cabinet attained a vote of confidence on 12 August.

Cigaal's coming to power brought with it optimism for both internal and foreign affairs. Domestically, he appeared to have bridged the gap between North and South and to have rid Somalia her regionalism problem. On the international scene Cigaal proceeded to try and bridge the gap between the country and her immediate neighbors at the expense of the Pan-Somali Movement.

As we mentioned earlier, the Pan-Somali Movement was in opposition to the Pan-African Movement when both philosophies met on the international scene. Such opposition had been manifested in armed conflicts between Somali and Ethiopia in 1964[76] and between Somalis who live in the former Northern Frontier District of Kenya and Kenyan government forces between 1963 and 1967.[77] In late August of 1967, Cigaal's government began to face Somalia's neighbors with a different philosophy. Attempting to ease tensions with her neighbors, the new government was given a full mandate by Parliament to continue with its initiatives toward finding a peaceful solution to the problem of the Somali territories under the Ethiopian and Kenyan governments.[78] Following this mandate several conferences were held between Somalia and her two independent neighbors, some of which were mediated by representatives from Zambia.

Cigaal's new approach to Somalia's neighbors was not well received by everyone at home. The losses in the Pan-Somali Movement were only one of the growing number of complaints which were being vocalized in the country, as a steady undercurrent of unrest began to mount gradually. Each new conference which inevitably saw no border changes caused Cigaal's popularity to decline sharply. At first, the prime minister seemed capable of redeeming himself with Parliament and public. Later, as the parliamentary election date neared, the question of whether Cigaal would be able to retain his power was raised.

During the final months of 1968 and the beginning of 1969, Premier Cigaal's popularity, especially in northern Somalia, seemed to be at its lowest ebb. By the time the general parliamentary elections came in March of 1969, several incidents had occurred which cast serious doubt on his leadership. Rumors of corruption at polling stations and political assassinations reached the capital. An apparent feeling of little confidence in the government from the general public was mocked by Parliament's 116 to 1 vote of confidence for Cigaal's new Council of Ministers on 19 June 1969. Moreover, rumors contributing to the growing unrest did not cease with the elections.

Matters came to a head on 15 October 1969, when President Shar-Ma-Arke was assassinated during a tour of the drought stricken north. Five days later, further rumors were abruptly halted with a new development on the political scene. At 4:00 am on 21 October, the army and police of the Somali Republic seized control of the government, abolished the constitution, and formed a Supreme Revolutionary Council (S. R. C.) to rule the country. All the ministers have since been held under house arrest in the president s villa at Afgooye awaiting their trials which (at the time of this writing), it is said, will be held in the parliament building in Muqdisho.

With the coming of the military to power came the revival of the political *heello* which had been suppressed by skillful censors during Cigaal's term of office. To be sure, one reason for the dominance of love as a major theme of heello before the coup was the work of these censors. One poem, originally composed in 1963, was revived and heard on the radio frequently during the first weeks of the coup.

Example 23:

I   M: 1   Hubka cadowga guba,

           2   Waa kuwa gurtee,

           3   Gaadiid noqdee,

           4   Kula garab-socdee,

               (repeat ll. 1-4)

      C: 9   Gobannimadayada,

          10   Geeshkaa hayee,

          11   Waxay Kuu galaan,

          12   Waa inaad guddaa,

               (repeat ll. 9-12)

II. M: 17   Goortaan arkaba,

         18   Waa geeddii oo,

         19   Iyo galab-carrow e,

         20   Gucla roorayee,

              (repeat ll. 17-20)

      C: 25 Gobannimadayada, etc.

III. M: 33   Kii Kaa gardaran,

         34   Aan gacan Ku siin,

		35	Gaaliyo Islaan,
		36	Kuuma oggolee,

(*repeat ll. 33-36*)

C:		41	Gobannimadayada, etc.
IV.	M:	49	Hubka cadowga guba, etc.

(*as stanza I*)

I.	M:	1	The weapons that burn the enemy
		2	Were those collected by them.[79]
		3	They are mobile and [heavily equipped].
		4	They march beside you.

(*repeat ll. 1-4*)

	C:	9	Our independence:
		10	The army holds it.
		11	For what they do for you,
		12	You must reward them.

(*repeat ll. 9-12*)

II.	M:	17	Whenever I see them,
		18	They are on the move.
		19	And whenever they move in the evening
		20	They trot, swinging their arms.[80]

(*repeat ll. 17-20*)

	C:	25	Our independence, etc.
III.	M	33	He who treats you unjustly,
		34	And who will not assist you,
		35	[Whether he be] infidel or Moslem:
		36	They do not allow him [to come near] you.

(*repeat ll. 33-36*)

	C:	41	Our independence, etc.
IV.	M:	49	The weapons that burn, etc.

(*as stanza I*)

The Poetry of the Third Period

As it was with the poetry during the second period, all of the poetry of period three was very similar in structure. The universality of a unified system of alliteration has an exception in only one poem in my collection (see above, pp. 131-33). Theme was also to remain unified in all the poetry of this period.

One of the most striking changes between the *heello* of Periods Two and Three occurred in length. The *heello* of period three became very long indeed, but length must not be overrated: it was not due to the composition of more lines of poetry, but to the extensive and more varied use of line repeating. Elimination of the line repeats from the poem on pp. 123-26, for instance, yields only 27 original lines of the 136 lines in the complete poem.

The systematic use of refrain was also continued with the *heello* of the third period. The refrain was sometimes sung by the soloist alone, sometimes by a male or female chorus or a combination of both. Together with line repeating, refrain lengthened the poem. Almost all the *heello* of period three contain a refrain, and the line repeat patterns at this time were expanded. We shall review these patterns in Chapter 7, for their development covers the entire period of the *heello*.

The imagery of the third period became much more sophisticated, although it was still overwhelmingly taken from the pastoral nomadic way of life. We shall cover imagery as a whole in the following chapter, for like line repeat patterns, imagery has developed over the entire period of the *heello*. One form of image—better still, system of imagery—became especially developed in this period: the hidden message.

We have seen how it is more difficult to design a hidden message against members of one's own society than against foreigners. This involves in fact more than poetic ability, as in the case of the radio official who played the poem "Leexo" at the crucial point in the election of the new president of the republic (see above, pp. 139-42). At one point during the administration of Prime Minister Cigaal, the officials at Radio Muqdisho were so skilled in deciphering hidden meanings that little political poetry was broadcast at all. A Somali acquaintance of mine remarked at the time that all the poems on the radio were only about love. To him there were no interesting ones, and by "interesting" he meant "political" and therefore controversial.

The antigovernment poetry of this period strongly resembles the anticolonial poetry before it, although poetry of the latter theme did not cease with independence. Example

24, composed around 1967 by Ciise Warsame (music by Cabdulla Sigsaag), is obviously antigovernment, although I was never able to uncover the exact subject of complaint. It is included here because it is undoubtedly the most popular *heello* to date.[81]

Example 24:

I 1 Is guhaadshayeey,
   2 Inta aan guntaday,
   3 Gucla roorayayeey,
   4 Godobtay nin qaba,
   5 Garan waayayeey,
      (*repeat ll. 1-5*)
  11 Anigu na garaadkay,
  12 Kaa gaabsan waayayeey,
  13 Adna garashadaadii,
  14 Ii garaabi waydaye,
      (*repeat ll. 11-14*)
  19 Dhibtaa aan gelaayona,
  20 I gargaari mayside,
  21 Gudcurkaan habeenkii,
  22 Dhaxanta iyo guuraa,
  23 Aaa, aawadaa gozdoomaa,
      (*repeat ll. 19-23*)
        29 Naftan gu iyo jiilaal,
        30 Biyii gaadhi wayday,
        31 Waa gaal-aroortaa,
        32 Sida geel horweynaha,
            (*repeat ll. 29-32*)
        37 Gelinna isma taagoo,
        38 Weli maan geyoobine,
        39 Waa Loo garaabaa,
        40 Ruux gaabinaaya e,
        41 Aaa, gacalnima eegoo,
            (*repeat ll. 37-41*)

II. 47 Inkastoo nin geesiyi,

48 Rag u geed-adaygyay,

49 Haddaan garabka Lala qaban,

50 Guri oodi maayo e,

(repeat ll. 47-50)

55 Gacmo madhan Illaah baa,

56 Guudkood xil saaray,

57 Sida geyi abaareed,

58 Cawl gooni-daaqaan,

59 Aaa, aawadaa gozdoomaye,

(repeat ll. 55-59)

65 Gufaacale rooboo,

66 Guuxiyo dabaylaa,

67 Meeluu i geeyoba,

68 Gacankiis i qaadaye,

(repeat ll. 65-68)

73 Garanna maayo meeshay,

74 Godobtu iga raacday,

75 Waxaan haystay mooyiye,

76 Ifka dhibi i gaadhdhaye,

77 Aaa, hadal wayga gozanyay,

(repeat ll. 73-77)

83 Naftan gu iyo jiilaal, etc.

I. 1 Lo I scolded myself,

2 And—having prepared myself—[82]

3 I began to run.

4 Who bears the guilt for my distress

5 I cannot tell.

(repeat ll. 1-5)

11 My understanding

12 Restrains me from speaking curtly to you.

13 But you, according to your understanding,

14   Have never shown sympathy for me.

(repeat ll. 11-14)

19   [Behold] the hardship which I bear:

20   You never give me assistance.

21   On a moonless night,

22   Through chill and travelling by night,

23   I am isolated because of you

(repeat ll. 19-23)

    29   This soul [of mine]—in Gu[83] and Jiilaal[84]

    30   Has never reached [the succor of] water—

    31   Has [never] got [past] the waiting line at the well.

    32   Like a herd of strong camels [in distant grazing lands].

    (repeat ll. 29-32)

    37   I never rest in night or day,

    38   Yet I never reach the place [to quench my thirst].

    39   One should find sympathy

    40   With a man who is slow.

    41   Remember [our] bond of brotherhood.

    (repeat ll. 37-41)

II   47   Though a brave man

48   Be the strongest and most enduring of men,[85]

49   Unless he is assisted by others,

50   He [can]not [even] construct a fence 'round [his] dwelling.

(repeat ll. 47-50)

55   To [a man with] empty hands, God

56   Always attaches shame.

57-58   Like a gazelle, grazing alone in a drought-stricken place, I

59   Have been isolated [from others] because of you.

(repeat ll. 55-59)

65   A heavy rain which has waves of showers,

66   [Roaring with] the sound [of thunder] and [strong] winds,

67   Wherever it takes me:

68   A wave [from it] has gripped me.

     (*repeat ll. 65-68*)

73   And lo, I do not understand what

74   I have done for [this] suffering to have followed me.

75   I do not know [what crimes I] have done.

76   But in this world, trouble has reached me.

77   And here my words end.

     (*repeat ll. 73-77*)

    83   This soul [of mine]—, etc.

Apart from poetry composed to protest against the government, other poems were concerned with domestic politics in general, such as Example 25 composed in 1963 by Cali Sugulle, and Example 26,[86] composed in (circa) 1965 by Caweys Geeddow. Mildly warning the government, these poems cannot be said to be in opposition to anyone and thus had no trouble with the censors.

Example 25:

I.	F:	1	Soomaalideennii, hadday sinnaatay,
		2	Soomaalideennii, hadday sinnaatay,
		3	Isu samafalkeedu na, waa dan iyo seetee,
		4	Isu samafalkeedu na, waa dan iyo seetee,
		5	Nin Lagu seexdow, ha seexan,
	C:	6	Toos!
	F:	7	Xil baad siddaa, ha seexan,
	C:	8	Toos!
	F:	9	Nin Lagu seexdow, ha seexan,
		10	Ha seexan, ha seexan,
		11	Ha seexan, ha seexan,
		12	Soo jeedoo, si weyn u feejigow,
	C:	13	Soomaalidii midowdoo,
		14	Saxalkii ka baxyoo samaatee,
		15	Soomaalidii midowdoo,
		16	Saxalkii ka baxyoo samaatee,
	F	17	Nin Lagu seexdow, ha seexan,

C: 18   Toos!

F: 19   Xil baad siddaa, ha seexan,

C :   20   Toos!

F: 21   Nin Lagu seexdow, ha seexan,

         22   Ha seexan, ha seexan,

         23   Ha seexan, ha seexan,

         24   Soo jeedoo, si weyn u feejigow,

II. F: 25   Subag weel ku daataa, sina uma xumaadee,

         26   Subag weel ku daataa, sina uma xumaadee,

         27   Waa subax wanaagsane, calanka na salaama,

         28   Waa subax wanaagsane, calankana salaama,

           29   Nin Lagu seexdow, etc.

III. F: 49   Waa seermaweydo iyo sebenbarwaaqee,

         50   Waa seermaweydo iyo sebenbarwaaqee,

         51   Saddexdii maqnaana, way soo socdaane,

         52   Saddexdii maqnaana, way soo socdaane,

           53   Nin Lagu seexdow, etc.

IV. F: 73   Sahanka laabtee, socdaalka dheer le,

         74   Sahanka laabtee, socdaalka dheer le,

         75   Saacuu arkaa baa, soof Lagu raraaye,

         76   Saacuu arkaa baa, soof Lagu raraaye,

           77   Nin Lagu seexdow, etc .

V.   F: 97   Saakana ammaana, way suubbanyiine,

         98   Saakuubna caaya, way saxalsanyiine,

         99   Waa laba sedleyniyo, sixir hadalladiinnee,

       100 Waa laba sedleyniyo, sixir hadalladiinnee,

         101 Nin Lagu seexdow, etc.

I.   F: 1   If we the Somalis have become equals [with the other nations of the world],

         2   If we the Somalis have become equals [with the other nations of the world],

         3   [Then] our good deeds to each other are a binding necessity.[87]

		4	[Then] our good deeds to each other are a binding necessity.
		5	O man, upon whom others rely,[88] do not sleep.
C:		6	Wake up!
F:		7	You carry responsibility; do not slumber.
C:		8	Wake up!
F:		9	O man, upon whom others rely, do not sleep.
		10	Do not slumber. Do not sleep.
		11	Do not slumber. Do not sleep.
		12	Be awake; be on the alert.
C:		13	The Somalis have become united:
		14	Misfortune has departed; [all] has become good.
		15	The Somalis have become united:
		16	Misfortune has departed; [all] has become good.
F:		17	O man, upon whom others rely, do not sleep.
C:		18	Wake up!
F:		19	You carry responsibility; do not slumber.
C:		20	Wake up!
F:		21	O man, upon whom others rely, do not sleep.
		22	Do not slumber, do not sleep.
		23	Do not slumber, do not sleep.
		24	O man, be awake; be on the alert.
II.	F:	25	Ghee which is spilt into a vessel does not become bad in any way.
		26	Ghee which is spilt into a vessel does not become bad in any way.
		27	'Tis a good morning; salute the flag.
		28	'Tis a good morning; salute the flag.
		29	O man, upon whom others rely, etc.
III.	F:	49	It is the Seermaweydo Season[89] and a prosperous period.
		50	It is the Seermaweydo Season and a prosperous period.
		51	The three that are absent will come to us.[90]
		52	The three that are absent will come to us.
		53	O man, upon whom others rely, etc.
IV.	F:	73	The camp guide who [makes] long journeys [of exploration] returned;

74   The camp guide who [makes] long journeys [of exploration]
       returned;

75   And the camp and animals are moved to the newly green pasture
       which he discovered.[91]

76   And the camp and animals are moved to the newly green pasture
       which he discovered.

77   O man, upon whom others rely, etc.

V.   F: 97   Praise [our leaders] this morning, [for] they are honorable, but

98   Insult them tomorrow,[92] [for] they will become troublesome;

99   [They are the ones] who take two shares. [O leaders], your
speeches [are like] sorcery.

100   [They are the ones] who take two shares. [O leaders], your
speeches [are like] sorcery.

101   Oh man, upon whom others rely, etc.

Example 26:[93]

I.   M: 1   Anilaa ballamee barbaareey,

2   Biyo waa La helee,

3   Aan baxnee badarkii abuurree,

4   Beerihii aan fallee,
       (*repeat ll. 1-4*)

9   Aan is barno,
       [Dong, dong, dong][94]

10   Inaan beer falannoo,

11   Aan ku baahi baxnee,
       (*repeat ll. 9-11*)

C: 15   Beer nin falaa,
       [Dong, dong, dong]

16   Ma bariyee,

17   Weligiisna ma baahoodee,
       (*repeat ll. 15-17*)

II.   M: 21   Barkin meel La dhigtoo,

22   La buurtoon, La baraarugineey,

        23   Barqadii La kacoo bilaashlee,

        24   La cun aan barannee,

        (repeat ll. 21-24)

          29   Aan is barno, etc.

III.   M: 41   Inaan baar aan tagnoo bilcantii,

        42   Aan la baashaalnee,

        43   Balwa aan tunno baallaa dheelnoo,

        44   Kuma baanaan karnee,

        (repeat ll. 41-44)

          49   Aan is barno, etc.

IV.   M: 61   Badarkoo badahaan Lagu keeno,

        62   Beledkoo ka baxee,

        63   Barbaxiis na waa ayaanee,

        64   Bil ma gaari karee,

        (repeat ll. 61-64)

          69   Aan is barno, etc.

I.   M: 1   Let me give you some advice, O ye youths,

        2   For water has been found.

        3   Let us go forth to plant the millet,

        4   And farm in the fields.

        (repeat ll. 1-4)

         9   Let us teach each other

           [Dong, dong, dong]

        10   So that we may operate our own farms—

        11   May satisfy our own needs.

        (repeat ll. 9-11)

      C: 15   [For] a man who farms [for himself]

           [Dong, dong, dong]

        16   Never begs

        17   And never falls into [acute] hardship.

        (repeat ll. 15-17)

II.   M: 24   We have become accustomed to taking our meals with others,

        21   To lying [idle] on a headrest,[95]

22 To having plenty to eat, to not waking up [early],

23 And to rising late in the morning.

(repeat ll. 21-24)

29 Let us teach each other, etc.

III. M: 44 We cannot cure [our ills]

41-42 By frequenting the bar and sporting with the women—

43 By singing *belwo* and dancing.

(repeat ll. 41-43)

49 Let us teach each other, etc.

IV. M: 61 Concerning grain imported from abroad,

62 Which grows in other countries—

63 Its satisfaction is [only] temporary

64 And will not last [even] a month.

(repeat ll. 61-64)

69 Let us teach each other, etc.

Other themes of period three emerged either because they matured as topics for modern poetry or because the time was right for them to appear. The debate over the role of women in the new society of post-1960 Somalia reached the public in more and more poems during this time. We have already quoted one poem on this subject (see above, pp. 7-11); Example 27 is taken from an entire play concerning this topic, *Shabeel Naagood*, by Xasan Sheekh Muumin. The poem was composed in 1968.

Example 27:

I. M: 1 Xaajadii qalloocan,

2 Qofkii ku xarragooda,

(repeat ll. 1-2)

5 Waa Lagu xariiraa,

(repeat ll. 1-5)

11 In Lagu xantaa,

12 Xaq, miyaa?

13 Xeer, miyaa?

(repeat ll. 11-13)

		17	Ma idiin xalaal baa?
		18	Idinkaa xujooboo,
		19	Xuduudkii ka tallaabsanaayee,
		20	Naa xishooda,
II.	F:	21	Annagoo xorownoo,
		22	Xaqayagii midhaystay,

(repeat ll. 21-22)

		25	Inaad na xakamaysaa,

(repeat ll. 21-25)

		31	Aad na xidhxidhaa,
		32	Xaq, miyaa ?
		33	Xeer, miyaa?

(repeat ll. 31-33)

		37	Ma idiin xalaal baa?
		38	Idinkaa xujooboo,
		39	Xuduudkii ka tallaabsanaayee,
		40	Xubin na siiya,
III.	M:	41	Inaad marada xayddaa,
		42	Xaglaha na qaawisaa,
		43	Inaad marada xoortaa,
		44	Xaglaha na qaawisaa,
		45	Xuub caarro huwataa,
		46	Inaad marada xoortaa,
		47	Xaglaha na qaawisaa,

(repeat ll. 46-47)

		50	Xuub aad huwataa,
		51	Xeradii ka baxdaa,
		52	Xag, miyaa?
		53	Xeer, miyaa?

(repeat ll. 51-53)

		57	Ma idiin xalaal baa, etc.

(as stanza I)

IV. F: 61 Xilagube haddii uu,

62 Xaslan waayo kiisa,

(repeat ll. 61-62)

65 Xaawalay dhamaanteed,

(repeat ll. 61-65)

71 In Lagu xantaa,

72 Xaq, miyaa?

73 Xeer, miyaa?

(repeat ll. 71-73)

77 Ma idiin xalaal baa, etc.

(as stanza II)

V. M: 81 Daad nimuu xambaaraa,

82 Badbaadada xusuustee,

(repeat ll. 81-82)

85 Hanadkaad u xilataa,

(repeat ll. 81-85)

91 Inaad xeeladisaa,

92 Xaq, miyaa?

93 Xeer, miyaa?

(repeat ll. 91-93)

97 Ma idiin xalaal baa, etc.

(as stanza I)

IV. F: 101 Marwadaad xodxodataa,

102 Inaad xagasha gooysaa,

(repeat ll. 101-102)

105 Oo dhashiina xortaa,

(repeat ll. 101-105)

111 Aad xanaanin waydaa,

112 Xaq, miyaa?

113 Xeer, miyaa?

(repeat ll. 111-113)

117 Ma idiin xalaal baa, etc.

(as stanza II)

I.   M: 2   The person who is openly guilty of

            1   Faulty behavior:

                (*repeat ll. 1-2*)

            5   One must treat him gently.

                (*repeat ll. 1-5*)

          11   To gossip about him secretly:[96]

          12   Is that just ?

          13   Is that lawful?

                (*repeat ll. 11-13*)

                17   Is it allowed [by our religion] for you [to do this]?

                18   You made an offense,

                19   And you crossed the boundary.[97]

                20   O women, be ashamed of yourselves.

II.   F: 21   As we became independent,

          22   Our right bore fruit.

                (*repeat ll. 21-22*)

          25   That you bind us strongly,

                (*repeat ll. 21-25*)

          31   [That] you keep us shut up [in our homes—]

          32   Is that just?

          33   Is that lawful ?

                (*repeat ll. 31-33*)

                37   Is it allowed [by our religion] for you [to do this]?

                38   You made an offense,

                39   And you crossed the boundary.

                40   Give us [at least] part [of our rights].[98]

III. M: 41   That you roll up [your] dresses

          42   [So that] the back of [your] knee is visible—

          43   That you cast aside [traditional] clothes,

          44   [So that] you make bare the back of [your] knees,

          45   And dress in [cloth as transparent as] a spider's web—

          46   That you cast aside [traditional] clothes,

          47   [So that] the back of [your] knee is visible—

                (*repeat ll. 46-47*)

50   And dress in transparent cloth—

51   You leave [the responsibility of your] homes.

52   Is that just?

53   Is that lawful?

(repeat ll. 51-53)

   57   Is it allowed, etc.

   (as stanza I)

IV. F: 61   If the man who mistreats his wife,

62   Fails to keep her contented,

(repeat ll. 61-62)

65   [Then this affects] all women [in the world]—

(repeat ll. 61-65)

71   To talk about her secretly:

72   Is that just?

73   Is that lawful?

(repeat ll. 71-73)

   77   Is it allowed, etc.

   (as stanza II)

V. M: 81   The man taken away by a flood

82   Thinks of rescue.

(repeat ll. 81-82)

85   You [always] appreciate an able man.

(repeat ll. 81-85)

91   To deceive him:

92   Is that just ?

93   Is that lawful?

(repeat ll. 91-93)

   97   Is it allowed, etc.

   (as stanza I)

VI. F: 101 Sometimes you court [women].

102 That you hamstring them—

(repeat ll. 101-102)

105 And cast aside your children,

   (*repeat ll. 101-105*)

111 And fail to care for them,

112 Is that just?

113 Is that lawful?

   (*repeat ll. 111-113*)

   117 Is it allowed, etc.

   (*as stanza II*)

Other topics which emerged at this time were due, even more than the debate over the role of women, to the right timing and maturity of the *heello*. With the appearance of the following poem in 1968 one might conclude that almost any theme was acceptable for modern poetry. Composed by Abu Hadre, this poem covers the topic of football (soccer), and is noted for the loan words that have come into the Somali language as a result of the adoption of this game by the peoples of the Horn.

Example 28:

   I.   C: 1   Ya! Ya! Ya!

   (*repeat l. 1, three times*)

   F: 5   Leebiyo gantaalaha, Laysula gabbanayee,

   6   Ay labada geesood, isla gaadayaanee,

   (*repeat ll. 5-6*)

   9   Waa gammuunkii gaashaanka jiidhee,

   (*repeat l. 9*)

   11   Waa gool!

   C: 12   Gool! Gool! Gool! Gool!

   (*repeat ll. 11-12*)

   F: 15   Waa gool!

   Spoken by F: 16   Waa gool!

   II.   C: 17   Ya! Ya! Ya!

   (*repeat l. 17, twice*)

   F: 20   Gurxanka aad maqalaysaan, guubaabo weeyee,

21 Tii gaabis noqotee, lista gaadhi waydaa,
(repeat ll. 20-21)

24 Galabtaynu eegnaa, taa guushu raacdaye,
(repeat l. 24)

26 Waa gool!, etc.

III. C: 32 Ya! Ya! Ya!
(repeat l. 32, twice)

F: 35 Gegidii cayaarta, golihii isboodhka,

36 Markii baa gozaankii, Loo geed fadhiistee,
(repeat ll. 35-36)

39 Guntiga adkayso soo qaad galaaska,
(repeat l. 39)

41 Waa gool!, etc.

IV. C: 47 Ya! Ya! Ya!
(repeat l. 47, twice)

F: 50 Gudub ula rooroo, geesta ka laaboo,

51 Guji yaanay lumine, goolka ku beegoo,
(repeat ll. 50-51)

54 Shebegga ku gooyoo, birtu ha gariirtee,
(repeat l. 54)

56 Waa gool! etc.

Spoken by F: 61 Waa gool! Waa gool! Gool!

I. C: 1 *Ya! Ya! Ya!*[99]
(repeat l. 1, three times)

F: 5 Dodging each other with [their] star players,[100]

6 Both teams [are] creeping up on each other.
(repeat ll. 5-6)

9 There goes the star player[101] crashing through the defense[102]
(repeat l. 9)

11 It's a goal!

C: 12 Goal! Goal! Goal! Goal!
(repeat ll. 11-12)

	F:	15	It's a goal!
Spoken by F:		16	It's a goal!
II.	C:	17	*Ya! Ya! Ya!*

(*repeat l. 17, twice*)

> F: 20   The roar which you are hearing is encouragement [from] the crowd.
>
> 21   The team which becomes [too] slow will fail to reach success.[103]
>
> (*repeat ll. 20-21*)
>
> 24   This evening we shall see which one victory shall accompany.
>
> (*repeat l. 24*)
>
> 26   It's a goal., etc.

III.   C: 32   *Ya! Ya! Ya!*

(*repeat l. 32, twice*)

> F: 35   [On to] the playing field. [On to] the sports field!
>
> 36   When the score has been decided—[104]
>
> (*repeat ll. 35-36*)
>
> 39   Prepare yourself,[105] and go to receive the cup.[106]
>
> (*repeat l. 39*)
>
> 41   It's a goal!, etc.

IV.   C: 47   *Ya! Ya! Ya!*

(*repeat l. 47, twice*)

> F: 50   Run across [the field] with [the ball] toward [the goal], and dodge [the opponents] from side to side.
>
> 51   Pass it so that it will not get lost; aim it into the goal.
>
> (*repeat ll. 50-51*)
>
> 54   [Kick it so hard that it] will cut through the net; let it shake the [very] goal posts.[107]
>
> (*repeat l. 54*)
>
> 56   It's a goal!, etc.

Spoken by F: 61   It's a goal! It's a goal! Goal!

Aside from their involvement in Pan-Somalism and Pan-Africanism, period three also saw Somalis looking abroad to other nations and continents and comparing other countries' plights with those of Somalia and Africa. Example 29, composed in 1967 by

Cabdullaahi Qarshe, is an example of a poem having international implications.[108]

Example 29:

I. 1 Dawladii gumaysiga,
    2 E dul-ahaanba Afrika,
    3 Waagii ay damaaciyayeen,
    4 Shirkii ay u dalbadeen,
    5 Magaaladay u soo dirteen,
    6 Kobtii ay ku doodayeen,
    7 Baarliin daya,
    8 Bal daya,
    9 Derbaa dhex yaal,
    10 Bal daawada,
II. 11 Durbaday noo soo galeen,
    12 Lugtay raggeennii dabradeen,
    13 Sidii dameero ay rarteen,
    14 Ay karbaash ugu dareen,
    15 Ay darkii buuxiyeen,
    16 Dushafkii daaddaadiyeen,
III. 17 Markay madowgii damqadeen,
    18 Durbaannaday garaacayeen,
    19 Dawankii ay yeedhiyeen,
    20 Gabayaday ku diirayeen,
    21 Ay heesaa isu direen,
    22 Waa tay duhur xusuusteen,
    23 Badi wada dareeriyeen,
IV. 24 Nabsiga aan daahinow,
    25 Ee aan dakaaminow,
    26 Dawga Loo tilmaaminow,
    27 Ee aan cidi diranninow,
    28 Degdegga aan oqoonninow,
    29 Marmar na aan daahinow,
    30 Diinka ka dheerayninow,

	31	Dayuuraduhu aanay gaadhinow,
	32	Tan iyo waagii dura,
	33	Dalkayaga in La maqnaa,
	34	Duqiiyow waa sidee,
	35	Xaqayagu ma duudsaa,
V.	36	Waxaan ku soo duubayaa,
	37	Hadalka aan ku daynayaa,
	38	Waxaan uga danleeyahaan,
	39	Idin dareesiinayaa,
	40	Shimbirahaa duulayaa,
	41	Ee dushaa meerayaa,
	42	Marleyba way daalayaan,
	43	Daafta way imanayaan.

	1	The colonialist governments
I.	2	Of the whole of Africa—
	3	When they coveted it—
	4	The meeting[109] they arranged for this,
	5	The city where they sent [delegates],
	6	In the exact section [of town] where they debated—
	7	Look at Berlin,
	8	All of you look!
	9	A wall is splitting it—
	10	Look and be entertained!
II.	11	As soon as [the colonialists] invaded us,
	12	They shackled our men's legs,
	13	And loaded them like donkeys,
	14	And whipped them,
	15	They filled the trough [with them],
	16	And made the camps to overflow.
III.	17	When the black men felt the pain [and revolted]:
	18	The drums which they beat,
	19	The bells which they rang,
	20	The poems which stirred them,

21   And the songs which they sent to each other:

22   [All] this they remembered one afternoon,

23   And they drove most [colonialists from Africa].

IV. 24   O Nabsi,[110] you who never tarry,

25   And who never get exhausted,

26   And whom no one directs,

27   And whom no one instructs,

28   And who never know haste,

29   And yet who sometimes are not late;

30   O you who [can] be as slow as a tortoise,

31   [Yet] whom airplanes [can] never overtake;

32   From time immemorial

33   Our lands[111] have not been our own—

34   O Elder,[112] how it is [that you do not act]?

35   Is our right[113] to be forfeited?

V. 36   The point on which I end [my poem],

37   And on which I would terminate my discourse,

38   And what I mean by it,

39   I will reveal to you:

40   The birds which are flying

41   And gliding about above

42   Will some day tire [and need rest]

43   And descend to earth.[114]

Since period three is still in process, no definite conclusions can be drawn about it or about the future of the *heello* as a whole. We have covered the modern poem from an historical point of view and have observed characteristics of its development through time. Such an approach, however, cannot cover the total picture of the *heello*, since some of its features run through all these periods and are not necessarily related to the parallel history of the country. A complete observation of the modern poem must include a discussion of some characteristics which emerged during all these periods of development.

NOTES

1. Lewis (1965) has been revised twice, once in 1980, published by Longman, and again in 1988, published by Westview Press. The revised editions include two new chapters, bringing historical coverage of Somalia up to the latter 1980s.

2. Lewis 1965, p. 162.

3. Ibid., p. 154.

4. Date of Somali independence.

5. *Luggooyada.* "Disaster"; literally, "the cutting of legs." This image is often used as a curse in Somalia.

6. *26 June 1960.* Date of the independence of the former British Somaliland Protectorate.

7. Somalis churn milk for *ghee*, the clarified butter, which is used as a sauce for meat, rice, etc. This metaphor indicates great prosperity, for *ghee* is made from milk only during periods of rain and abundance. During drier seasons ghee is made by boiling meat. This line could read: "When did we gain prosperity?"

8. *12:00 midnight.* Literally, "6:00 midnight." This is the system of counting time, common in Moslem, Jewish, and Coptic areas, where 1:00 = 7:00; 2:00 = 8:00, etc. The independence of British Somaliland came at midnight.

9. I. E., when British and Italian Somalilands became the Somali Republic.

10. The poet means the missing territories of Greater Somalia, of which there are three, not two. It is probable that the poet needed an "L" word (e. g., *labadii*, "the two") for alliteration purposes.

11. *Haweeyo.* Panegyric name. It means "The Best One of All."

12. "Cast aside freedom." I. E., by joining the southern regions.

13. *Geeddi.* The move of a Somali *reer* ("family encampment") from one site to another.

14. *Abaar.* "Drought." The implication is that the joining of the northern and southern regions would cause a political drought for the northerners.

15. *Golmoon.* "Lean"; literally, the condition of the abdomen when it is shrunk in; this is caused by severe hunger.

16. Frothing milk denotes prosperity.

17. *Nabsi.* See pp. 114, note 49.

18.   This line implies that the poet rejects the future advice from his elders who wanted the joining of the northern and southern regions to take place. The poet feels that the problem is one for the younger generation to solve.

19.   For a complete history of this historic decision, see Andrzejewski (1974b).

20.   This poem was translated by Muuse X. I. Galaal and edited by me and Michael Cushman Walsh. (See Preface.)

21.   In his confusion the singer cannot find his fellow singer. The metaphoric implication of this line is: "Where are you, O students of Somalia? What are your goals in education? What has foreign language to do with Somali education?"

22.   I. E., acceptance of the use of foreign languages.

23.   I. E., by foreigners.

24.   Lewis 1965, p. 156.

25.   Ibid., p. 166.

26.   Ibid., p. 174.

27.   This formula is borrowed from the traditional Somali genre called *guux*. The *guux* originated, like the *belwo*, in the area of Boorame west of Hargeysa, and was used as a recitation at night to keep the men guarding camels awake.

28.   *Hir* and *hilaac*. "Distant shapes of clouds" and "lightning" respectively. These are harbingers of rain, the universal Somali symbol of prosperity. (The opposite symbol can be seen in line 27.) Lines 7-9 announce the coming of independence to the Somali Republic.

29.   I. E., the freedom that the poet expected with independence did not come.

30.   *Hadh gal*. "To rest"; literally, "to enter the shade." Somali idiom which means, among other things, "to stop for mid day meal."

31.   *Ya*. Exclamation of emotion, here sorrow.

32.   I. E., the support I had was weak and of little use.

33.   *Way*. Exclamation of emotion, here sorrow

34.   I. E., there is still hope. The milking of the camel is done on the left side. Milk shares the implications of rain in Somali imagery.

35.   I. E., why are you now idle ? I am in jail and can do nothing, but you, O Northern Somalia, are not.

36.   I. E., support, action.

37. In Somali society women occupy a position inferior to men. Thus the handicapped North is symbolized by a woman.

38. This line is from a Somali folk narrative, the genre of which always ends in a proverb. There was once a man who had a she-camel. Another man came to him and claimed that the she-camel was really his. The two men went to a traditional Somali court to have their case heard by the elders. (Somali Customary Law is called *xeer* and is conducted by respected clan elders who know the customary jurisprudence.) Neither man could produce proof of ownership and the elder in charge said to the original owner: *Hubsiino hal baa La siistaa.* "Certainty is bartered for a she-camel." In short: "It is better to lose a she-camel and be certain, than to keep it and risk hell fire on Judgment Day." The line in the poem implies: "It is better to let a guilty one go free than to punish the innocent."

39. *Dhadhiin.* Place name. Dhadhiin is located in the Sheekh Pass between Sheekh and Berbera in the North. The implication of this line is obscure. Dhadhiin literally means "a pool of water."

40. I. E., I searched for a plan very carefully.

41. I. E., when the coup was taking place, why did you not assist me? Note that the question is phrased in the present tense in the original.

42. Praise directed to the lieutenants.

43. I. E., forces from the Somali government.

44. I. E., lack of support and strength.

45. I E., the man responsible for carrying out the details of God's will is one's father. The father here symbolizes the northern members of Parliament. He might also symbolize General Dazuud.

46. I. E., the northern M. P.'s failed to support the coup.

47. I. E., the man with power tries to preserve it.

48. *Hadh gal.* "To find rest"; literally, "to enter the shade." See note 30 above. This line implies that those in power are well off.

49. *Aroori.* Place name. A large, treeless, and desolate plain south of Burco in northern Somalia. This plain is often referred to in poetry and has come to mean "desert" or "a desolate place." This line implies: "I was helpless and poor."

50. These lines are delivered with sarcasm. The government is "right" because it has might.

51. *Fidhin laan gobeed.* Long, carved, wooden comb made from the branch of the Gob Tree (*zizyphus spina christi* or *zizyphus mauritania*) and used by Somali women. The Somali bow is also made from this tree, and the tree also bears edible fruit. The Gob is said to have its roots in heaven, and if a clan is called "*gob*," it means that it is made up of clever and honorable men. (*Gun*, "bottom," is the opposite of *gob* in this context.) This line is also sarcastic because the government is aligned with intelligence and honor. Stanza VIII, taken as a whole, implies that the lieutenants and their coup have failed. Northern Somalia then says to the government in Muqdisho: "You are right only because you have the power."

52. The various battles in Burco and Hargeysa in the civil war in the North in 1987 have sharply reversed the sentiment of this sentence written in 1960. Whether regionalism or clan conflicts between the Daarood and the Isaaq, this strife has led to the unilateral formation of the Somaliland Republic, roughly encompassing the old British Somaliland Protectorate.

53. This poem is from Cali Sugulle's play of 1962 entitled *Indha-Sara-Caad*, an ambiguous term in Somali which can mean any of the following: "That which Dazzles the Eyes," "The Distant Mist/Haze/Dust," "That which Dims the Sun," "A Cataract on the Eye." All these interpretations imply some sort of political deception or confusion. The play was extremely popular and was reported to have run nineteen consecutive nights in Muqdisho. It is said that (then) Prime Minister Shar-Ma-Arke, who attended the play more than once, wept with emotion during the performance.

54. The reference here is to the young men of the countries that are enemies of Somalia.

55. I. E., the children of the Somali nation who are under foreign control.

56. I. E. we are cowards.

57. Lines 7-10 imply, "If our own people are maltreated, I cannot reject death; in such circumstances I must not think of the claims of my clan, of wealth and prosperity."

58. Meaning implied. Note the similar structure in the Somali animal story in Omar Au Nuh, 1970 (number ii, p. 9).

59. "You" are the parts of Somalia outside the Republic.

60.   *Qoqobka.* "[Political] boundaries"; literally, the fence inside a Somali corral to divide the animals. The image is that the corral is Greater Somalia while the fences divide its five parts.

61.   *Dhammees yahay.* "Is complete/whole"; literally, "is born on schedule."

62.   The implications of these lines are as follows. The five points of the star on the Somali flag (see page 116, note 67) represent all five parts of the Somali nation, but only two of these parts make up the present Democratic Republic of Somalia. The poet is implying that national fulfillment (represented by the moon) was born prematurely, for the five Somalilands are not yet united. Although this is the situation (symbolized by the mirage), then (as the chorus states) the poet is dishonorable if he rejects death, claims clan ties, etc. Note that the word for an astrological star (*xidig-ga*: masculine) is used instead of the word for an astronomical star (*xidig-ta*: feminine) to describe the star on the flag.

63.   I. E., of those Africans who sided with foreigners.

64.   Lewis 1965, p. 201.

65.   *Soco.* "Agree"; literally, "to go/proceed."

66.   It would not be surprising if *Leexo* became known as "the poem that overthrew two governments." Martin Orwin has written to me that after much interoffice debate in January, 1991, Saciid Cali Muuse, an announcer in the Somali Section of the B. B. C. in London added a new chapter to the history of this poem. During this month and several preceding it, the civil war had been raging in Muqdisho, and the forces of President Maxamed Siyad Barre were weakening daily. To air this poem would be seen by many as taking sides in the conflict, but finally permission was given, and *Leexo* was broadcast at about 5:30pm (East Africa time). Unknown to the Somali Section staff at the B.B.C., about one hour later on the same day, Maxamed Siyad Barre fled the capital for the last time, and his government officially fell to the rebel forces. It is not likely that the broadcast of *Leexo* at this time (heard by many in Somalia) had much to do with the toppling of the Barre regime, but it is likely that this event will add to the aura which already surrounds this poem.

67.   This poem was translated by Muuse X. I. Galaal and edited by me and Michael Cushman Walsh. (See Preface.)

68.   *U loog.* Literally, "to slaughter an animal for the refreshment of a guest."

69.   *Leexo.* This Somali morpheme has a broad semantic range. It could mean any of the following: "swinging/momentum/pendulum force"; anything which causes the above, as in the poem, "light breezes." The image is derived from the children's amusement of swinging on the branch of a tree.

70.   *Laac.* An indistinct object or thing on the horizon and not necessarily the typical mirage of the desert, which is *dhalanteed* in Somali.

71.   This is a reference to the Somali belief in *Nabsi.* See pp. 114, note 49.

72.   Feet = actions; breast = feelings; i. e., you did not do as your conscience directed.

73.   *Him.* An unknown enemy who had attacked the poet in the past. The same enemy is now attacking the person to whom the poet addresses his verse.

74.   *Abundance.* Literally, "the milking."

75.   *Garanuug.* Waller's gazelle.

76.   Lewis 1965, p. 201.

77.   For a collection of articles and essays concerning the Ethiopia-Somali-Kenya Dispute, see Hoskyns 1969.

78.   *Somali News*, no. 356, 24 November 1967, p. 1.

79.   *Them. Xoogga Dalka.* The Somali national army.

80.   A reference to the style of marching in Somalia. The line also implies that the army is not lazy.

81.   This poem was translated by Muuse X. I. Galaal and edited by me and Michael Cushman Walsh. (See Preface.)

82.   *Gunto.* "To prepare oneself"; literally, "to tighten the knot in one's garment," i. e. in preparation for vigorous activity.

83.   *Gu.* The primary rainy season in Somalia.

84   *Jiilaal.* The primary dry season in Somalia.

85.   *Geed-adayg.* "Most enduring of men"; literally, "the hardest wood."

86.   This poem was translated by Muuse X. I. Galaal and edited by me and Michael Cushman Walsh. (See Preface.)

87.   Compare the Somali proverb:

      Dani waa seeto.

      Necessity is a hobbling rope.

88. *Lagu seexdo.* "Upon whom others rely"; literally, "upon whom others sleep"; i. e., "who is watchful so that others may sleep peacefully." This expression is often used in nomadic life where night guards are posted during a time of danger, and when old women have to look after the fires (against wild beasts) at night. If a person is a reliable guard, then he is someone "on whom one can sleep." The person upon whom others are relying is Aadan Cabdulla Cusmaan, the first president of the Somali Republic.

89. *Seermaweydo Season.* The time in the middle of the primary rainy season when abundance abides. This is the time for marriages and the other festivities of the rainy season.

90. *Saddexdii.* "The Three." Reference to the three parts of Greater Somalia outside the state of Somalia.

91. This image refers to the independence of the Somali Republic.

92. *Saakuub.* "Tomorrow"; literally, "the third day from today"; i. e., in the future; because they will become corrupted by their power.

93. This poem was composed in the Benaadir Dialect of Somali.

94. Three rings of a cow bell, used as a rhythmic interlude.

95. *Barkin.* "Headrest." A carved, wooden headrest, used as a pillow by the interior people in Somalia. Similar headrests dating back over seven thousand years can be found in the Egyptian section of the British Museum.

96. To gossip about someone secretly and to spread malicious rumors about him, even if the rumors are true, is considered one of the most offensive acts that can be committed against a person. Moslem ethics require that the person be approached in private and his offense be discussed in secret with him.

97. I. E., of reason.

98. This line could also mean, "Concede us a point [in this discussion]."

99. *Ya.* Exclamation of emotion, here excitement.

100. *Leebiyo gantaalaha.* "The star players"; literally, "the arrow and the arrows." These terms are used as metaphors for the best players of each team. The arrow is considered the most fearful weapon in Somalia, especially because it is often poisoned.

101. *Gammuunka.* "Star player"; literally, "the arrow." See note 100 above.

102. *Gashaanka.* "The defense"; literally, "the shield."

103. *Lista.* "Success"; literally, "list," from Italian *lista.*

104. *Geed fadhiisto.* "To decide"; literally, "to sit under a tree." The traditional Somali method of deciding about a clan's affairs is conducted under a large tree, which then becomes the symbol of *xeer*, Somali traditional law.

105. *Guntiga adkayso.* "To prepare oneself"; literally, "to tighten one's garment." See note 82 above.

106. *Galaaska.* "The cup"; literally, "the glass." A loan word from English.

107. *Birta.* "The goal post"; literally, "metal/iron," from which the goal posts are constructed.

108. This poem was translated by Muuse X. I. Galaal and edited by me and Michael Cushman Walsh. (See Preface.) Because no tape was available for this poem, it was not possible to reproduce the line repeat and refrain pattern.

109. *The meeting.* The Berlin Conference of 1884-85, a turning point in the European scramble for Africa. The powers (Britain, France, Portugal, Germany, and King Leopold of Belgium—who was working to gain a personal empire unrelated to the government of Belgium—) revealed to each other here that a quick partition of Africa was inevitable: the scramble for Africa had officially begun.

110. *Nabsi.* See pp. 114, note 49.

111. *Our lands.* The Somalilands outside the Somali state. This image could also refer to the whole of Africa.

112. *Elder*, i. e., *Nabsi.*

113. *Right*, i. e., Somalia's right to her missing lands.

114. I. E., *Nabsi* will eventually come. The colonialists and what they wrought (the division of Somalia and Africa) cannot last forever.

7

CHARACTERISTICS OF THE HEELLO: ALL PERIODS

Themes Common to All Periods

Many of the themes in the poems we have quoted thus far are topical; they relate to specific events in Somali history or social interaction. But other themes, four of which are very common, have been consistently employed over the entire developmental period of modern poetry. These themes have been quoted in the text earlier, but for other reasons. Attention should be given to them, not as unrelated to social or historical developments, but as consistent themes which have inspired poets of the *heello* since 1948.

By far the most common theme in modern poetry is love. Inherited from the Family of Miniature Genres, this theme has been a favorite from the beginning. More than half the poetry in my collection is concerned with love; this theme is even sometimes used to conceal more subtle messages having political and social overtones. As a topic per se, love is condemned by many traditional and conservative Somalis, but its frequent use on the radio bears witness to its popularity, especially among Somali youths and the new elite.

As a theme, love may be divided into two subthemes. Lovers are sometimes hopeful, successful in their endeavors, and optimistic about the future. They may, as Maxamed Suleebaan Bidde does in Example 30, praise their love for her spiritual and physical features. The following poem was composed in 1968.

Example 30:

I.	1	Sida geed caleenliyo,
	2	Ubax guud ka qariyeen,
	3	Oy gooni laamaha,
	4	Ay midiba geesteed,
	5	Hoobaan is gaadhiyo,

6   Guntin midha ah leedey,
      (*repeat ll. 1-6*)

13   Oo soo gandoodoo ,

14   Galka faraqa soo daray,
      (*repeat ll. 13-14*)

17   Oo godan barwaaqo ah,

18   Durduraan gudhayniyo,

19   Gacan webi ku yaallaan,
      (*repeat ll. 17-19*)

23   Oon Gu iyo Jiilaal,

24   Midab guurin baad too,
      (*repeat ll. 23-24*)

     27   Gabadhyahay kal-gacal baan,

     28   Goortaan Ku eegaba,
         (*repeat ll. 27-28*)

     31   Qalbiga iga gelisaa,
         (*repeat ll. 27-31*)

     37   Waxse aanan garanayn,

     38   Ii gunudday caashaqee,

     39   Halka aad i gaadhsiin,

II.   40   Sidaad tahay gammaan faras,

41   Sange geesi daaqsaday,

42   Uu gal-duur miray,

43   Soddon bil iyo gawdeed,

44   Uu goobay farawgii,

45   Sararta iyo gaaddada,
      (*repeat ll. 40-45*)

52   Oo galangalcooboo,

53   Cuduuduhu gammuurmeen,
      (*repeat ll. 52-53*)

56   Oo galabba Loo raro,

57   Sida ramag Guyaal dhalay,

58   Hadba kaynta geeda leh,
      (*repeat ll. 56-58*)

62   Oon guluf colaadiyo,

63   Weli socoto dheer gelin,

     (*repeat ll. 62-63*)

     66   Gabadhyahay kal-gacal baan, etc.

III.   79   Sida Gubanka qaarkii,

80   Uu gorgoor ku simanyay,

81   Ama maadh galbeedoo,

82   Gubatiyo ku taal Hawd,

83   Oo labagardhooboo,

84   Badh ba gees u seexday,

     (*repeat ll. 79-84*)

91   Dharabka iyo geedaha,

92   Quruxdooda gaarka ah,

     (*repeat ll. 91-92*)

95   Ama haro gingimanoo,

96   Guud ka xarfanaysoo,

97   Shimbiro ka giigeen,

     (*repeat ll. 95-97*)

101   Oon Gu iyo Jiilaal,

102   Midab guurin baad too,

     (*repeat ll. 101-102*)

     105   Gabadhyahay kal-gacal baan, etc.

I.   1-2   [You are] like a tree hidden [from view] by [its] leaves and flowers;

     3 & 6   And [each] separate branch has a cluster of fruit,

     4   Which, on every side [of the branch],

     5   Has reached overripeness.

     (*repeat ll. 1-6*)

     13   And [the fruit] leans downward [in its ripeness],

     14   And dips [its] sides into a cool pool of water.

     (*repeat ll. 13-14*)

     17   [The tree] is in a prosperous valley,

     18   By a stream which does not dry up,

19   And which is situated by a tributary of a river,
     (*repeat ll. 17-19*)

23-24   And you are [like a tree] which does not lose its color in Gu or Jiilaal.[1]
        (*repeat ll. 23-24*)

27   O girl, I love thee [as my own kin];
28   Whenever I see you,
     (*repeat ll. 27-28*)

31   You cause [love] to enter [my] heart.
     (repeat ll. 27-31

37   But the thing I do not know is
39   The place to which you will lead me,
38   Because you knotted the love in me.

II.   40   As you are like a colt,
41   A stallion that has been raised by a brave man:
42   He grazed it every night in a thicket,
43   For thirty [days]: a complete month.
44   It became covered with fat
45   In the ribs and on the breast.
     (*repeat ll. 40-45*)

52   And [the horse] became fat and bulky,
53   And [its] upper legs became fat and solid.
     (*repeat ll. 52-53*)

56   And [the horse] is moved every evening
58   To the forest which has [good] grass,
57   Like she-camels which give birth during the rainy season.
     (*repeat ll. 56-58*)

62-63   And [the horse] has not yet been used by a party of raiders or on a
        long march.
        (*repeat ll. 62-63*)

66   O girl, I love thee, etc.

III.   79   [You are either] like the parts of Guban,[2]
80   [Where] the *gorgoor*[3] grows,
81   Or [like] *maadh*[4] in the evening,[5]
82   That grows in Gubato[6] and in the Hawd,[7]

178

83 And which [grows] in rows,

84 Some of it swaying [as though it were] asleep.

  (*repeat ll. 79-84*)

91 [You are like] the dew and the grass:

92 Their special beauty.

  (*repeat ll. 91-92*)

95 Or [like] the full lake,

96 Which has ripples on [its] surface,

97 [And where] birds quench their thirst.

  (*repeat ll. 95-97*)

101-102 And you are [like the tree], which does not lose its color in Gu or
    Jiilaal.

  (*repeat ll. 101-102*)

105 O girl, I love thee, etc.

Poems do not always express successful love. For instance, in Example 31, composed in 1969, the poet employs an unsuccessful approach to love. He asks his beloved many questions about love, but what he really implies is that all these things have happened to him. We might add a final line to the poem, thus: "Did love do all these things to you, as it did to me for your sake?" This poem is also unusual because it has no refrain, but compensates the absence of a refrain by beginning each stanza with the same line.

Example 31:

I. 1 Qummaneey jacayl,

  2 Marna jaar ma noqoteen,

  (*repeat ll. 1-2*)

  5 Jid ma wada lugayseen,

  6 Ma la cuntay jidiin,

  7 Jahaad ma isku aragteen,

  (*repeat ll. 5-7*)

  11 Jiiddaad ka dhalatiyo,

  12 Ma Kaa jaray dadkii,

13   Gooni-joog ma Kaa dhigay,
    (*repeat ll. 11-13*)

II.   17   Qummaneey jacayl,

18   Weli jiif ma Kugu helay,
    (*repeat ll. 17-18*)

21   Dhudhub ma isku jiidhdheen,

22   Jiljilada ma Kaa galay,

23   Hadba jinac ma Kuu riday,
    (*repeat ll. 21-23*)

27   Jiidh durugsanaa iyo,

28   Qalbi meel fog Kaa jiray,

29   Iyagii ma jaaddeen,
    (*repeat ll. 27-29*)

III.   33   Qummaneey jacayl,

34   Weli jalaw ma Kuu yidhi,
    (*repeat ll. 33-34*)

37   Jara adag ma Kugu xidhay,

38   Reeryo jaan ma Kugu raray,

39   Jilbaha na ma Kuu riday,
    (*repeat ll. 37-39*)

43   Jibaadka iyo taahii,

44   Jeenfad ma oydoo,

45   Ilmo jabaq ma Kaa tidhi,
    (*repeat ll. 43-45*)

IV.   49   Qummaneey jacayl,

50   Weli jar iyo buur dheer,
    (*repeat ll. 49-50*)

53   Ama jaranjar hoosteed,

54   Ma Ku geeyay jiiroo,

55   Guryo jaan ma Kula galay,
    (repeat ll. 53-55)

59   Waxaad jeefad socota ba,

60   Intuu jalawgii Kula dhacay,

61   Jilbahaad ku socotiyo,

62 Ma Kuu laabay jeenyaha,
(*repeat ll. 59-62*)

V. 67 Qummaneey jacayl,

68 Weli jabaq ma Kula yidhi,
(*repeat ll. 67-68*)

71 Jabad ma isku aragteen,

72 Dadka kaad ka jamatiyo,

73 Jaallahaa ma kulanteen,
(*repeat ll. 71-73*)

77 Halkaad uga jid bixi layd,

78 Juuqba ma iska waydoo,

79 Hadalkii ma Kaa jaray.
(*repeat ll. 77-79*)

I. 1 O Qumman,[8] did love

2 And you ever become neighbors?
(*repeat ll. 1-2*)

5 Did you travel together?

6 Did you have a meal with him?

7 Did you meet him in battle?[9]
(*repeat ll. 5-7*)

12 Did [love] isolate you from [your] people and

11 From the land in which you were born ?[10]

13 Did he isolate you?
(*repeat ll. 11-13*)

II. 17 O Qumman, did love

18 Find you while you slept?
(*repeat ll. 17-18*)

21 Did you encounter him in a narrow place?

22 Did he enter you through [your] foot?[11]

23 Did he [cause] you to sway sideways?
(*repeat ll. 21-23*)

27 A person in a distant place, and

28   A heart which is far from you:

29   Did you [and love] go to them?

   (*repeat ll. 27-29*)

III.   33   O Qumman, did love

   34   Rush suddenly upon you?

   (*repeat ll. 33-34*)

   37   Did he bind you with a strong halter?

   38   Did he put the burden of jinns upon you?

   39   Did he bring you to your knees?

   (*repeat ll. 37-39*)

   43-44   [After] long clamor, groaning and moaning, did you weep profusely?

   45   Did tears fall from your eyes?

   (*repeat ll. 43-45*)

IV.   49   O Qumman, did love

   50 & 54   Ever bring you to a steep slope, a cliff, a tall mountain,

   (*repeat ll. 49-50*)

   53   Or to the foot of a ladder?[12]

   55   Did he enter the houses of jinns with [you]?

   (*repeat ll. 53-55*)

   59   While you walked tiredly along,

   60   And while he beat you with a stick,

   61-62   Did he make you bend your knees, with which you walk, and the
       limbs [of your body]?

   (*repeat ll. 59-62*)

V.   67   O Qumman, did love

   68   Run with you?

   (*repeat ll. 67-68*)

   71   Did you see him in the bush?

   73   Did you meet your friend,

   72   The one you yearn for from among the people?

   (*repeat ll. 71-73*)

   77   While you should have talked with him,

   78   Did you fail to find even one word?

79   Did [love] make you lose your voice ?
      (*repeat ll. 77-79*)

But the themes in Somali love poetry must not be taken as necessarily related to real life situations. Many *heello* are merely compositions by poets of good imagination and ability. Furthermore, it is a well-known practice—or so I am told—for Somali professional poets to create an image of themselves as great lovers.

Along with love, political themes can be observed in all periods of development, but the political themes can also be subdivided. Following are examples of the three most common political themes of the *heello*.

Although not as popular as love, anticolonialism has been one of the most popular themes of the *heello* and did not cease as a topic of inspiration when Somalia attained her independence. The following poem depicts Africa as a sleeping woman with whom the poet, Axmed Yuusuf Ducaale (?), is pleading to awake. It was probably composed in 1963.

Example 32:

I.   1   Hohey Afrikaay huruddooy,

      2   Cadow Ku heeryee huruddooy,

      3   Halyeyadaadii huruddooy,

      4   Haad baa cunaayee huruddooy,
            (*repeat ll. 1-4*)

      9   Haamaa La saaraa huruddooy,

      10   Hayin sidiisaa huruddooy,

      11   La hogaaminayaa,
            (*repeat ll. 9-11*)

      15   Dulli Lama hullaabtee,

      16   Away hanaddadaadii,
            (*repeat ll. 15-16*)

      19   Doqon baa habawsan,

      20   Weligeed hallaysan e,

      21   Sida xoolihii baa,

22   Xerada Lagu hooyaa,

    (repeat ll. 19-22)

II.   27   Habeenno badan baan huruddooy,

    28   Hammuun ku seexdee huruddooy,

    29   Hirtaanyo awgeed huruddooy,

    30   La hadli waayee huruddooy,

    (repeat ll. 27-30)

    35   Naa caanihii hashaydaan huruddooy,

    36   Haleeli waayee huruddooy,

    37   La iga hor-joogaa,

    (repeat ll. 35-37)

    41   Dulli Lama hullaabtee, etc.

III.   53   Horor waraabahaa huruddooy,

    54   Waxyaha Ku haysta huruddooy,

    55   Oo hantidaadii huruddooy,

    56   Kaa hirqanaayee huruddooy,

    (repeat ll. 53-56)

    61   Hadina waydee huruddooy,

    62   Hadmaad ogaane huruddooy,

    63   Aad hagaagi doontaa,

    (repeat ll. 61-63)

    67   Dulli Lama hullaabtee, etc.

I.   1   Hohey Africa, you sleeping [woman]—

    2   O Sleeping One, an enemy has put a pack saddle mat [on your back];

    3   O Slumbering One, your champions

    4   Are being devoured by birds of prey, O Sleeping One.

    (repeat ll. 1-4)

    9   O Sleeping One, water vessels are put [on you],

    10   O Slumbering One, like an obedient camel,

    11   Which is led forth on a lead.

    (repeat ll. 9-11)

    15   One does not wrap oneself in disgrace;

16   Where are your Great Men?
      (*repeat ll. 15-16*)

19   Fools are [always] lost,

20   Always in a confused state,

21   Like the animals

22   Being led into the corral.
      (*repeat ll. 19-22*)

II.   27   O Sleeping One, many nights

28   I slept in bitter thought, O Slumbering One.

29   O Sleeping One, because of great anger,

30   I could not speak, O Slumbering One.
      (*repeat ll. 27-30*)

35   O Sleeping One, the milk of my own she-camel,

36   I could not afford [to drink], O Slumbering One.

37   They[13] stand against me.
      (*repeat ll. 35-37*)

    41   One does not wrap oneself, etc.

III. 53   O Sleeping One, the bold hyenas,[14]

54   Hold your body [in subservience], O Slumbering One,

55   And, O Sleeping One, your possessions

56   Have been denied you, O Slumbering One.
       (*repeat ll. 53-56*)

61   O Sleeping One, you failed to understand;

62   O Slumbering One, when shall you know,

63   And proceed in the right path?
      (*repeat ll. 61-63*)

    67   One does not wrap oneself, etc.

Like anticolonialism, patriotism did not cease to be used as a theme in modern poetry when independence was attained. Although the period 1959-61 saw the largest number of patriotic poems, such poetry is still composed. Example 33 is another poem by Cabdullaahi Qarshe; composed in 1961. It was so popular that Radio Muqdisho employed it as a signature tune until "Dhulkayaga" replaced it (see above, pp. 83-84 and 88-90). Example 34 was composed in (circa) 1964 by Cabdullaahi Cabdi Shube.

Example 33:

I.   M: 1   Oqoon lazaani waa iftiin lazaaneey,

            2   Oqoon lazaani waa iftiin lazaaneey,

            3   Waa aqaliyo ilays lazaaneey,

            4   Waa aqaliyo ilays lazaaneey,

     C: 5   Ogaada, ogaada, dugsiyada ogaada,

            6   Ogaada, ogaada, walaalayaal ogaada,

               (repeat ll. 5-6)

II. M: 9   Waa oommanaan iyo abaarey,

           10   Waa oommanaan iyo abaarey,

           11   Omosiyo oon biyo lazaaney,

           12   Omosiyo oon biyo lazaaney,

     C: 13   Ogaada, ogaada, etc.

III. M: 17   Indhaha oon kala qaadnay,

           18   Indhaha oon kala qaadnay,

           19   Ifka ugu ilbaxsanaannee,

           20   Ifka ugu ilbaxsanaannee,

     C: 21   Ogaada, ogaada, etc.

I.   M: 1   [To be] without knowledge is [to be] without light;

            2   [To be] without knowledge is [to be] without light;

            3   It is a house without illumination;

            4   It is a house without illumination;

     C: 5   Know it! Become aware of the schools; know it!

            6   Know it! Know it, brothers and sisters, know it!

               (repeat ll. 5-6)

II. M: 9   It is suffering of thirst and drought;

           10   It is suffering of thirst and drought;

           11   [It is] desert and thirst, [being] without water;

           12   [It is] desert and thirst, [being] without water;

     C: 13   Know it, etc.

III. M: 17   [So that] we [may] open [our] eyes

           18   [So that] we [may] open [our] eyes

19 [In order] to become modern and progressive in this world,

20 [In order] to become modern and progressive in this world,

C: 21 Know it, etc.

Example 34:

I. 1 Dibi geesaliyo,

2 Ido gorod madow,

3 Waa waxa dhulkeena

4 Laynagu gartaa,

5 Maantay galladi,

6 Noo soo gashee,

7 Gobannimadayada,

8 Guullow adkee,

(repeat ll. 5-8)

II. 13 Geed qodhax leh iyo,

14 Gudin iyo hangool,

15 Waa waxa dhulkeena u gaarehee,

16 Laynagu gartaa, etc.

III. 25 Wiil geel-jiroon,

26 Gaajadu karayn,

27 Waa waxa dhulkeena u gaarehee,

28 Laynagu gartaa, etc.

IV. 37 Dhul guduudan,

38 Aan gogol doonahayn,

39 Waa waxa dhulkeena u gaarehee,

40 Laynagu gartaa, etc.

V. 49 Reer-guuraayiyo,

50 Gaashaan xardhani,

51 Waa waxa dhulkeena u gaarehee,

52 Laynagu gartaa, etc.

I. 1 The bull with horns, and

2 The black-headed sheep

3   Are animals special to our country:

    4   We are famous for them.

    5   Today, happiness

    6   Has come to us.

    7-8 O God, the Victorious, strengthen our independence!

        (*repeat ll. 5-8*)

II.   13   The thorn tree, and

       14   The *gudin*[15] and *hangool*[16]

       15   Are things special to our country:

         16   We are famous for them, etc.

III.   25   Boys who herd camels, and whom

       26   Hunger cannot [disable]

       27   Are something special to our country:

        28   We are famous for them, etc.

IV.   37   The red earth,

       38   Which needs no *gogol*[17]

       39   Is something special to our country:

        40   We are famous for it, etc.

V.   49   Nomadic settlements, and

       50   Decorated shields

       51   Are things special to our country:

        52   We are famous for them, etc.

The idea of Greater Somalia is far from dead on the Horn of Africa and has, like the above mentioned themes, served as inspiration to *heello* poets consistently over the developmental periods of modern poetry. As in Example 35, composed in 1960 by Maxamed Suleebaan Bidde (?), Pan-Somalism is often the main theme of a poem, but references are also made to it in poems composed on other topics.

Example 35:

I.   1   Wajeerta hoose,

    2   Wajeerta hoose,

    3   Inay soo wareegtoo,

    4   Inay soo wareegtoo,

5   Warshado u sameeyoo,

6   Wax walba u dhammeeyoo, hey!

7   Ayaan wacad ku qaaday,

8   Ayaan wacad ku qaaday,

9   Waddaankayga wanaagsan,

10   Waddaankayga wanaagsan,
     (*repeat ll. 7-10*)

II.   15   Soomaaloo wanaagsan,

16   Soomaaloo wanaagsan,

17   Giddigeed walaal ah,

18   Giddigeed walaal ah,

19   Warshado u sameeyoo, etc.

III. 29   Inaan wiida diido,

30   Inaan wiida diido,

31   Obokh soo walwaaloo,

32   Obokh soo walwaaloo,

33   Warshado u sameeyoo, etc.

IV.   43   Inuu cadowgu waashoo,

44   Inuu cadowgu waashoo,

45   Oo aan Hawd ka weedhoo,

46   Oo aan Hawd ka weedhoo,

47   Warshado u sameeyoo, etc.

I.   1   The lower Wajeer:[18]

2   The lower Wajeer:

3   That it will come to our side,

4   That it will come to our side,

5   [That I] will build factories [for it],

6   [And] complete everything, hey!

7   I have made a solemn promise.

8   I have made a solemn promise.

9   Concerning my good country.

10   Concerning my good country.
     (*repeat ll. 7-10*)

II. 15   The Somalis who are good, and

 16   The Somalis who are good, and

 17   [Who are now] brothers and sisters,

 18   [Who are now] brothers and sisters,

 19   [That we] will build factories [for them], etc.

III. 29   That I shall reject the *oui*,[19]

 30   That I shall reject the *oui*,

 31   That I obtain Obokh,[20]

 32   That I obtain Obokh,

 33   [That I] will build factories [for it], etc.

IV. 43   That the enemy go insane,

 44   That the enemy go insane,

 45   That I shall drive him from the Hawd,

 46   That I shall drive him from the Hawd,

 47 [That I] shall build factories [for it], etc.

Along with these recurring themes, some elements of structure are best treated outside the historical approach to the development of the *heello*. Let us consider these elements in detail.

Structural Characteristics and Development Common to all Periods

Although not separate from Somali history and social development during this time, some characteristics of structure, such as the gradual refinement of poetic language and the addition of more musical instruments, are not bound to any one period. Furthermore, other features, such as imagery and the influence of media on the *heello*, were common to all periods and not the result of any one period.

The relative ease of translation of the early *heello* compared to the classical poems of the Somali past is certainly one method of discovering that the language of modern poetry is more simple and closer to contemporary spoken Somali than that of such genres as the *gabay*.

Comparing the latest *heello* with the earliest *heello*, one finds that the language used has become more refined, though the difference is not nearly as profound as between the *gabay* and the *heello*. Earlier *heello*, still close to the tradition of the miniature poem, tend to use direct concepts in place of metaphoric imagery or symbolism. Some examples are: greed, success, distress, difficulty, independence, love, poverty, misfortune, disgrace, enemy, hatred, foolishness, justice, death, victory, defeat, evil, hardship, virtue. Later *heello*, as we shall shortly see, used more subtle and complex images. When independence was attained and poems against the government were composed, the device of the hidden messages (see pp. 38-41) had to be employed more imaginatively to fool the Somali censor but still be understood by the general public.

We mentioned that line repeating patterns expanded in the third period. But these patterns gradually developed over the entire duration of the *heello*. We might categorize these patterns as follows, beginning with these poems having little or no repetition at all:

1) Little or no line repeating in the text, followed by a refrain (as in the poems on pp. 128-33 pp. 135-36 and pp. 139-42).

2) Single lines repeated in the text, followed by a refrain (as in the poems on pp. 120-22, pp. 150-53).

3) Couplets repeated in the text, followed by a refrain (as in the poem on pp. 123-26).

4) Triplets repeated in the text, followed by a refrain (as in the poem on pp. 134-35).

5) Quatrains repeated in the text, followed by a refrain (as in the poem on pp. 144-45). More complicated systems are found in the following poems:

6) A quatrain repeated and a pentastich repeated alternately in the text, followed by a refrain (as in the poem on pp. 147-50).

7) A quatrain repeated in the text, with a refrain of two triplets repeated, one sung by the soloist and one sung by the chorus (as in the poem on pp. 153-55).

6) A couplet, followed by a single line repeated in the text, followed by a refrain (as in the poem on pp. 160-62). Still further complicated systems are exhibited in the following patterns:

9) A couplet repeated, followed by a single line, followed by a complete repeat of this again in the text, followed eventually by a refrain. This system yields the following pattern: A B A B C A B A B C, or:

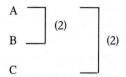

A
B
C

(2)

(2)

(as the poems on pp. 118-20, pp. 155-60).

10) A sexain repeated in the text, followed by a refrain made up of a couplet repeated three times and a couplet repeated once (as in the poem on pp. 137-39).

The list goes on, but the above catalogue will give an idea of the variety of line repeating patterns found in the modern poem. What is important to remember about these patterns is that, although the *heello* resemble each other in their patterns, there is no set rule for how the pattern is to be accomplished. It is left to the poet or composer of musical accompaniment to choose which lines to repeat and how to work out the pattern. But line repeating is not the only innovation of form which developed. We mentioned another form of repetition pattern on p. 105. In Example 36 below, composed by Xasan Diiriye in 1967, an even more profound example of this type of repetition pattern can be seen. In it the following pattern occurs:

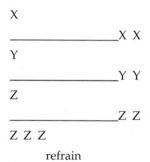

X

_____X X

Y

_____Y Y

Z

_____Z Z

Z Z Z

refrain

Example 36:

I. 1 Gurxamayey,

2 Sidii aar gantaal qaba, gurxamayey, gurxamayey,

3 Geydhamayey,

4 Guuxa iyo reenkii, geydhamayey, geydhamayey,

5 Gilgilayey,

6 Timaha guudka iga baxay, gilgilayey, gilgilayey,

7 Waan gilgilayey, gilgilayey, gilgilayey,

8   Waxay gubay adoo gobaad ii gargaari waydee.

9   Waxay gubay adoo gobaad ii gargaari waydee.

II.   10   Guntadayey,

11   Sidii geesi raacda ah, guntadayey, guntadayey,

12   Gurmadayey,

13   Gucla-roorka orodkii, gurmadayey, gurmadayey,

14   Dhex galayey,

15   Geeri iyo nolol walaala ah, dhex galayey, dhex galayey,

16   Waan dhex galayey, dhex galayey, dhex galayey,

17   Waxay gubay, etc.

III.   19   Gar-naqayey,

20   Sidii oday guddoonshe ah, gar-naqayey, gar-naqayey,

21   Gabbadayey,

22   Guhaad iyo colaaddii, gabbadayey, gabbadayey,

23   Guud marayey,

24   Wixii ila gudboonaa, guud marayey, guud marayey,

25   Waan guud marayey, guud marayey, guud marayey,

26   Waxay gubay, etc.

IV.   28   U gudayey,

29   Sidii gaadh ilaala ah, u gudayey, u gudayey,

30   Gaatamayey,

31   Sidii goray gabbal u dhacay, gaatamayey, gaatamayey,

    (repeat ll. 30-31)

34   U gozayey,

35   Gaajiyo oon i gowracay, u gozayey, u gozayey,

36   Waan u gozayey, u gozayey, u gozayey,

37   Waxay gubay, etc.

I.   1   I growled

2   Like a male lion with an arrow [in its flesh], I growled, I growled.

3   I became wild

4   [With] roaring and grunting, I became wild, I became wild.

5   I shook

6   The hair which grows on my head, I shook, I shook.

7   I shook, shook, shook.

   8   What burned me was that you, who are of noble birth failed to support me.

   9   What burned me was that you, who are of noble birth failed to support me.

II. 10   I prepared myself[21]

11   Like the brave searcher of lost animals, I prepared myself, I prepared myself.

12   I came to the aid of those in distress.

13   Trotting and running, I came to the aid of those in distress, I came to the aid of those in distress.

14   I came close[22]

15   [To where] life and death are brothers, I came close, I came close.

16   I came close, came close, came close.

   17   What burned me, etc.

III. 19   I mediated

20   Like an old arbitrator, I mediated, I mediated.

21   I dodged

22   The scolding and enmity, I dodged, I dodged.

23   I failed[23]

24   [To do] what I was supposed [to do], I failed, I failed.

25   I failed, failed, failed.

   26   What burned me, etc.

IV. 28   I walked in the night

29   Like an observant guard, I walked in the night, I walked in the night.

30   I walked stealthily

31   Like the male ostrich at sunset, I walked stealthily, I walked stealthily. (*repeat ll. 30-31*)

34   I became weary

35   With hunger and thirst that cut [my] throat, I became weary, I became weary.

36   I became weary, became weary, became weary.

   37   What burned me, etc.

Together with refinement in language and patterns of repetition came development in musical accompaniment. But to transcribe the text of an oral poem is not as difficult as transcribing its musical accompaniment. Furthermore, the musical part of the *heello* is outside the scope of this book. Suffice it to say that development in music can go a long way from a petrol tin drum to the present orchestra of Radio Muqdisho. And finally, the melodies of the present day *heello* are as varied and interesting as those in modern Western pop music.

Language and music, then, have become more refined: music through the addition of more and more musical instruments and of more complex melodies, and language through the use of more complex structure and imagery. Direct concepts have been illustrated (see above, pp. 190-91). But what of more complex images?

Many images have one special, metaphoric or allegoric meaning only within one particular poem. Thus *gantaal* ("arrow") represents a star football player in the poem on pp. 160-62, but not necessarily elsewhere. Many other images can be said to represent one idea only. They occur so frequently in a single metaphoric or allegoric sense (e.g., rain and drought) that their use may be regarded as a set convention of Somali poetic diction. Still other images have a range of meanings, although very limited. The audience, however, is rarely left in doubt as to which meaning to choose. The context of that image usually assists the listener in discerning the right meaning.

Very few images are new to Somali poetry as a whole. For example, the airplane in the poem on pp. 163-65 (line 31) is not a traditional image. The use of different words for arrow (*gantaal, leeb, gammuun*) to represent the star football player in the poem on pp. 160-62) is a novel device, as is the use of the Somali shield (*gaashaan*) that stands for defense in the same poem. Most images, however, are traditional and have come to modern poetry either from traditional poems or from the traditional way of life. Four main categories cover the majority of conventional images used in the *heello*.

Positive Images   For a nation that depends upon rain to such a great extent as Somalia, it is hardly remarkable that one finds so many images related to rain in the poetry.[24] The rainy season brings to the nomad happiness, abundance, prosperity, ease of tensions, marriage, and the birth of new animals to replenish his flocks. All of these things and more are represented by images linked to the rainy season. Some poems, like the ones on pp. 175-79 and pp. 201-02, are virtually dripping with wet images Following is a list of the more common of these images:

1.   *Gu*, the primary rainy season

2.   *Dayr*, the secondary rainy season

3.   Rain

4.   Water

5.   Milk

6.   Green grass or the greenness of the bush (*nimco*)

7.   The Sign of *Sagal* (see below, pp. 201-02, line 17)

8.   Cool pool of water, often with a mention of the ripples in the pool

9.   Cool, damp sand (*rays*)

10. The new buds

11. The fruit of a tree or bush

Another important group of images is representative of wisdom, truth, knowledge, and more recently, formal education (see p. 37). Various forms of light symbolize these ideas, which are highly respected among the Somali. Light itself as well as the sun and the sunrise are often used. Moreover, images such as the moon and the beacon fire are popular, for they are forms of light which occur during the night. Conversely, darkness represents ignorance and falsehood.

Beauty is expressed in Somali poetry by several images . The beauty of the landscape is often expressed with the same symbols as those related to rain, and some of these, like the flower and the newly emerging buds, depict female beauty. A woman's beauty is often compared to that of a horse . Horses are less often used to represent wealth, but the camel commonly symbolizes this. The ownership of one hundred camels denotes great wealth, while the possession of only one she-camel is used to show a person's poverty.

Light is not the only product of the sun. Shade from its heat is a metaphor for rest and solace in many poems. Because it is blue, the daylight sky symbolizes the Somali flag.

Parts of the body figure prominently as positive images. For example, strength and power are traits prized by the Somalis, and the upper arm and lower leg symbolize them. The lower leg, however, is more often used to symbolize weakness because of the associated mutilation of hamstringing. The right hand, in contrast to the Moslem consideration of the left hand as ritually unclean, adds emphasis to a deed.

Negative Images   As images relating to rain make up so many positive symbols, so
                      images relating to drought comprise a large number of the negative
ones. Rivers, streams, and even camels often dry up in *heello,* representing a disaster of
some sort, poverty, or want. Thirst and the two dry seasons, *Jiilaal* and *Xagaa,* are sister
images to drought and express the same feeling. Other common images symbolizing
disaster are the black hole and the cliff. Sudden disaster is symbolized by the flood. When
water comes to Somalia it is not always in the form of gentle rain. Torrents of rain often
cause flash floods, which in turn bring death and disaster. It is said that in Burco a large
net is strung across its seasonal river (*tog*) in the rainy season to catch the bodies of unlucky
people who are swept away by the floods.

The thorn is yet another symbol for disaster; in this case it signifies hindrance along
a set path to a goal. The worst disaster of all, death, is sometimes symbolized by the snake
or serpent.

The mirage, common enough on the plains of the Horn, is an image of trickery and
deceit.

The colonialist in Somali poetry is represented by the hyena and the buzzard,
animals considered unclean because they feed on carrion. Conversely, the colonized
African is sometimes depicted as a beast of burden, either camel or donkey. This image
occurs in the classical poem when referring to a clan reduced to vassalage by another.

Sleep often symbolizes ignorance or neglect of duty, but being awake at times when
one should be asleep is not an opposite symbol. Sleeplessness is an image used to express
the negative side of love.

As we have seen in several poems, love is considered an illness, a disease, or a state
of insanity.[25] *Jeex qudhacya waaweyn,* "[Love is] a valley of big thorn trees," cries the poet.
The poet in love sometimes compares himself to the gazelle who wanders alone, away
from his fellow gazelles. This symbol of loneliness is supplemented by the roar of the lion,
representing grief.

Mixed Images   Parallel to the images which, in most circumstances have but one
                   meaning, is a group of images which have two or more references.
The dual condition of these symbols, however, rarely leads to confusion among the Somali
audience, for the context of the poem usually defines the image. Clouds, for example, are
sometimes a positive symbol since they bring rain. On the other hand, they can be negative

symbols, since they also blot out the sun, the light, wisdom.

Not all these images are positive-negative mixtures. Some are one sided but still have two references. Lightning is sometimes the announcer of rain and sometimes the bringer of light, both positive interpretations. Fire is another bringer of light, but it has a negative meaning as well, for it can burn painfully. The audience, however, would rarely be left in doubt as to which way to interpret fire, as we can see in these lines:

> Mar sidii ilayskii ololkaa,
> Iftiinkaagu i jiidhay.

> Once, like the light of the flame,
> Your light hit me.

The tree, like the above mentioned images, falls into the dual interpretation category, at one time symbolizing the beauty of women, at another, the law of traditional Somalia. [26] Old and ugly women in Somalia are often bent from many years of toil and labor. If a woman is compared to a tree, the element of beauty emphasized is straightness of limb, or youthfulness. What is meant by the second interpretation, law, is derived from the time when the elders of a clan used to hold their meeting (*shir*) to discuss traditional law (*xeer*) in the shade of a tree. When the poet declares

> Gurmagozan La jaray e,
> Guudkii saraan,
> Ku gabboodsadaa.

> I am on top of[27]
> The stump of a tree that has been cut down,
> [Where] I am being sheltered.

the listener knows that law, reason, the systematic life, have collapsed and that the poet is experiencing a state of anarchy.

Two images which are commonly employed in modern poetry remain neutral, but their effect on the individual is sometimes positive, sometimes negative. The seat of emotion symbolized by the abdominal region of the body (heart, liver, stomach, diaphragm) sometimes houses happiness, at other times sadness. Likewise, the Somali belief in *Nabsi* (see p. 114, note 49) occasionally works in one's favor, but it can also work against one.

Along with images that usually have only two meanings, we find those which have more than two interpretations. Wind, for example, will dry things out and cool them off, but it also can announce the coming of rain. Other images, such as the wound (disaster, death, colonialism, the pain of love) and the arrow (death, star football player, the satellite) are employed for their general characteristics and can symbolize any number of things.

Situational Imagery   Apart from the relatively tangible images are those which make up a situation or condition.[28] A large part of this imagery is taken from the pastoral way of life and has come to modern poetry from traditional sources. The use of such images as the movement of the family group (*reer*) from one camp site to another (*geeddi*) is employed in a number of ways (see pp. 120- 22 lines 9-11). The scout (*sahan*) who looks for this new camp site also symbolizes preparing the way and announcing prosperity or a better condition (see pp. 150-53, lines 73-76).

To remain on the left side of the camel (an image from the poem on pp. 128-33, line 38, meaning to remain hopeful) is also from the nomad's experience. Yet another image from the traditional way of life is the cleansing of one's emotions (stomach) as the milk vessel is cleaned (see pp. 110-11, lines 15-17). To love a woman as though she were a kinsman is an image that shows how strong clan ties are in traditional society.

The nomad's environment also offers a rich supply of images for his poetry. The moon and star symbol in the poem on pp. 134-35, lines 41-43 is an example.

A common group of images representing disaster, loss of power, or a state of instability is the reference to swaying, flying, being neither of this world nor of the next. (See pp. 139-42, lines 8, 9, 27, and pp. 179-83, line 23.) Also representing the above conditions is the image of isolation from society and kin. Poets often find themselves having been exiled by their kinsmen because of love or political alliance. It must be stressed, however, that this image is almost always employed as a poetic convention. Actual expulsion from one's clan is rare and is regarded as one of the most dreadful things that can happen to a man. Related to this state of being is another complaint used by many poets: the world, my peers, or my generation has passed me by, and I am held back.

Unified Imagery   Each image in a Somali poem contributes to the total picture of the poet's message in the minds of the listeners. These images are usually easy to understand, for where the listener has not been preconditioned, context will usually solve the problem. Taken as a whole, however, the images employed by any one *heello* often form a system, a unified conceptual framework, a second level of meaning which reinforces the first or linguistic level of the poem. This of course is not always the case, as images are many times unconnected by any unifying feature. In the poem on pp. 120-22 however, the same basic statement is made in each stanza, each time using different images. This message might be reduced to the following:

A.   While one is in a good condition,

B.   One does not deliberately push oneself into a bad condition.

In Example 37 we see this substructure or unifying framework of imagery operating in a different manner. This poem, composed in 1965 by Maxamed Suleebaan Bidde, uses two sets of positive images extensively. The first set is made up of images relating to rain; the second set relates to light. The poet compares his love to the beauty and prosperity of rain and the wisdom and truth of light. He claims that he sees these characteristics in his environment in such a way that he actually confuses them with the person of his beloved. Furthermore, each stanza represents a different time of day, each stanza progressing to the next period. Thus we have the following system:

Stanza I: Sunrise

Stanza II: Midmorning

Stanza III: Noon

Stanza IV: Sunset

Stanza V: Nighttime

Example 37:

I.   1   Geed iyo ruux markaynu kala garanno,

       2   Qorraxdoo gees kastaba fallaadho gantay,

          3   Yaad geddeedii tahoon LaGaa garan,

          (*repeat l. 3, twice*)

II.   6   Daruur goor barqo ah, Ku guud-timi,

       7   Oo intay biyo gelisay kala gurataad,

          8   Yaad geddeedii tahoon LaGaa garan,

          (*repeat l. 8, twice*)

III.   11   Gugoo dazay, geedahoo baxay,

       12   Gelgelimaad xareedda oo galacloo,

          13   Garaarole baan LaGaa garan,

          (*repeat l. 13, twice*)

IV.   16   God-fiiday godkeeda jeex la gashay,

       17   Guduudka Sagalkee u gaarka ah,

          18   Yaad geddeedii tahoon LaGaa garan,

          (*repeat l. 18, twice*)

V.   21   Dayaxoo goor caweysin soo guday,

       22   Oo geyigu nuuray gelin dhaxaadkii,

          23   Yaad geddeedii tahoon LaGaa garan

          (*repeat l. 23, twice*)

I.   1   When [it is light enough] for us to tell a tree from a man—

       2   When the sun shoots its arrows [of light] in every direction:[29]

          3   You are [so] similar [to this] that one is confused.

          (*repeat l. 3, twice*)

II.   6   When a cloud passes over you at midmorning,

       7   And fills [the air] with water, and [then] disperses:

          8   You are [so] similar [to this] that one is confused.

          (*repeat l. 8, twice*)

III.   11   When Gu [brings] rains, and the green grass grows—

       12   [When] rain water reflects [light][30] in the pool,[31]

13   And [on its] ripples, one is confused.
     (*repeat l. 13, twice*)

IV.   16   When part of the evening sun entered its hole,[32] and
      17   [The other half gave] the redness special to the Sign of Sagal:[33]
           18   You are [so] similar [to this] that one is confused.
                (*repeat l. 18, twice*)

V.   21   The moon which came forth[34] in the late evening,
     22   And the earth reflected [its light] at midnight:
          23   You are [so] similar [to this] that one is confused.
               (*repeat l. 23, twice*)

In Example 38, composed in 1964 by Xuseyn Aw Faarax, we see the unifying framework of imagery operating in yet another way. The poet is praising his love by comparing her to a tree. Many images from the rainy season are employed here, and the stanza progression is also unique, exhibiting the following pattern:

Stanza I: The root
Stanza II: The trunk
Stanza III: The branch
Stanza IV: Things on the branch and below the trees: flowers, seeds, leaves, grass
Stanza V: Something which comes from the outside and becomes a part of the tree: mistletoe

Example 38:

I.   1   Dhirta xididka hoosaa,
     2   Dhulka Loogu beer e,
         (*repeat ll. 1-2*)
     5   Way dhicilahaayeen e,
     6   Dhismahooda weeyee,
         (*repeat l. 6, three times*)
     10   Kii dhabah jacaylku na,
     11   Kii dhabah jacaylku na,
     12   Halkii kama dhaqaaqoo,

13   Dhidib baa u aasan e,

     (repeat ll. 10-13)

II.   18   Sida dhumucda weeyaan,

    19   Jirridda iyo dhuuxa e,

       (repeat ll. 18-19)

    22   Dhererkiyo laxaadka na,

    23   Waa Laysku dhaabee,

       (repeat l. 23, three times)

    27   Kii dhabah jacaylku na,

    28   Kii dhabah jacaylku na,

    29   Lama kala dhantaaloo,

    30   Lafuhuu dhammeeyaa,

       (repeat ll. 27-30)

III.   35   Sida dhudaha weeyaan,

    36   Isu dheelli-tiraanoo,

       (repeat ll. 35-36)

    39   Mid ba dhan u baxaysee,

    40   Dhinaca isa saaree,

       (repeat l. 40, three times)

    44   Kii dhabah jacaylku na,

    45   Kii dhabah jacaylku na,

    46   Waa dhaqan wadaagiyo,

    47   Isu dhalasho daacada,

       (repeat ll. 44-47)

IV.   52   Sida dhalanka weeyaan,

    53   Dheehaa caleentu ye,

       (repeat ll. 52-53)

    56   Ubax wada dhalaaliyo,

    57   Dhimbiishaa hadhaysee,

       (repeat l. 57, three times)

    61   Kii dhabah jacaylku na,

    62   Kii dhabah jacaylku na,

    63   Waa dhool hillaac iyo,

64 Dhibic-roob ku haysee,
(repeat ll. 61-64)

V. 69 Waa sida Dhillowyahan,

70 Intuu laan iskaga dhegey,
(repeat ll. 69-70)

73 Dhexda Loogu marayoo

74 Dhakhso uga baxaayee,
(repeat l. 74, three times)

78 Kol hadduu dhab naga yahay,

79 Kala dhuuman maaynnoo,

80 Kala dhuuman maaynnoo,

81 Waagaa dharaar noqon.
(repeat ll. 78-81)

I. 1-2 The trees are planted in the earth so that the roots are below;
(repeat ll. 1-2)

5 [Otherwise] they would have fallen,

6 [But this] is their structure
(repeat l. 6, three times)

10 And love which is true

11 And love which is true

12 Does not move from its place;

13 And it has a central staff[35] secured in the ground.
(repeat ll. 10-13)

II. 18 [Love] is like the thickness

19 Of the trunk and [its] juices;[36]
(repeat ll. 18-19)

22 The height and the strength

23 Are intertwined in them.
(repeat l. 23, three times)

27 And love which is true,

28 And love which is true,

29 Cannot be split,

30   [For] it permeates [deep]³⁷ into the core.
        (*repeat ll. 27-30*)

III.   35   [Love] is like the slender trees,

        36   [For] they are balanced by each other.
                (*repeat l. 35-36*)

        39   Each [branch] grows in one direction,

        40   Leaning on other [branches] side by side.
                (*repeat l. 40, three times*)

        44   And love which is true

        45   And love which is true

        46   Is sharing ways of life and

        47   Being born for each other in honesty.
                (*repeat ll. 44-47*)

IV.   52   [Love] is like the newborn grass:³⁸

        53   The color of the leaves.
                (*repeat ll. 52-53*)

        56   The glittering of all the flowers,

        57   And the shading of the seed pods.
                (*repeat l. 57, three times*)

        61   And love which is true

        62   And love which is true

        63   Is the rain cloud [with] lightning

        64   The rain drops falling on it.
                (*repeat ll. 61-64*)

V.   69   [Love] is like the mistletoe³⁹

        70   After it has fixed itself onto a branch,
                (*repeat ll. 69-70*)

        73   And wrapped around it,

        74   Growing quickly upward.
                (*repeat l. 74, three times*)

        78   Once love is true for us

        79   We cannot hide from [one another].

        80   We cannot hide from [one another].

81   [Then] the dawn will become the day.[40]

(*repeat ll. 78-81*)

Perhaps imagery plays the major role in the diction of the modern poem, but it is not the only device used. Another, panegyric naming, we have seen before in the Family of Miniature Genres.

Inherited mainly from the Family of Miniature Genres, panegyric naming does not have the major role in modern poetry that it has in the miniature poem. Perhaps the reason for this has to do with the length of the *heello*. Other devices, such as the extensive development of imagery possible in a longer poem, have come into play. Panegyric naming, however, must not go unmentioned. Everything said of this device in the section on the miniature poem (see pp. 42-43) is true of the *heello*, so we shall not repeat it here, except to give some examples of these names taken from modern poems. Following is a list of panegyric names used in the *heello* of my collection:

1.   *Raalliya*. The One-Who-Pleases

2.   *Dawo*. The One-Who-Cures-All-Ills

3.   *Dul-Mare*. The One-Who-Passes-above-All-Others (i.e., The Best One)

4.   *Guud-Haldhaaleey*. The One-with-Hair-Like-the-Feathers-of-the-Male-Ostrich

5.   *Hibo*. The One-Who-Has-Received-Everything

6.   *Xalan*. The Clean One

7.   *Amarran*. The Blessed One

8.   *Qumman*. The Perfect One

While a discussion of the imagery in the modern poem is most important in describing its diction, other devices employed must not be overlooked. Personification, for example, occurs often where a woman, sometimes the poet's lover, personifies the country or part of the country of Somalia (see pp. 120-22 and pp. 128-33); or sometimes she represents a politician to whom the poet speaks (see pp. 139-42 and pp. 147- 50).

Juxtaposition of images is a popular device and finds many methods of expression in the *heello*. Compare the following lines from different poems:

1.   Dayaxoo goor caweysin soo guday,
      Oo geyigu nuuray gelin dhaxaadkii.

      The moon which came forth in the late evening,
      And the earth reflected [its light] at midnight.

2.   Ma idlaado, ma abaadoo. . .

      [Love] never wears out, nor lasts a long time. . .

3.   Janno ubax leh weeyee,
      Marna jahanna naariyo. . . .

      [Love is like] a heaven of flowers,
      And at other times, a hellfire. . . .

4.   Jidiinkaa i engegay jirkoo dazayoo . . .

      My throat is parched whilst heavy rains fall . . .

5   May hoorin, may hoorin,
      May hoorin, weli hogoshii Dayreedey.

      It has not [yet] rained; it has not [yet] rained;
      Still the cloud of Dayr[41] has not [yet] rained.

One other common device found in modern poetry is the use of a proverb or part of a proverb as a situational image (see p. 109, line 13, and pp. 179-83, lines 5-7). Less often the punch line of a folktale will be employed (see pp. 128-33 line 53).

Along with the characteristic themes and structure, another feature common to all periods demands detailed attention in this chapter. The effect of media upon the modern poem is of major importance in understanding its development. The tape recorder, for instance, has exerted some influences on the oral poem in Somalia in a manner similar to the influence that writing has on poetry in literate societies. Indeed, without the impact of media the *heello* would have no doubt taken a very different form.

The Impact of Media on Modern Poetry

Unlike writing, which had no apparent effect on the modern poem, (and many modern poets can read and write in English or Italian and/or Arabic) the radio and tape recorder have had a considerable impact. At times they play a simultaneous role, for example, when tapes are played on the radio. At other times they are separated, as when a live performance is broadcast or when tapes are played at a tea shop. In any case, both have exerted influence on four features of the *heello*, causing it to deviate from the usual characteristics of oral art in Somalia. More correctly, these two media have added to the usual features of Somali oral art and have affected its structure, performance, transmission, and preservation.

At least two elements of structure were greatly influenced by the radio and the tape recorder. In the early days of the *heello*, the policy of the radio station in the British Somaliland Protectorate was to determine the price to be paid for a poem by its length. Although the means of measuring were not perfectly exact, a definite relationship was established: the longer the poem, the more money paid to the poet. As a result, poems became longer and longer. The easiest way to lengthen a poem was through line repeating and refrain, and thus these devices eventually became regular features of the *heello*.

Another influence which the tape has exerted on modern poetry is oddly related to a similar influence that writing has on literate societies. When a poem is written down, it can have no variation, and an original, "authentic" version of the poem comes into being. The same situation has occurred with the "freezing" of oral poetry on tape in Somalia. Variation certainly is less possible with the modern poem. Not only is there an "authentic" version of each recorded poem, but it is played time and time again over the radio in this one version only. If anyone attempts to memorize the poem—and many Somalis do just this—one is constantly reinforced by hearing a single version of the poem. The same version heard on tapes played in tea shops—important social gathering places—adds still more reinforcement.

The *heello* is performed in a number of places and in several circumstances. Here again, the media have exerted their influence. With the ability to "freeze" a poem on tape, live performances cease to be of ultimate importance. One may, as many Somalis do, listen to poems on the radio in a tea shop or on a tape recorder with friends at a *Qat* party.[42] One may also listen to this poetry privately. No longer is social intercourse necessary to the enjoyment of oral poetry, to the very performance of it, although private listening must not be overstressed. The ownership of a tape recorder brings social prestige; many of these machines are privately owned now. Social gatherings such as weddings, national holidays, and religious festivals, moreover, make ready use of the *heello*.

Another milieu in which modern poetry was performed was the political party meeting. Not only were tapes used, but live recitations over another type of medium, the public address system, were common before the abolition of political parties by the Barre regime.[43] This recitation was occasionally performed inside a building and away from the visible presence of the audience; it could also be done from inside a moving vehicle, such as a taxi. Live performances before an audience, in the traditional man-ner, were also common. Poems extolling the qualities of the candidates were used alongside popular *heello*, presented for their entertainment value only.

Finally, the modern theater in Somalia must not be omitted from this discussion. Inside the newly developed drama of the country, the *heello* can be found alongside other, traditional poetry. The theater, which had its beginnings at about the same time as the modern poem, has provided an important outlet and impetus for it and continues to do so to an even greater extent today. In the theater the tape recorder also plays a role. Lacking the facilities of writing (i. e., for the stage, lacking a script), the playwright often teaches the actors the poems to be used in the drama by playing recordings of them over and over until they have been memorized.[44]

The influence of the radio and tape recorder upon the spatial dispersion of the modern poem is almost too obvious to present. The poem stretches as far as radio reception is possible. But the older influences of Somali poetry must not be ignored. Clearly the *heello* is carried from place to place by human memory as well as by the media.

When a modern poem loses its space on the air, its dispersal in time, like the traditional poem, depends upon its popularity with the public. One reciter, however, cannot deliver a poem along with the orchestration accompanying it. The preservation of a modern poem in its "original" form (soloist, orchestra, chorus) is not so much dependent upon its popularity and the influences of traditional oral art as it is upon the condition of the tape on which it is recorded and the place where the tape is stored. The very question of an original form has only come into being with these media.

The text of a modern poem can, however, continue from generation to generation as a traditional poem does. The *heello* has not been in Somali culture long enough for this to have happened, but another aspect of the preservation of particular poems in Somalia is becoming more common. There are a small number of Somali scholars who record poetry in writing. Whatever the limitations of transcription, which records only one facet of an oral poem (e.g., the text, leaving out the music, melody, circumstances of performance, etc.), it might be argued that at least the text of the poem is preserved.

The radio and tape recorder have exerted a heavy influence on modern poetry; but one other medium, musical instruments, has also had its effect. Indeed, the addition of an entire orchestra is one of the major differences between modern and traditional poems.

Finally, the media as a whole have succeeded in bringing about new social statuses in Somalia: those of the professional poet and reciter, both of which exist as nonprofessional statuses in traditional society even today. Moreover, the media have also brought about two entirely new statuses: those of the professional composer of musical melody and the professional musician. Note also that any one person may embody one or all of these talents.

Before the advent of radio in Somalia a poet usually participated in the economic pursuits of his area. Now, with an organized and financed outlet for his poetic abilities, the poet can make a living at his art. Indeed the establishment of the Radio Artistes Association in about 1968 bears witness to the professional atmosphere in which the present day Somali poet finds himself.[45]

NOTES

1. *Gu & Jiilaal.* The principle rainy and dry seasons in Somalia.

2. *Guban.* The range of mountains south of the branch of the rift valley in northern Somalia.

3. *Gorgoor.* A type of grass in Somalia, maybe *eleusine floccifolia*.

4. *Maadh.* A type of grass from which Somalis make mats for the walls of their portable huts (*aqal*), maybe *aristida sp.*

5. *Maadh* in the evening reflects many beautiful colors.

6. *Gubato.* Place name. Gubato is somewhere near the Hawd in eastern Ethiopia.

7. *Hawd.* The northeastern part of the Ogaadeen in Ethiopia.

8. *Qumman.* Panegyric name. See p. 206, number 8.

9. Lines 5-7 allude to a Somali proverb:

> Ninkaad taqaanno, waa inaad jid la martaa,
> Jidiinna la cuntaa, jahaad na la gashaa.

> If you are really to know a man, you must first travel with him,
> Eat a meal with him, and enter battle with him.

    What the poet is asking the girls is: "Do you really understand love?"

10. The reference here may be to a Romeo and Juliet situation.

11. *Jiljilada.* The area of the foot above the heel (*cidhibta*), behind the ankle (*canqawga*), and in front of the Achilles tendon (*seedda*).

12. I. E., love sometimes throws you up, sometimes down.

13. The colonialists.

14. The colonialists.

15. *Gudin.* Somali axe used for cutting thorn bushes which are used for the construction of fences and corrals. The *gudin* has an iron head and a wooden handle.

16. *Hangool.* See page 93, note 27.

17. *Gogol.* Sleeping mat or skin. This line means that because the red earth is so soft, one does not need bedding in order to rest on it.

18. *Wajeer.* One of the principal towns in the N. F. D. in Kenya, which is inhabited and claimed by Somalis.

19. *Wiida.* "The *Oui* (yes)" refers to the positive vote on the referendum in Jabuuti (1958, 1967). An affirmative vote is for France to remain in the colony.

20. *Obokh.* Town in the French Territory of Afars and Issas (French Somaliland).

21. *Gunto.* See page 171, note 82.

22. I came close. Literally, "I entered into the center of."

23. I failed. Literally, "I passed over the top of"; i. e., "I made an attempt but failed/I was never able to get to the bottom of it/I was prevented from fully explaining the matter [because of hostile reception]." A Somali term of debate.

24. Compare the use of rain in the *heello* with that of the miniature poem. See pp. 34-35.

25. Compare the use of illness in the *heello* with that of the miniature poem. See p. 35.

26. Compare the use of the tree in the heello with that of the miniature poem. See pp. 35-36.

27. Note that the poem translates easier when the first two lines are transposed.

28. Compare this discussion with the discussion of the miniature poem on pp. 35-36.

29. The sunbeams are caused by moisture in the air. This adds to the overall positiveness of the poem because one sees sunbeams only in the rainy season.

30. I. E., water is so abundant that one sees its reflection in many pools. This also shows the listener that it is noon, for sunlight which is directly overhead in Somalia is reflected in the pool.

31. *Gelgelimaad.* "The place where animals dust themselves." A place picked out by animals to dust themselves in order to keep the insects off. These places have no grass growing in them and are used so often for this purpose that they fill up with water, forming little pools.

32. Somalis have a traditional belief that the sun enters a hole in the horizon at sunset, passes through the earth, and comes out of the hole at the other end of the horizon at sunrise.

33. "Sign of *Sagal.*" A red sunset which is a sign of coming rain in Somali weather lore.

34. *Gud.* "To come forth"; literally "to walk at night."

35. *Dhidib.* A fixed pole used as the central pivot to support the weight of the portable hut (*aqal*). The line reads literally: "A staff is buried in the ground for [love]."

36. *Dhuuxa.* "Juices," i. e., "sap"; literally, "bone marrow."

37. *Dhammee.* "Permeates [deep]"; literally, "completes."

38. *Dhalan.* Minute plants growing under other plants and eaten by sheep. Glover (1947) identifies them as *danthaniopsis barbata*.

39. *Dhillowyahan.* Glover (1947) identifies this as anything from *oranthus Fischer* to *oranthus curriflorus*. See his book, pp. 361-62.

40. I. E., our lives together (dawn) will mature (become the day).

41. *Dayr.* The secondary rainy season in Somalia.

42. *Qat (Catha edulis).* A green leaf chewed for its effects as a drug. It is often chewed at social gatherings in the north of Somalia. Poetry is often recited at these "*qat* parties," which are attended mostly by men.

43. Party rallies and other political gatherings during the Barre regime continued to provide a milieu for live poetry recitals, where public address systems were utilized.

44. For a history of the development of the theater in Somalia, see Andrzejewski (1978).

45. The establishment of a national troupe, the *Waaberi* ("Dawn") artists, after the 1969 coup also bears witness to this professional atmosphere.

43. Party rallies and other political gatherings during the Barre regime continued to provide a milieu for live poetry recials, where public address systems were utilized.

44. For a history of the development of the theater in Somalia, see Andrzejewski (1978).

45. The establishmenbt of a national troup, the *Waaberi* ("Dawn") artists, after the 1969 coup also bears witness to this professional atmosphere.

8

CONCLUSION

The Inheritance of the *Heello*

It would be absurd to contend that the present form of the *heello* is final; its entire history so far has been one of change. What follows can only be a definition of the *heello* as it is at the time of this writing, for it may yet evolve into new and different forms. To describe the modern poem, it is most useful to summarize its characteristics, beginning with their historical origins. Indeed it is for this reason that this book has been organized largely from the historical point of view.

Inheritance from Classical Poetry — From the classical poetry of the traditional Somali pastoralist the *heello* inherited its length and unity of theme. Alliteration is a characteristic of all Somali poetry, and the unity of it throughout the whole of the modern poem comes also from the classical model. The dialect of Somali used, as well as the imagery, has also been inherited from the nomad. The prestige of the modern poem is largely a result of its use in the political and social arena, this also having been taken from classical pastoralist poetry.

Inheritance from the Miniature Poem — Together with these features from classical poetry, the *heello* has inherited some features from the Family of Miniature Genres, especially its last form, the *belwo*. The very name of the genre, *heello*, comes from an introductory formula associated with this family. The theme of love, the most common in modern poetry, has its origin here. Some elements of its diction, including panegyric naming and images concerning love, are from the miniature poem. And finally, its use in less formal situations, such as at weddings and festivals, comes from the miniature family.

Borrowed Features — Along with characteristic features inherited from indigenous sources the *heello* has borrowed some of its features from abroad. Musical instruments and the musical setting of the poem are from foreign sources. Although the melodies used by the *heello* are indigenous, the use of one individualized melody for each poem in the genre is a foreign device, as is the use of formalized refrain and line repeating in the structure of the poem. And finally, its use over the radio, itself a foreign borrowing, is the result of foreign influence.

Intrinsic Development   The inheritance of features from foreign and indigenous sources is not all that has shaped the modern poem. Once the stage is set, there remain the acts of the drama to be performed, and several features of the *heello* were developed from the process of its own evolution. Themes like anticolonialism and the debate on the role of women in modern society belong exclusively to the *heello*. Its use in political rallies and in the theater in Somalia are results of its passage through time. Its modern diction, notably lacking in archaic language, is also a characteristic of maturation.

Forces Behind the Success
and Development of Modern Poetry

Considering what happened in the developmental period between the *belwo* and the *heello*, the *belwo* itself had a mild beginning indeed. What happened, then, to cause this unprecedented development? The main causes are outlined below.

Changes in the Social Setting   As pointed out earlier, the social scene in urban Somali life began to change a great deal after the British returned to the Horn in 1941. The new administration brought about several basic changes, including the successful establishment of formal education. The nomadic way of life was not greatly affected by these new programs, but then the modern poem neither began nor developed among the nomads; it was an urban poem from the beginning.

Along with changes brought about by foreigners came a new attitude toward change on the part of Somalis themselves, as witnessed by the success of the education program. Other areas of development were to have the same success as the education program. The names of these Somalis who played important roles in other areas could be given, but it is not the purpose of this book merely to describe history. The important point is that Somalis began to face change. Change was no longer out of the question. Traditional methods of accomplishing social functions were weakened as more modern programs, such as the township committees and town planning boards (see p. 52), were established.

This new attitude of progressiveness was reflected in the artistic endeavors of Somali poets. It was no longer out of the question to have musical accompaniment to miniature poems. Cabdi's petrol tin drum was not only to survive opposition but it was to prepare a way for the tambourine, the flute, the violin, and the lute. Later, the clarinet, saxophone, and organ were to become acceptable as part of modern poetry recitals. Furthermore, it was now acceptable for each poem of the new genre to have its own melody. If the modern poem were faced with traditional poetic rules, we might conclude that each *heello* is a genre unto itself.

So changes became acceptable, and although brought about by foreigners, change was to be, had to be carried out by Somalis themselves. From another source change was to be initiated as new media came onto the Somali scene.

The Use of New Media   New media brought about the possibility of new variation from tradition. If the petrol tin drum could work its way into poetry where accompaniment was rare before, then other changes would become easier. Add the flute to the drum and tambourine, and still more possibilities of change open up. One can only beat rhythm on the former, but on the latter melody becomes possible. With the addition of more and more musical instruments, more and more possibilities of variation and combination arise. The grounds were laid for the technical aspects of change. Then came the addition of Indian and Western music as models from which the new poem could develop. Eventually the concept of one melody per poem arose in Somali poetry as it exists in Arabic, Hindi, Italian, and English songs— four types that Somalis had access to.

The radio played an important role in the rapid dissemination of the *belwo*. Indeed it influenced its very structure. We have seen that a refrain and the use of line repeating developed out of the administration's method of paying for the use of a poem by its length. The *belwo* and later the *heello* were very useful to the radio station, for they could be used as fillers between programs. Different lengths of time gaps could be filled by *belwo* and *heello* of varying lengths. Programs centered around their recitation came to occupy a major part of radio time on the air.

The radio also gave the modern poem prestige, for the new elite apparently lent its tacit support and obviously approved of its use. It became even more popular when the colonial government let it slip by uncensored of the political implications hidden in its imagery.

And it was the radio which provided the source of the foreign songs which became part of the model for the *heello*. As mentioned above, Somali poets were exposed to Arabic, Hindi, Italian, and English songs. Hargeysa, Muqdisho, and Aden all had radio stations where this music could be heard.

Adding to the popularity of the *heello* was also its use in drama. The modern theater in Somalia, which had its beginning during this period uses modern and traditional poetry in much the same way as Western operetta and musical comedy. Poetry was used with Somali drama from the beginning, and this marriage of play and poem added to the dissemination, popularity, and ultimate preservation of the new genre.[1]

Identification with Politics   When the *heello* adopted political themes, the future of modern poetry was secured. The *belwo* had been chiefly concerned with intimate love and thereby lacked the status of classical poetry. With political themes came the prestige needed for the *heello* to be considered a serious work of art. It rapidly became the voice of patriotism and anticolonialism. In fact, it later became such a popular device for delivering political viewpoints that the political *heello*, as we mentioned earlier, was suppressed during the administration of Prime Minister Cigaal. Prior to the coup of October 1969, though, the *heello* was consistently important to party politics, for if a party was to gain widespread support, it had to secure the services of a good poet. During an election year especially, *heello* could be heard from the loudspeakers of party headquarters and at political rallies.

Timing of the *Belwo* and *Heello*   Unlike the other miniature poems, the *belwo* went through a period of metamorphosis and emerged as the *heello*. This change in traditional poetics paralleled a new Somali attitude of accepting change in the development of such social activities as education and road building. New media and the adoption of the theme of politics at the right time in the drive toward independence gave the *heello* a secure place alongside other genres of

Somali poetry.

It was to this historical period that the *belwo* was added and the *heello* emerged. At a time when dynamic innovation was beginning on the Horn, the *heello* became the voice of that innovation. Having begun as a result of change, the *heello* now will possibly bring about some change in the society from which it emerged. With such poems as the ones on pp. 7-11 and pp. 155-60, for example, the role of women is gradually being redefined by the elite.

The *heello* in Somalia is a modern phenomenon, something new in Somali culture; it is based on something old and influenced by elements from outside Somali culture. But the modern poem is very much a Somali work of art. The metamorphosis of the *belwo* to the *heello* was an aesthetic purification and expansion process, which took a genre of miniature poetry that had caught the public fancy at a period of stress and change in Somali history and converted it into a structure more closely resembling the classical poem, the ultimate in oral beauty and meaning to the Somali. Today the *heello*, like its classical sisters, is a long poem. Its alliteration is unified and its themes deal with ideas and events, social problems, and beliefs which were formerly treated by the genres of *gabay, jiifto, geeraar* and *buraambur* alone. Indeed the modern poem appears to have replaced these genres in some situations of urban Somali life. But the *heello* is also different from classical poetry. The theme of private love, inherited from the Family of Miniature Genres, has not been lost. Each *heello* has its own particular identifiable melody. It is a blend of old and new, of indigenous and foreign. It is a new shoe on an old foot.

NOTES

1. See Andrzejewski's essay on Somali theater and translation of *Leopard Among the Women: Shabeel Naagood* (1974). For a broader history of the development of the theater in Somalia, see Andrzejewski (1978).

APPENDIX OF SOMALI PROPER NAMES

In the following appendix, only a selected list of proper Somali names appears. Those names which I have never seen in written form or the popular spelling of which I am unsure have been omitted from the list. The name "Bidde," for example, has no doubt appeared in written form, but I have never seen it. On the other hand, the name "Hibo" is very likely spelled the same in most orthographies. The one obvious excep-tion to the method of spelling all Somali words within the orthographic system used in this book is the proper name "Somali," which would otherwise be spelled "Soomaali." Because of the widespread use of this name, it was felt best to employ the popular spelling.

Somali Form	Popular Form	Somali Form	Popular Form
Aadan	Adan or Aden or Adam	Baydhabo or Baydhaba	Baidoa
Abokor	Abokor or Aboker	Benaadir or Banaadir	Benadir
Afgooye or Afgoy	Afgoi	Berbera	Berbera or Barbara
Afmeer	Afmer		
Axmed	Ahmed	Boorame or Boorama	Borama
Aroori	Arori		
Aw	Au	Bowndheri	Bowndheri or Bonderi
Awaare	Awareh		
Awdal	Audal	Buraambur	Burambur
Ban Balcad	Ban Balad	Burco	Burao
Baraawe Baraawa	Brava	Bur Hakaba	Bur Hacaba
		Caaqib	Aqib
Barre	Bare	Caasha	Asha

221

Somali Form	Popular Form		Somali Form	Popular Form
Cabdi	Abdi		Dharaar	Darar
Cabdille or	Abdilla or		Diiriye or	Diria or
Cabdulle or	Abdulla or		Diiriya	Deria
Cabdalle	Abdalla		Dirir Dhabe or	Dira Dawa or
Cabdi-Rashiid	Abdi Rashid or		Dirir Dhaba	Diredawa
	Abd ar-Rashid		Ducaale	Duale
Cabdi-Risaaq	Abdi Rizak or		Faarax	Farah
	Abd ar-Razak		Gaaroodi	Garodi
Cabdullaahi	Abdullahi or		Gadabuursi	Gadabursi
or Cabdillaahi	Abdillahi		Garoowe	Garowe
Cadale	Adaleh		Geedow	Gedo
Cali	Ali		Geelo	Gelo
Camuud	Amud or		Geryaad	Geriad
	Amoud		Habaas	Habas
Caweys	Aweis		Hargeysa	Hargeisa or
Cawo or	Awo or			Hargeisha
Cawa	Awa		Hawd	Haud
Ceerigaabo	Erigavo		Hobyo	Obbia
Cigaal	Egal		Ibraahiin	Ibrahim
Ciise or	Issa		Ismaaciil	Ismail
Ciisa			Jaamac	Jama or
Cilmi	Ilmi			Djama or
Cismaaniya or	Ismania or			Giama
Cusmaaniya	Osmania or		Jaaraa-Horato	Jara Horato
	Osmaniya		Jabuuti	Jibuti or
Cumar	Omar			Djibouti
Cusmaan or	Osman or		Jiilaal	Jilal
Cismaan	Isman		Jowhar	Johar
Daarood	Darod		Jubba or	Juba or
Dalays	Dalais		Juuba	Giuba
Dazuud or	Daud		Khadiiya or	Kadija
Dhadhiin	Dadin		Qadiija	

Somali Form	Popular Form	Somali Form	Popular Form
Kismaayo or Kismanyo	Chismayo or Kisymayu	Siciid	Saeed
Laas Caanood	Las Anod	Sayid	Sayyid
Maxamed	Mohamed or Muhammad or Mahammad	Seylac	Zeila
		Shabeelle	Shebelle
		Shar-Ma-Arke	Shermarke or Shirmarke
Maxmuud	Mohamud or Mohamoud or Mahamud or Mahamuud	Sheekh or Sheykh	Sheikh
		Shire or Shira	Shira or Shirreh
Maryan	Mariam	Sigsaag	Zigzag
Mudug	Mudugh	Sinimo or Sinime or Sinima	Cinema
Muqdisho or Muqdishow	Mogadishu or Mogadiscio		
Muumin	Mumin	Siyad	Siad or Syad
Muuse or Muusa	Musa	Sugulle	Suguleh or Seguleh
Naji	Naji or Neji	Suleebaan or Suleemaan	Suleiman or Suleman
Nuux	Nuh	Taleex	Tale or Taleh
Nuur	Nur		
Obokh or Oboq	Obock	Tog Wajaale	Tug Wajale
Ogaadeen	Ogaden	Ugaas	Ughaz
Qarshe	Qarshi or Karshe or Kharshe or Gharshe	Wajeer	Wajer
		Warsame or Warsama	Warsama
Reer	Reer or Rer	Xaaji	Haji or Hagi or Hajji or Hadji
Saahid	Sahid		
Saciid or	Said or	Xasan	Hassan

Somali Form	Popular Form
Xawo or Xawa	Hawo
Xirsi	Hirsi
Xoogga Dalka	Hoga Dalka
Xuseyn or Xuseen	Hussein or Husseyn
Yuusuf	Yusuf

BIBLIOGRAPHY

Andrzejewski, B. W. "Speech and Writing Dichotomy as the Pattern of Multi-lingualism in the Somali Republic." In *Report of the C. T. A. /C. S. A. Symposium on Multilingualism in Africa*. Brazzaville, 1962, pp. 177-81.

----------. "Somali Stories." *Selection of African Prose*: 1. *Traditional Oral Texts*. Edited by W. H. Whiteley. Oxford Library of African Literature. London: Clarendon Press, 1964, pp. 134-63.

---------. "The Art of the Miniature in Somali Poetry." *African Language Review* 6 (1967): 5-16.

----------. "Reflections on the Nature and Social Function of Somali Proverbs." *African Language Review* 7 (1968): 74-85.

----------. "The *Roobdoon* of Sheikh Aqib Abdullahi Jama: A Somali Prayer for Rain." *African Language Studies* 8 (1969): 21-34.

----------. "The Role of Broadcasting in the Adaptation of the Somali Language to Modern Needs." *Language Use and Social Change: Problems Multilingualism with Special Reference Eastern Africa*. Edited by W. H. Whiteley. London: Oxford University Press, for the International African Institute, 1971, pp. 262-73.

----------, trans., ed., *Leopard Among the Women: Shabeelnaagood: A Somali Play by Hassan Sheikh Muumin*. London: Oxford University Press, 1974a.

----------. "The Introduction of a National Orthography for Somalia." *African Language Studies* 15 (1974b): 199-203

----------. "Modern and Traditional Aspects of Somali Drama." *Folklore in the Modern World*. Edited by Richard M. Dorson. The Hague: Mouton, 1978, pp. 87-101.

Andrzejewski, B. W., and Lewis, I. M. *Somali Poetry: An Introduction*. London: Clarendon Press, 1964.

Andrzejewski, B. W., and Muusa Hhaaji Ismaaciil Galaal. "A Somali Poetic Combat." *Journal of African Languages* 2 (1963): 15-28, 93-100, 190-205.

----------. "The Art of the Verbal Message in Somali Poetry." Edited by Johannes Lukas. *Hamburger Beiträge zur Afrika-Kunde* 5 (1966): 29-39.

Andrzejewski , B. W., Strelcyn, S., and Tubiana, J. *Somalia: The Writing of Somali*. Paris: U. N. E. S. C. O., 1966.

Armstrong, Lilias E. "The Phonetic Structure of Somali." *Mitteilungen des Seminars für orientalischen Sprachen zu Berlin*. 37:3 (1934): 116-61.

Cerulli, Enrico. *Somalia: Scritti vari editi ed inediti.* 3 Vols. Rome: Amministrazione Fiduciana Italiana, 1957, 1959, and 1964.

Drysdale, John G. S. *The Somali Dispute.* Pall Mall World Affairs Special Series, no. 1. London: Pall Mall Press, 1964.

Finnegan, Ruth. *Oral Literature in Africa.* Oxford Library of African Literature. London: Clarendon Press. 1970.

Glover, P. E. A. *Provisional Check-List of British and Italian Somaliland Trees, Shrubs and Herbs (Including the Reserved Areas Adjacent to Abyssinia).* London: The Crown Agents for the Colonies. 1946.

Hess, Robert L. "The Poor Man of God--Muhammad Abdullah Hassan." *Leadership in Eastern Africa: Six Political Biographies.* Edited by Norman R. Bennet. Boston University, African Research Studies No. 9. Boston: Boston University Press, 1968.

Hoskyns, Catherine, ed. *Case Studies in African Diplomacy, Number II: The Ethiopia-Somali-Kenya Dispute, 1960-67.* Dar Es Salaam: Oxford University Press for the Institute of Public Administration. 1969.

Information Office [of the British Somaliland Protectorate], The. *War Somali Sidihi.* Mimeographed. Hargeysa, 1953-1960.

Jaamac Cumar Ciise, Sheekh. *Diiwaanka Gabayadii: Sayid Macamad Cabdulle Xasan.* Muqdisho: Wasaaradda Hiddaha iyo Taclinta Sare. 1974.

Johnson, John William. "A Bibliography of Somali Language and Literature." *African Language Review* 8 (1969):279-97.

----------. "The Family of Miniature Genres in Somali Oral Poetry" *Folklore Forum* 5:3 (1972):79-99.

----------. "Research in Somali Folklore." *Research in African Literatures* 4:1 (1973): 51-61.

----------. "Somali Prosodic Systems." *Horn of Africa* 2:3 (Summit, New Jersey: Horn of Africa Journal, 1979): 46-54

----------. "Recent Contributions by Somalis and Somalists to the Study of Oral Literature." in *Somalia and the World: Proceedings of the International Symposium Held in Mogadishu, October 15-21, 1979,* ed. Hussein M. Adam (Mogadishu, Somali Democratic Republic: Halgan Editorial Board, 1980a): 117-31

----------. "Somalia." *The New Grove Dictionary of Music and Musicians* (London: Macmillan, 1980b): Vol. 17, pp. 472-73

----------. "Recent Researches into the Scansion of Somali Oral Poetry." in *Proceedings of the Second International Congress of Somali Studies,* ed. Thomas Labahn (Hamburg: Helmut Buske Verlag, 1985): 313-31

Johnson, John William. "Set Theory in Somali Poetics: Structures and Implications." in *Proceedings of the Third International Congress of Somali Studies,* ed. Annarita Puglielli (Rome: Il Scientifico Editore, 1988): 123-33

----------. "Somali Poetry." *The New Princeton Encyclopedia of Poetry and Poetics* (Princeton, N.J.: Princeton University Press, 1993): 1164-65

----------. "Musico-Moro-Syllabic Relationships in the Scansion of Somali Oral Poetry." in *Voice and Power: The Culture of Language in North-East Africa: Essays in Honour of B.W. Andrzejewski. [African Languages and Cultures: Supplement 3].* Edited by R. J. Hayward and I. M. Lewis (London: School of Oriental and African Studies, University of London, 1996): 73-82

----------. "Music of Somalia." in *Garland Encyclopedia of World Music* (New York: Garland Pub. Co., ca.1996) [in the press]

Laurence, Margaret. *A Tree for Poverty: Somali Poetry and Prose.* Nairobi: The Eagle Press for the Somaliland Protectorate, 1954.

Lienhardt, Godfrey. *Social Anthropology.* London: Oxford University Press, 1964.

Lewis, I. M. *Peoples of the Horn of Africa: Somali, Afar and Saho.* Ethnographic Survey of Africa: North Eastern Africa, Part I. London: International African Institute, 1955.

----------. "Sufism in Somaliland: A Study in Tribal Islam." *Bulletin of the School of Oriental and African Studies* 17:3 (1955): 581-602; 18: 1 (1956): 146-60.

----------. "The Gadabuursi Somali Script." *Bulletin of the School of Oriental and African Studies* 21 (1957a): 134-56.

----------. *The Somali Lineage System and the Total Genealogy: A General Introduction to Basic Principles of Somali Political Institutions.* Mimeographed. Hargeysa: The Secretariat Office [of the British Somaliland Protectorate], 1957b.

----------. *A Pastoral Democracy: A Study of Pastoralism and Politics Among the Northern Somali of the Horn of Africa.* London: Oxford University Press, 1961.

----------. *The Modern History of Somaliland from Nation to State.* New York: Frederick A. Praeger Co., 1965.

----------. "From Nomadism to Cultivation: Expansion of Political Solidarity in Southern Somalia" *Man in Africa* Edited by Mary Douglas and Phyllis M. Kaberry London: Tavistock Ltd. 1969.

----------. *The Modern History of Somalia: Nation and State in the Horn of Africa.* London: Longman, 1980.

----------. *The Modern History of Somalia: Nation and State in the Horn of Africa.* [Revised] Boulder, Colorado: Westview Press, 1988.

Lord, Albert B. *The Singer of Tales.* Cambridge, Massachusetts: Harvard University Press, 1960.

Maino, Mario. *La Lingua Somala strumento d'insegnamento professionale.* Allesandria: Tipografia Ferrari, Occella and Co., 1953.

Mohamed Farah Abdillahi and Andrzejewski, B. W. "The Life of Ilmi Bowndheri, a Somali Oral Poet who is Said to have Died of Love." *Journal of the Folklore Institute* 4:2/3 (1967): 73-87.

Muusa Hhaaji Ismaaciil Galaal. *The Terminology and Practice of Somali Weather Lore, Astronomy and Astrology.* Mimeographed. Mogadishu, 1968.

Muusa Hhaaji Ismaaciil Galaal and Andrzejewski, B. W. *Hhikmad Soomaali.* Annotated African Texts IV: Somali. London: Oxford University Press, 1956.

Omar Au Nuh. *Some General Notes on Somali Folklore.* Mimeographed. Mogadishu: 1970.

Somali Government. *Somali News: National Weekly.* Mogadishu: Published by the Ministry of Information at the National Press. (Last issue as a weekly, 26 September 1969. Name changed to: *Somali News: Government National Daily,* Published from 1 October to 18 October 1969.)

[Suleiman Mohamoud Adam]. *The Development of Broadcasting in Somalia.* Mogadishu: Ministry of Information, 1968.

Touval, Saadia. *Somali Nationalism.* Cambridge, Massachusetts: Harvard University Press, 1963.

Trimingham, J. S. *Islam in Ethiopia.* London: Clarendon Press, 1952.

----------. *Islam inEast Africa.* London: Clarendon Press, 1964

Wellek, Rene, and Warren, Austin. *Theory of Literature.* London: Jonathan Cape Publishers, 1949.

Yaasiin Cismaan Keenadiid. *Ina Cabdille Xasan e la sua attività letteraria.* Naples: Instituto Universitario Orientale, 1984.

INDEX OF FIRST LINES TO THE *HEELLO*

GENERAL INDEX

Aadan Cabdulla Cusmaan, 139, 172n

Abu Hadre, 160

Abu Jahal, 8, 11, 23n

Adam and Eve, 9, 22n, 23n

agriculturalist, 1, 23n, 72n

Axmed Suleebaan Bidde, 139

Axmed Yuusuf Ducaale, 183

alliteration, 12, 15, 45n, 92n, 166n

    disunified in modern poetry, 77, 80, 83, 97, 107, 112n

    in mega-miniature poetry, 77

    in miniature poetry, 30, 33, 34, 41

    in traditional poetry, 12, 24n, 215

    unified in modern poetry, 19, 83, 107, 146, 215, 219

animals as image in poetry, 6, 30, 34, 36, 39, 40, 41, 42, 46, 48, 84, 91n, 153, 169n, 170n,
    185, 188, 194, 195, 197, 212n

anticolonial theme in *heello*, 19, 108, 146, 183, 185, 216, 218

antigovernment theme in *heello*, 20, 34, 38, 117, 146, 147

arrow as image in poetry, 172n, 193, 195, 199, 201

Boorame, 19, 49, 51, 53, 54, 55, 56, 57, 59, 72n, 75, 99, 100, 113n, 167n

boundary shift, xvi, 19, 52-53, 95-97, 113n 143

British

    and border shift, xv-xvi, 19, 52-53, 95-97

    and development of Protectorate, 49, 50, 52, 58, 112n, 216-17

    changes in social and political scene, 44, 49-53, 58, 71n, 117-18, 127-28, 169n, 216

    government, 37, 64, 92n, 173n

    in World War II, 50-52, 95

    Somaliland Protectorate (British Administration), xv-xvi 43n, 49, 55, 82, 92n, 103,
        113n, 114n, 116n, 166n, 208